UNBEATABLE

Up The Dubs!
Ernie Hau...

ERIC HAUGHAN is a multimedia sports journalist with RTÉ Online. He has been involved with his local St Finian's Newcastle club since childhood, and he now coaches their ladies' team. Eric's idea of a day well spent is hitting the road with his daughter to catch the Dubs in pre-season mode at an obscure provincial ground. This is his first book.

UNBEATABLE
Dublin's Incredible Six in a Row

Eric Haughan

THE O'BRIEN PRESS
DUBLIN

First published in 2024 by The O'Brien Press Ltd,
12 Terenure Road East, Rathgar, Dublin 6, D06 HD27 Ireland.
Tel: +353 1 4923333; Fax: +353 1 4922777
E-mail: books@obrien.ie; Website: obrien.ie
The O'Brien Press is a member of Publishing Ireland.

ISBN: 978-1-78849-520-2

Text © copyright Eric Haughan, 2024
The moral rights of the author have been asserted.
Copyright for typesetting, layout, editing, design © The O'Brien Press Ltd
Cover and internal design by Emma Byrne.
Cover and internal images courtesy of Sportsfile.

All rights reserved. No part of this publication may be reproduced or utilised in any form or by any means, electronic or mechanical, including for text and data mining, training artificial intelligence systems, photocopying, recording or in any information storage and retrieval system, without permission in writing from the publisher.

8 7 6 5 4 3 2 1
28 27 26 25 24

The author and publisher would like to credit the following for references throughout this book: Mediahuis/Independent Newspapers; *The Meath Chronicle*; *The Mayo News*; *The Connacht Tribune*; *The Irish Examiner*, *Gaelic Life*; Boylesports; RTE.ie; the GAAgo Ratified podcast; and The Hop Ball podcast. Our thanks to Reach Sport for permission to reprint extracts from *The Hill*, Bernard Brogan's autobiography; to Gill & Macmillan for extracts from *Until Victory Always*, the autobiography of Jim McGuinness; and to Penguin UK for extracts from *Dublin v Kerry* by Tom Humphries and *Dublin: The Chaos Years* by Neil Cotter.

Printed and bound by Nørhaven Paperback A/S, Denmark.
The paper in this book is produced using pulp from managed forests.

This book is dedicated to every man and woman
who has ever worn a jersey.
And to the men and women who write about them.

And to Abbie.
Wherever in the world this life takes you,
we'll always have the Dubs.
Love, Dad.

CONTENTS

	Foreword by John O'Leary	9
Chapter One	Day Zero: 2014	17
Chapter Two	Back on Top: 2015	26
Chapter Three	Mayo Mayhem: 2016	50
Chapter Four	The 60-Second Kickout: 2017	73
Chapter Five	Twelve Minutes: 2018	104
Chapter Six	So Long, Jim. And Thanks: 2019	132
Chapter Seven	Oh, The Weather Outside Is Frightful: 2020	166
Chapter Eight	Hell or Connaught: The 2,540th Day: 2021	184
Chapter Nine	Reflections	205
Chapter Ten	Where to Now? 2022–2024	212
Chapter Eleven	Best of the Best: Dubs v Rest of World	233
Chapter Twelve	Lies, Damned Lies, And …	240
Chapter Thirteen	The Games: (About) A Decade of the Dubs	246
	Index	289
	Acknowledgements	299

Foreword

BY JOHN O'LEARY
**Dubs goalkeeper, 1980–1997,
double All-Ireland winner**

What happened to me will never happen again. I made my senior debut for Dublin in the 1980 Leinster football final. The right place at the right time. I was lucky. I had won a minor All-Ireland the year before and was invited along to a training session at Parnell Park on the Saturday morning before the provincial decider with Offaly. Stephen Rooney, who was an O'Dwyers man like myself, was on the panel as well. He'd played midfield with Brian Mullins in 1974 when Dublin came from nowhere to win the All-Ireland.

Mick O'Brien, a soccer goalie with Athlone Town who was famous for swinging on the crossbar, was knocking around. Mick Kennedy had played in goal in the first two rounds of the championship, but Mick was a corner-back. So I did the training session, took a few kickouts. Thought it went okay. Kevin Heffernan told me to bring my gear the next day. I thought this was great – I'd have the best seat in the house to watch the Leinster final.

On the day of the match, I walked up Clonliffe Road with Tommy Drumm, one of our more senior players at the time. He turned to me and asked if I'd like to be playing. Looking back, Tommy might have had an idea I was starting and wanted to feel me out to see if I was ready. Of course I said, *oh yeah, I'd love to*. Standard answer. Then in the dressing room, I had the number 1 jersey thrown to me. 'You're in today,' Heffernan said, simple as that. I was Dublin's goalkeeper for the next 18 years.

So I go all the way back to the man himself. Heffo. I played with the greats of the 1970s. I captained the 1995 side that produced so many brilliant servants to the Dublin senior football team, including Pat Gilroy, Jim Gavin and Dessie Farrell – the three men who finally began delivering All-Ireland titles for the capital again after 16 long, barren years.

Look at their day jobs. Pat was a businessman, running his own company. He brought with him structure and organisation. Jim had a career in the army, with all the discipline of the air corps. He got to grips with the team, brought them together, convinced them they were not going to lose. He made them feel like a unit, gave them a culture and an image. It was planning, planning, planning with military precision. Planning for every eventuality. Planning for chaos. Dessie, who is a GAA man to the core, continued where the others left off. They gave us that solid structure, and if you have that, you can bring people on. Not every player who's coming into the squad is at the same level.

The best manager I ever had was Kevin Heffernan. His ability to put his arm around one fella and give the next fella a kick in the arse was exactly what was needed at the time. He could multitask and be flexible. He was a natural diplomat and had an innate ability to bring the players

FOREWORD

on. I get the sense that Dublin now has a structure filled with people who have those skills.

Over the years that this book covers, there's no getting away from it: Dublin were incredibly lucky with some of the draws we got in big games. I feel really sorry for Mayo in that period. I've got great admiration for Mayo – they just kept coming back. That takes some commitment. It would have sickened a lot of teams. It's a long drive from Castlebar to Croke Park, and I love how the Mayo fans follow their team year after year. They were so, so close, but there was something about the way that Dublin team just kept their heads. Call it resilience or plain old stubbornness, but Dublin got stronger from winning all those close games.

It comes from the coaching, the conversations, the leadership – the setup within the unit that Jim brought in, leaning on his military background – but clearly the lads were putting in a lot of hard work as well. Those early days were known to be tough. Under old regimes, they were flaky against the better teams; they were turned over in games they should have been winning. They didn't have that backbone. Jim and Pat Gilroy brought that in. I'd love to have been a fly on the wall during that time. It must have been such an incredible environment.

I played in 70 championship matches in a row, starting with that Leinster final debut – which we lost, by the way, with Faithful legend Matt Connor's goal giving Offaly a 1-10 to 1-8 win. Bobby Doyle got our goal, I'm sure. That 70-match run was a record, until it was broken by a young man named Stephen Cluxton. I like to joke that I 'discovered' Cluxton when I was a selector under Tommy Carr between 1997 and 2001. Tommy asked me about this young keeper, and I just liked everything about him. It was his attitude, his demeanour, his approach and his temperament. He was good – and I knew he was good. He had a way of 'being there'. I liked the way he behaved in the group.

People say Stephen reinvented goalkeeping, particularly the kickout, but we had a certain kickout strategy as far back as 1995, basic and straightforward though it was. If you look at my first kickout in that 1995 final against Tyrone, I took it short to Keith Galvin and he nearly missed it! In those days, our wing-backs Paul Curran and Mick Deegan would walk in from their positions and if the forward didn't follow them, I'd pop it short; if the forward came with them, I'd knock it over them into space for Paul Clarke or Jim Gavin to run onto from wing-forward.

Cluxton is a phenomenal talent. He's going straight over the top with kickouts. He's going over the middle. He's hitting it over an opponent's head, dropping it in to someone in a little tight spot, areas you wouldn't usually see keepers try to use. He's like a golfer with a short iron, pitching onto a green.

Football is pretty simple: you get the ball, three steps, hop, keep going forward. What we see now is very different. The way they play the game is always evolving. Back in the 1979 minor final, Kevin Barry, an Erin's Isle man, handpassed the ball over the bar for the winning point and provoked the establishment of a rule where you weren't allowed score with a handpass for the next 10 years.

I like the way Dublin are currently motoring, but the juggernaut has to go on. They have been really good at their work since 2011, and now it'll be a new team of fellas in. We were very lucky with the skill we had within that 'golden generation' squad, but there is also a structure in place that allows the individual players to do what they want to do – which is probably not typically the case in a lot of other counties. So, you had a Brogan or a Flynn who were able to play to their strengths and express themselves, as they did over those five or six years.

We tend to get a bit of mud thrown at us in Dublin. Croke Park. Sponsors. Population. Whatever. My attitude was always, if you're hearing that, you're doing something right.

You just keep going, it's only chatter and it never bothered me when I played. Dublin got a fantastic secretary in the recently retired John Costello who put a lot of things in place within the county board, and they had guys like Jim Gavin come in and make the most of it. Everything else that's going on around us helps, absolutely. Dublin haven't hidden behind that. Pat Gilroy has come out and said that we have these structures in place and we went after it from a sponsorship point of view. Jim has said the same, and he said every county should do it. Is it the case that counties are not really looking inwardly, they're looking at it saying 'We can't compete with them' because of the perceived advantages? Look at yourself. It really all starts with yourself.

I'm the answer to a quiz question. Which former Dub played with the fathers of Jack McCaffrey (Noel), the Brogans (Bernard Snr), Con O'Callaghan (Maurice), James McCarthy (John) and, of course, Dean Rock (Barney)? Another old teammate, John Caffrey, has a daughter, Leah, starring for the Dublin ladies' side, who are regular All-Ireland winners themselves.

If I was to go about picking the best 15 from the players I played with and the current generation, I'd have some job on my hands. I more or less played with three generations of Dublin players. You'd have to think Brian Mullins and Brian Fenton would be in midfield. And the likes of Barney Rock and Kieran Duff would be in with a great shout. We'd have a problem at half-back trying to fit in Keith Barr, Jack McCaffrey, Paul Curran, Mick Deegan and James McCarthy, to name just a few. Then in the forwards you've got Anton O'Toole, Bobby Doyle, Paul Clarke. You'd have to look at someone like Ciarán Whelan, who played for ten years and never got an All-Ireland but had a brilliant Dublin career. Eamonn Heery was as tough as it gets at half-back but, like Ciarán, his time with the Dubs fell between the All-Ireland wins of 1983 and 1995. Tommy Carr was similar, as was Noel McCaffrey, who missed 1983 but played in losing finals in 1984 and 1985. Noel's son Jack and daughter Sarah have both gone on to win several All-Irelands between them. That's how it goes.

The one position that's easy to pick, believe it or not, is goalkeeper: it's Paddy Cullen. I was 13 years old when I saw Paddy save that penalty against Galway in the 1974 final. A real lump-in-the-throat moment, I'll never forget it. That's where it all started really. Jimmy Keaveney, Gay O'Driscoll, Anton O'Toole, all those guys. That 1970s squad carried us through 1983 and made the 1995 team. And so many of the 1995 guys moulded the 2011 team. The Dublin squads from 1974 to 2024 are inextricably linked. Inseparable. It all began with Heffo's Army.

That 1995 winning team has been particularly good at giving back and showing the way forward. Not just in terms of providing managers like

FOREWORD

Tommy, Pat, Jim and Dessie, but guys like Paul Clarke, Mick Deegan, Jason Sherlock and Mick Galvin have been around for a while. Declan Darcy was on the 1994 Leitrim team that we beat in the semi-final, and he, of course, went on to play with Dublin. He was alongside Jim for his seven years as manager. So that 1995 generation has been successful at keeping the legacy going.

It'll be interesting to see where the next leadership group is going to come from. It has to come from the 2011 team. That 2011 breakthrough win still feels so recent, but it's really a long time ago now. There's not many from the 1995 team left who are young enough to step into it. It's time to start pulling from that 2011 group and watching Dublin's legacy continue to grow. It's their turn.

How would I sum up this golden generation of players we've watched take the game to unprecedented heights over the last decade? They're simply a team I would've loved to have played with!

Up the Dubs.

John O'Leary

CHAPTER ONE

Day Zero
2014

Croke Park, Sunday, 31 August 2014: All-Ireland semi-final day. Defending champions Dublin lead 2012 winners Donegal by eight points to four. The game ebbs into the 24th minute. Dublin, in their second season playing under Jim Gavin's total football mandate, look irresistible. Donegal, with pragmatic master-motivator Jim McGuinness in the dugout, appear to be gasping for air.

Alan Brogan in possession, head up as always, eases down the right sideline and finds the cutting Cormac Costello, who takes off straight for the posts. The Whitehall Colmcille forward's instant-attack instinct has been a hallmark of his play since the first time he appeared in a blue jersey.

Gliding towards the Hill 16 goal, just inside the barrelling Costello, Diarmuid Connolly, as menacing as Steven Spielberg's shark in *Jaws*, eases ominously into the picture. Connolly already has two scores to his name at this point: the first, a nonchalant right-footed drive from 50 metres slightly right of the goal that shows outright disdain for

Donegal's much-vaunted blanket defence; the second, a simply stunning left-footed curler from under the Hogan Stand that even has Kevin McStay – who hands out compliments to the Dubs sparingly, at best – purring in the RTÉ studio.

Costello does what any sensible athlete should do when they notice the best player of their generation making a line towards goal beside them: he slips Connolly the football. The Hill leans forward in anticipation. Connolly feints left and checks back, allowing the last remaining defender to slide past. Turning onto his favoured right foot, he now has only the sizeable presence of Donegal keeper Paul 'Papa' Durcan left to negotiate.

In August 2014, if the goalkeeper then standing at the Canal End goal, Stephen Cluxton, was the undisputed best number 1 in the country, it's fair to say Durcan was 1A. Equally, in August 2014, if you needed a footballer to bury a gilt-edged goal chance in order to save your life, you were most likely dialling Connolly's number.

Connolly, in the form of his life, one on one with Durcan. A goal seemed inevitable. The Hill would explode. The Dubs would lead by seven. Donegal would need a bigger boat.

The St Vincent's man's effort, however, is scuffed. Durcan saves. Donegal clear. The shark's fin disappears beneath the gloom once more.

Four minutes later, Christy Toye – wearing number 10 on his back, having been named in the initial starting 15 – replaces Pat McGrath. Donegal, after surviving near death, begin to show a faint pulse.

A pair of Ryan McHugh goals – one just before and one just after half-time – turn the game on its head. Donegal, unthinkably, prevail.

The dastardly Dubs are vanquished. Dublin 0-17 Donegal 3-14.

This would prove to be one of the most influential sliding-doors moments in recent GAA history. The Ulstermen laid bare a chink in the swashbuckling Sky Blues' armour; a gaping tactical hole which Jim Gavin immediately set about filling.

Dublin would not lose a championship game again for 2,540 days …

* * *

'[The Dubs] had owned every team they met over the summer, and they appeared to be getting stronger with every game. You regularly heard the word "invincible" mentioned in radio discussions about them. It is a dangerous word, that …'

Jim McGuinness, *Until Victory Always*

This whole thing is Donegal's fault, ya know. Day Zero. Ground Zero. Dublin were demolished by a Donegal side they were supposed to overwhelm. Worse still, they'd conceded 3-14 while doing so.

On the face of it, a decade later, it's easy to look back at this semi-final – this result – and wonder what all the fuss was about. The tournament holders took on the champs of the previous year in the final four. Hardly a David-versus-the-other-fella situation, on paper at least.

But Dublin had arrived into Headquarters that Sunday afternoon on the back of a 2013 that saw them bring sexy football to a level we hadn't seen in years, if ever. In the spring of 2014, they took care of Cork with seven points to spare in the National League semi-final and demolished Derry in the final. Speaking about Stephen Cluxton, whose kickouts had largely dictated the game, then-Derry manager Brian McIver admitted afterwards, 'We thought we had our homework done. But he's the master.' Donegal, incidentally, had lost the Division 2 league final to Monaghan by six points.

Dublin simply consumed every team they faced in the 2014 Leinster Championship, scoring seven goals in three games as first Laois (2-21 to 0-16) then Wexford (2-25 to 1-12) and Meath (3-20 to 1-10) were humiliated. Next up, they devoured Monaghan in the All-Ireland quarter-final by 2-22 to 0-11 on the same day that Donegal edged Ulster rivals Armagh by 1-12 to 1-11 in their own last-eight clash. The Ulster pair's combined score on the day would have been just enough to pip the Dubs' total by a point.

So Dublin won their first National League since 1993 in Jim Gavin's first season and then stormed to All-Ireland glory that summer before successfully defending that league title with room to spare in 2014. In a championship preview in the *Irish Independent*, Vincent Hogan painted a stark picture: 'Nothing short of a falling comet would seem equipped to stop Dublin.' Handwringing became a national pastime – even more so than usual. Joe Duffy's phonelines were jampacked. (Probably.)

Nobody saw it coming. This beautifully timed Donegal ambush. Well, almost nobody.

Jim McGuinness probably did. And Brendan Devenney, the Donegal manager's old county teammate. In fact, he predicted it. The week before the quarter-finals, Devenney laid his cards on the table. 'Donegal would win, no doubt about it,' he told the *Irish Independent*'s Donnchadh Boyle when asked about the prospects of a Dublin/Donegal semi. 'When a tough defence meets a tough attack, it's easier to lock down a 45 than open it up. And this strength in depth that Dublin have – if their top six can't break the defence, the other lads coming in aren't going to have much joy. When there's players coming off the bench, it suits when a game is opening up. But with Donegal, it never does open up. There is a lot of hype. Donegal will be saying "we're going to stop your forward line".'

Paddy Andrews, a scoring substitute for Dublin on the day, saw the same problem in hindsight. 'Our philosophy under Jim … We won the All-Ireland in 2013 playing this really attacking style,' the St Brigid's man told a GAAgo podcast almost a decade later. 'As players, it was magic to play. We would go training, and training is 15 on 15. Go and play, beat your man. We loved it, absolutely loved it. We had this mentality that we were going to be the team to break the blanket defence. That was our north star … The reality was, Jim McGuinness and other teams were looking at us going, well Dublin play this way, we know they're going to attack … You get your feedback on the pitch. And we got it.'

All these years later, Devenney can look back at the dynamic between the two sides. 'Dublin were going full-gun attack. Jim Gavin was saying "this is how I play football and I'm going to stick to my principles" – which I love, I admired him for that. It wasn't in any way naïve because Dublin were coming up towards a level, as a team, that we'd never seen.

'Dublin, this huge force. Donegal, this brick that you have to break down. Now if the brick gets on top of the team that's going all-out attack, then they're going to wither and die. This brick, they're going to stick to their tactic because that's all they know. It's the same mantra, it's the same thing, over and over, it's drilled into them. Whereas Dublin are playing with a bit of spontaneity. They're trying to break this down. But if this [brick] gets on top of you, you're beat.

'That said, in the opening ten minutes of the game, Dublin nearly blew Donegal away. The famous [Connolly] goal chance. In my heart of hearts, nothing to do with being from Donegal, but I just thought tactically Donegal were going to stick to their game plan and if the game's tight, it's going to go against Dublin.'

The terror of those opening ten minutes was not lost on Jim McGuinness on the Donegal sideline either. His team had spent weeks preparing for this. He himself had had this game in mind for nine months. But nothing could ready a man for the blistering heat of a Dublin side that moved at a pace most county teams were unaccustomed to. Mike Tyson said something about everybody having a plan until they get a dig in the face.

'We played too deep for the first five minutes,' McGuinness wrote in his autobiography. 'I think it was because of the start that Dublin made and the power and the crowd and noise … It was a barrage and it was relentless. Dublin got their goal chance and Papa made a great save. If that had gone in, it would have been very difficult for us. And we went 0-9 to 0-4 down. Standing on the sideline, we were so disappointed. We felt that there was a possibility that we could implode here. Maybe this is a bridge too far. And if that happened, so be it. That's the game. That is why we play.'

'We got ahead of ourselves,' Paddy Andrews remembered. 'We weren't focused. We became everything that we hated in teams. We were ill-disciplined. We were arrogant. We didn't respect Donegal. We thought we were going to win that game comfortably.'

Andrews replaced Alan Brogan in the game and managed two points. But the damage was done. The Dubs may have handed back their crown that day, but they arguably took home something far more valuable than an All-Ireland final spot – the harshest of lessons learned.

'That game became the seminal moment for that group,' Andrews added. 'We didn't lose a championship match after that game for the next five years because of everything we took from it. It was just a massive lesson for everyone.'

Devenney again: 'I'd say Jim Gavin was fuming because, at the end of the day, the tactics of another manager had beaten this dream team of his. So he went back to the drawing board and ripped it up. And that's a huge question in the recent history of the GAA – what would have happened had Dublin beat Donegal? Or let's say they avoided a team like Donegal for a couple of years and were just playing the Mayos and Kerrys of this world, would they have kept playing this swashbuckling football? It would have changed everything about how they'd played in the following years … Gavin would have kept playing that way until something happened and you would have had such a different set of All-Irelands in those years.'

Those of a blue persuasion are at times convinced the rest of the island, shall we say, doesn't care all that much for them and their precious football team. 'Anyone but de Dubs', we're sure we hear them whisper – and occasionally shout. Just because they say you're paranoid doesn't mean they're not all out to get you. The increasing enmity towards Dublin in 2014 might not have been as pointed as some would have you believe, but it certainly wasn't all a figment of capital imaginations. The prospect of an unbeatable force in blue may have occasionally brought out the worst in some of our country cousins.

'It was a very absorbing game and in the mix of it, you have the whole "Dublin thing",' Devenney explained. 'I don't really get it, but there was this idea that Dublin were about to boss the All-Ireland and, for "wee Donegal", there was this David and Goliath thing attached to it because of the GAA monster that Dublin were about to become ... It was as if Donegal kind of put them back in their place, which is unfair. I'm not into that at all.'

The Dubs' boss, meanwhile, was in no doubt about what needed to be done and who, precisely, needed to do it. 'I accept full responsibility for that performance,' Jim Gavin said in the aftermath. 'One result won't change the core philosophy of how Dublin play football. But it's been a learning experience, that's for sure.'

Gavin wasn't the only member of the backroom team who took the defeat personally. His selector and former teammate Declan Darcy would later reveal, 'I put 3-14 on the inside of my locker – the score we conceded that day ... 3-14 on my laptop, 3-14 on my printer. Every day I woke up, it was on my locker. It grounded me. I knew when I had to go to work, I knew what was at stake. It definitely gave me huge motivation.'

In his *Irish Independent* column in April 2022, the retired-but-not-retiring Philly McMahon recalled, 'We stuck to our process in 2014 in the All-Ireland semi-final against Donegal. We pushed up on them even higher in the second half than the first, but they caught us out tactically. We were out-thought. In that case, the process failed us rather than the other way around. We had to rebuild our faith in that dynamic and we became more flexible. We worked on specific scenarios and formations within games. But they were just additional elements of the process, not deviations. We were finely drilled in all scenarios and knew exactly when to employ them. Every year, we'd just add stuff. No player was ever left wondering what he was supposed to be doing in a particular situation in a game. Nobody took the matter into their own hands and embarked on a heroic solo run.'

Newspaper columns and blogposts everywhere spoke of how Donegal had 'broken the unbeatable Dubs'. Jim Gavin was tasked with fixing them.

CHAPTER TWO

Back on Top 2015

2015 National League Division 1

Played 9, Won 6, Drew 1, Lost 2

Final position: League winners

The style of Dublin's dismissal of Cork in the league final on 26 April 2015 – and Jim Gavin's words afterwards – provide an insight into what had changed since September the previous year. 'To keep Cork to such a low score from play was satisfying for the defence,' Gavin said after the 1-21 to 2-7 win. 'And in attack, in the second half, to score 12 from 14 shots is a very good return for our forwards and probably a reflection of the work they are doing on the training field.'

It was the first hint of the efficient, streamlined, analytics-driven model we would bear witness to over the coming years. Dean Rock sent over 10 points, three from play, but the Man of the Match award went to Jack McCaffrey, who was about to embark on a Footballer of the Year season that would see him if not reinvent wing-back play, certainly take it to a whole new level.

The win/loss/draw columns may have looked identical, and the ultimate reward may have been the same, but the Dublin teams that secured National League titles in 2014 and 2015 were two very different entities altogether. Sure, the personnel hadn't changed in any serious way. The man at the helm of it all, Jim Gavin, was as particular, focused and driven as ever. But on the pitch, there was an innocence missing. The joie de vivre that had been there in 2013 and 2014 as the Dubs run-and-gunned their way up and down pitches all over the country had been replaced by a still-dashing but certainly more pragmatic approach. Donegal had stolen that innocence and in doing so, had done Dublin a massive favour.

Gavin made some key moves within his playing reserves, most notably shifting Cian O'Sullivan to the holding centre-back position that he would make his own. We also saw Dean Rock finally nail down the starting freetaker role. He burst onto the scene during the 2013 National League, coming off the bench in the final to kick two points from play as Dublin edged Tyrone 0-18 to 0-17 in a humdinger at Croke Park. Rock played in all five championship games during the 2014 campaign, but he started only the Leinster semi-final cakewalk against Wexford, a game in which he was upstaged by his half-time replacement, Cormac Costello, who came in and scored 1-5 from play.

By February 2015, however, Dean Rock was the man. He would go on to shatter Dublin scoring records over the next nine seasons, earning eight All-Ireland medals. Rock overtook the great Jimmy Keaveney as the capital's leading marksman in 2020 and kept on scoring right up until his final act, stroking over the game-sealing free of the 2023 All-Ireland final against Kerry.

Rock's career is a triumph of will and perseverance. 'I was dropped off the panel in 2010, then tore my hamstring off the bone in 2011,' he told RTÉ Sport's Des Cahill after announcing his retirement in January 2024. 'In 2012 I managed to come back and had a really strong campaign with the DCU Sigerson Cup team, and Pat [Gilroy] actually asked me up to the senior panel then. I got a few league games, but that summer he dropped me again … That was a really hard call to take.'

Rock led Ballymun Kickhams to Leinster Club glory in the winter of 2012, a ride that took them all the way to the All-Ireland Club final, where they would be edged out by Roscommon blue bloods St Brigid's by a single point, 2-11 to 2-10, on St Patrick's Day. But by then, his name had been made. He top-scored in that season's Club championship and the fact that his Ballymun manager was Jim Gavin's 1995 All-Ireland-winning teammate, Paul Curran, probably didn't hurt either. 'Jim got the [Dublin] job and it kind of snowballed ever since,' Rock said himself.

At the other end of the spectrum in 2015 was Alan Brogan. The Oliver Plunkett star had started all five championship games the previous year but been replaced in all of them. No shock. Brogan turned 33 in January of 2015 and had led the Dublin attack for over a decade. In what would turn out to be his final season in blue, he moved into the perfect impact-sub role, coming off the bench in all seven of Dublin's championship games before, as Rock would do eight years later, firing over the final point of the game in the All-Ireland final. Upon Rock's 2024 retirement, Brogan tweeted: 'I recall a 19-year-old Dean Rock coming to me after a [training] session asking what he could do to improve. Fair to say my advice obviously worked.' A pair that will go down in Blue history.

In the 2014 and 2015 league seasons, Dublin finished with the same record: played nine, won six, drew one, lost two. They added their tenth and eleventh National League titles with a convincing win over first Derry in 2014 (3-19 to 1-18) and the aforementioned 1-21 to 2-7 defeat of Cork a year later. But in many ways, that's where the comparison ends. In their seven group matches in 2014, Dublin hit opponents for nine goals and 99 points yet conceded 8-94 at the other end. In nine total games, they shipped 11 goals altogether. Just 12 months later, post-Donegal, Dublin scored 7-93 in their seven group games but conceded a mere 2-78. A score difference of +30, compared to the +8 of the year before. The Dubs' eight goals – including Diarmuid Connolly's strike in the final against Cork – would be spread fairly evenly, with only Bernard Brogan accounting for more than one. Jason Sherlock, the darling of 1995, had been brought in as forwards' coach. The two goals shipped against the Rebels in a league final which they still won comfortably doubled the amount they conceded in the whole competition. Dublin had tightened up. They wouldn't be caught with their pants down again. And if they weren't already, the rest of the country should have been gravely concerned.

***

Day 273: Sunday, 31 May 2015
Leinster quarter-final, Croke Park (attendance 33,544)
Dublin 4-25 Longford 0-10

It was summer in Leinster, and that meant one thing: the death knell for the provincial championship must be rung ad nauseum. The fans, it seemed, were voting with their feet.

It's hard to know where the Leinster Championship lost its way. Long gone were the classics of yesteryear which saw Meath, Dublin, Kildare, Offaly and Laois play out blood-and-guts battles in the days of the knockout, win-or-go-home All-Ireland structure. Dublin and Meath's breathless four-game saga of 1991 is often credited with reminding a now soccer-mad country, still drunk on the champagne of Italia '90, just how satiating the beer and chips of Gaelic games can be.

In 2002, a Dublin team which included Stephen Cluxton and Alan Brogan beat Kildare in a Leinster final classic to end a seven-year provincial famine under Tommy Lyons. Three years later, Tomás 'Mossy' Quinn slotted over two late-placed balls at the old stadium to hand Dublin a one-point win over Laois and a 45th provincial success, prompting a period of unparalleled dominance that not even the most romantic Dublin heart could see coming. Although the Dubs continued to win the province on an almost annual basis – Mick O'Dwyer led Laois to provincial glory in 2003, Westmeath won their only Leinster title in 2004 and Meath would 'Donegal' the Dubs in the 2010 semi-final – the deciders remained close-run, entertaining affairs. Until, that is, Jim Gavin's first-season Dubs saw off the Royal County 2-15 to 0-14 in 2013. After that, the competition seemed to fall off a cliff.

In 2015, Dublin were at their merciless best in their first championship encounter since the Donegal defeat. On the field, Bernard Brogan looked back to Player of the Year form. Writing in the *Irish Independent*, Colm Keys described the St Oliver Plunkett Eoghan Ruadh forward's display as his 'best since the 2013 All-Ireland final'.

Brogan helped himself to 1-6 from play. Dean Rock matched his output, while Jack McCaffrey wore out the whitewash on the wing and Stephen Cluxton's goal remained intact throughout. Tougher tests lay ahead, but every thousand-mile journey starts with a single step.

* * *

Day 301: Sunday, 28 June 2015
Leinster semi-final, Croke Park (attendance 50,324)
Dublin 5-18 Kildare 0-14

DUBLIN TURN ON POWER TO DEMOLISH LILYWHITES: 'Kildare obliterated as super-slick Dubs qualify for 10th Leinster final in 11 seasons.' The *Irish Independent* reached into its bag of war-time adjectives to convey the sheer devastation visited on Jason Ryan's shell-shocked Kildare troops at Headquarters.

Bernard Brogan and Diarmuid Connolly wreaked havoc in the Dubs' fluid inside forward line, accounting for 2-3 each; between them, the pair outscored the Lilywhites by four points. This game also saw a first championship start of the season for Cian O'Sullivan. If Dublin's big adjustment in reaction to the Donegal debacle looked simple on paper – stick a sweeper on the 45 and leave him there – it represented quite a diversion in the footballing philosophy of Jim Gavin. Sweepers were nothing new in Gaelic games in the summer of 2015. We'd come to expect them. In fact, at this point, we'd even been introduced to the dreaded double-sweeper, which would blight games up and down the country for years to come.

There are many who feel that the Gaelic football sweeper is a somewhat overrated title, a position that can make heroes of footballers who, in reality, are required to do very little other than mark space. However, Cian O'Sullivan – who'd started the Donegal defeat in midfield – would do more than anyone to convince those sceptics of the merits and intricacies of the holding half-back role. He would perfect that holding role and help marry Dublin's all-out-attacking instinct with a resilience and solidity that eventually created an indestructible GAA monster.

Since the retirement of the ironman Keith Barr many years before, successive Dublin managers had searched high and low for an adequate number 6. Bryan Cullen proved arguably the best of them, captaining Pat Gilroy's squad to that breakthrough title in 2011 – but, frustratingly for some, the Skerries Harps man didn't always man the defensive 45 for Dublin. In an era where the Boys in Blue were shorn of natural half-forwards, Cullen could more often be found in the 10, 11 or 12 shirt rather than the number 6. Indeed, on that beautiful day against

Kerry in 2011 when the dam finally burst ('McManamon dodging, McManamon scoringgg!'), Cullen was stationed at wing-forward with Ger Brennan manfully covering the centre-back position.

O'Sullivan's clubmate Jonny Magee, who himself anchored the Dubs' defence on many occasions in the early noughties, explained to the *Evening Herald*'s Niall Scully just what made O'Sullivan the quintessential modern anchorman. 'Cian is so good at reading the play, marking the space. Protecting the fullback line. He also has the speed and intelligence to drive forward and make the pass. He made the position his own. Other teams have tried to emulate it but not to the same degree. Cian has the ability to marshal everything around him.'

O'Sullivan himself addressed his role in an interview with Conor McKeon of the *Irish Independent* in 2017. 'You have a good standing point [at number 6] to see the opposition's transitions develop. And you're trying to assess, okay, what's the threat here? Are they gonna run the ball down the middle? In which case I may need to press out on a man and maybe get a tackle on him. Or are they going to dump a big high ball into a target man and the backline? In which case I might need to get a little bit closer to the guys in the fullback line, or a crossfield ball or whatever. So you're looking at the play evolve further out the pitch and trying to predict, okay, where's the ball going to end up? But I'm comfortable enough doing that job. I like doing that job.'

While commentators and pundits alike continued to ring the death knell of the Leinster Championship, Kildare veteran Paul Cribbin helped us trace the timeline of a competition that had gone from ultra-competitive to the monopolised domain of one county. 'I was probably quite naïve coming into the team in the early part of my career because in 2010, I left the senior panel and went to Australia to play AFL,' he recalled. 'Up until that point, I think in 2009 Kildare played Dublin in a Leinster final and there might have only been a couple of points in it [July 12, 2009: Dublin 2-15 Kildare 0-18]. So, when I left GAA, that's where Kildare and Dublin were at, they were very, very close. And then fast-forward to when I returned in 2013, we played Dublin in a semi-final and it was a completely different animal altogether.'

Our conversation with the experienced Cribbin took place a couple of short weeks before a 2023 Leinster semi-final in which Kildare almost caught Dublin napping. In hindsight, there were some clues that the Lilywhites were determined to make a point about Dublin's Croke Park logistical situation – having first made their point on the Croke Park pitch. 'They have a major advantage being able to play the majority of their home games in Croke Park,' Cribbin said plainly, without a hint of a whinge. It is what it is. 'Croke Park is different to other pitches, in terms of the dimensions. It's bigger than many of the other regional pitches you play in. The atmosphere fuels Dublin more than other counties because they outnumber them in support.'

* * *

Day 315: Sunday, 12 July 2015
Leinster final, Croke Park (attendance 49,840)
Dublin 2-13 Westmeath 0-6

Championship Really Starts Now After Leinster Farce. No, not a disgruntled Gael from down the country but Dublin legend Paul Curran writing in his *Herald* column.

Nobody either inside the camp or out was under any illusions that the demons of Donegal would be exorcised by July.

On the pitch, the insatiable Bernard Brogan kept his goal streak ticking along with a palmed finish from close range. Jack McCaffrey sprang forward for the other green flag while Man of the Match Diarmuid Connolly lit up an otherwise ho-hum occasion with three points from play as well as his trademark kickpassing. One particularly beautiful on-a-sixpence effort right onto Ciarán Kilkenny's lap from the St Vincent's forward shortly after the hour mark led to Dublin's 12th point.

Westmeath, unsurprisingly, set up in ultra-defensive mode and frustrated Dublin for large periods of the first half. John Heslin, the Lakemen's marquee forward who scored half of Westmeath's six points on the day, recalled a relentless Dublin squad. 'Coming up against the Dubs, we knew they were very strong. There was no doubt about it. We focused on curtailing them and we worked so hard at doing that in the first half.'

At half time, Westmeath were holding Dublin to their lowest points total of Jim Gavin's nine Leinster Championship games as manager, but the Dubs largely controlled the second period. Heslin puts that down to 'good management. They looked at the way the opposition were set up and – sure, ultimately, we set up the same in the second half – they had to make some small changes and they were back at us, you know?'

The Dubs cast a sizeable shadow over their provincial neighbours. If some teams felt they were beaten before they even got on the bus, it was easy to see why. The Dubs prepared for Westmeath the same way they prepared for Kerry or Mayo – by leaving nothing to chance.

Heslin: 'When we played the Dubs, we certainly weren't playing in awe of them, and our preparation wasn't to be in awe of the Dubs. But it felt as if Dublin gave everyone the attention to detail that they needed. They identified the weak spots in the opposition, and they prepared for them. In 2015, they adjusted to the way we played and came out and beat us. But the other thing to remember is the strength in depth they had. That if you did have an off day, that's okay. You're part of a team. Today is not your day. And the management changed things around and brought on other people, you know. It wasn't just up to a core 15 or a core 20. They had lads that they could just bring in and out and maybe play them today to suit a particular team.

'They weren't wanting for resources. Ultimately, that has to be significantly mentioned too. They wouldn't have won six All-Irelands in a row if they had the exact same people training Leitrim. If you think that's the truth, you know, you want to have a good look and talk to yourself.'

Post-Donegal, Dublin were morphing into a team that could take it any which way you gave it to them – and figure it all out on the move. The big blue machine rumbled on to the knockout stages.

* * *

Day 336: Sunday, 2 August 2015
All-Ireland quarter-final, Croke Park (attendance 58,680)
Dublin 2-23 Fermanagh 2-15

The test that Dublin supporters were waiting for arrived perhaps a round earlier than most would have envisioned. Fermanagh, with a late surge, gave Jim Gavin's side much to think about. The Dubs never looked like losing, but at least they got their hands dirty. Indeed, Stephen Cluxton's goal was breached for the first time that summer, not once but twice – by Sean Quigley and Thomas Corrigan.

'We've had adversity before and we never once bent the knee, buckled or rolled over for anyone, and we weren't going to roll over for Dublin today,' Fermanagh boss Pete McGrath declared afterwards.

The Fermanagh team had won over the hearts of supporters in their championship run that summer, and the day out in Dublin was the icing on the cake. May Fee of Enniskillen summed it up on the letters page of the *Fermanagh Herald*: 'What a fantastic day of human spirit exhibited by all members of the Fermanagh team. Moments of pure elation were afforded to a privileged audience of Fermanagh supporters. Lessons about mankind can be learned from this superb bunch of men and the cohort who manage them.'

Despite cameos from the likes of Alan Brogan, Kevin McManamon and the ready-to-fire Cormac Costello, Dublin's bench unusually failed to contribute a score. McManamon, in his defence, was instrumental in creating Dublin's late second goal. Bernard Brogan, too, was special. He finished with 1-6 from play, while his long-time running mate Paul

Flynn bagged the other goal. Jack McCaffrey's Connolly-like pinged pass for Brogan's green flag proved the highlight of the game.

Dublin had taken their spot in the All-Ireland final four, where Mayo (the small matter of overcoming Donegal aside) would eventually await. Fermanagh's late effort was a reminder that All-Irelands are never easily won.

* * *

Day 364: Sunday, 30 August 2015
All-Ireland semi-final, Croke Park (attendance 82,300)
Dublin 2-12 Mayo 1-15

Back in August 2014, after losing the All-Ireland semi-final replay to eventual champions Kerry, Mayo went into something of an off-pitch meltdown. James Horan stepped down as manager and was eventually succeeded by Pat Holmes and Noel Connelly. This came as something of a surprise to Kevin McStay, who thought he had the job despite sitting an interview where he felt he 'might have been too honest'. 'When I say the *interview*, it wasn't really an interview because I had the job, because I was the only candidate,' McStay later explained. 'Yet, 24 hours after that interview, one or two friends of mine in Mayo were able to tell me "You are not going to get that job". There were other people who were in the race but not saying it. That was very disappointing for me … Perhaps at the [interview], I said too much in terms of what my vision for the team was. That there might have to be some changes, and that was leaked to certain players. I would say that was an issue. It was a very difficult time for me personally. I had put all my hopes and dreams on [that job].'

Mayo began the 2015 National League on an upswing, with an eye-catching win in Killarney, 2-11 to 0-10, over the reigning-but-perhaps-still-recovering All-Ireland champions. That was arguably as good as it got for the springtime competition, however. They suffered a loss at home to Tyrone and were hammered 2-18 to 0-10 by those godforsaken Dubs in Castlebar a few days before Paddy's Day. Na Fianna stalwart Tomás Brady, something of a heavy ground specialist throughout several winter campaigns, would collect Man of the Match on that day after helping himself to three points from play. The goals came from Bernard Brogan, predictably, and Denis Bastick, not so predictably. Having won three of their first four league games, the Connacht men lost two and drew one of their last three to finish outside the top-four semi-final positions. As always, in Mayo, there seemed at least as many questions as answers.

McStay would finally be named Mayo boss in late August 2022. In between, a lot of water would flow under that red-and-green bridge.

Regardless of who was in the Mayo dug-out for this 2015 Championship semi-final, however, all the meaningful action was on the pitch – and it was thicker than a good gravy. When Jack McCaffrey slipped over a point at the Hill 16 end as the clock ticked towards the 61-minute mark to put Dublin seven points clear, a replay was the furthest thing from anyone's mind. We should have known better. There's rarely more than a hop of a ball between this pair. Dublin didn't score again, and, in the final quarter-hour of play, Mayo would question Stephen Cluxton's command of his kickout in a way no team had before. Colm Boyle dove desperately into a bunch of Dublin defenders to win a penalty – a decision that in the days of VAR (GAAR?) might well have been overturned. Cillian O'Connor converted. Fine margins. Andy Moran clipped over the equaliser, and, incredibly, it was Dublin hanging on at the end.

Denis Bastick replaced the black-carded Michael Darragh Macauley in the second half only to suffer a similar fate himself, eventually being replaced by Eric Lowndes. Bastick was very much a safe pair of midfield hands that helped see out many a game. On the day, his loss hurt Dublin in those crucial late stages when Mayo had gone into full nothing-to-lose mode.

Just before that McCaffrey point, super-sub Alan Brogan put Dublin 2-11 to 0-11 ahead with a beautiful score from near the left corner that prompted RTÉ's Dessie Dolan to exclaim, 'That's why the Brogan family are renowned in Dublin with a savage reputation', in a tone that sounded like the opening bar of a *Sunday World* crime podcast.

Bastick soared high to catch the kickout, was fouled, and immediately gave the ball to Philly McMahon, who found McCaffrey for the score. Dear ol' Dessie D was positively giddy now: 'It's so hard to nail [McCaffrey] down. His engine, his pace, a brilliant player having a brilliant season for Dublin.'

Colm Boyle never once waved a white towel in his Mayo career, and he drove forward here from centre-back to split the posts and make it a six-point game once again. The Connacht men clung to faint hope.

Moments later, one of Dublin's very best soldiers took on the kind of shot that was perfectly acceptable in 2015 but even just a few short years later seems almost out of place. James McCarthy won Cluxton's kickout after the Boyle score and was fouled. McMahon slightly over-hit the resulting free out wide to Paul Flynn in plenty of space, but tight to the Cusack Stand sideline. Flynn looked up and attempted to cut over a crowd-pleasing screamer from distance. A gift for the disciples of the Hill. It was a low percentage shot, however, well outside the 'scoring zone' we hear so much about in the modern era. The effort drifted harmlessly wide on the near side of the posts. Without wishing to beat a dead dog, it was a point attempt that, six points in the clear, you just don't see great players like Paul Flynn take now. These days, that ball is more likely to be worked back to the right-corner-back position than it is to be sent speculatively towards goal with the outside of a boot.

Flynn's wide 'may not matter at this stage of the match', suggested Darragh Maloney, beside Dolan in the RTÉ commentary booth. Oh, how we wished you were right, Darragh. Mayo's Keith Higgins – like Boyle, a player who took much punishment from Dublin over the years and spat back at it every time – collected the kickout and worked the ball through Lee Keegan and Aidan O'Shea before finding himself in scoring territory. Higgins didn't need a second invitation. The lead was now five, in the 64th minute. Then, near disaster. Cluxton dallied in possession, Andy Moran picked his pocket and looked sure to goal. John

Small brilliantly saved on the line, forcing the ball onto the post. The Dubs' backline was still afloat but taking on water. Cillian O'Connor shot wide. Mayo sent in Barry Moran to midfield who immediately won the Cluxton kickout and tangled with Bastick, leading to the Templeogue Synge Street player's black card. A minute later, another sub, Alan Freeman, cleaned up after Cluxton boxed Tom Parsons' point attempt clear. Dublin 2-12, Mayo 0-14.

Next, the penalty. Boyle went down; referee Joe McQuillan obliged; O'Connor converted. The Dubs clung to that one-point lead. Cluxton, inexplicably and uncharacteristically, struck his next kickout straight to Kevin McLoughlin. The ball was worked through O'Shea and O'Connor before Moran's equaliser.

Cluxton pushed a difficult late free wide at the Hill 16 end. Diarmuid Connolly saw red after a tussle with Lee Keegan. Aidan O'Shea claimed after the game that he had been head-butted by a Dublin player. 'Yeah, I was head-butted alright,' O'Shea stated, 'but, sure, that is not for me to enforce the rules of the game but there was plenty more things out there that the referee [Joe McQuillan] missed too ... I thought it was a good competitive game out there with some good one-on-one combat. I thought [McQuillan] had a good game for the most part. You are not going to get everything right.'

The final 10 minutes of the game were a snapshot of everything we love about these two rivals. Dublin were imperious for the first hour's play. Mayo were dead. We were sure of it this time. Dead as dead can be. They wouldn't suddenly sit bolt upright, Michael Myers style, for one final scare this time around. And yet, Mayo rose again. As the game ticked into injury time and their defensive structure fell apart, we were treated to another couple of examples of this Dublin team's enduring greatness. A greatness that, in moments of stress, can be held together by nothing more than stubbornness and survival instinct. A further reminder that, if you wanted to stand on Dublin's block, you were absolutely going to have to kill each and every one of them first.

In the 71st minute, with Mayo rampaging forward looking for a winner, Alan Freeman drove hard for a loose ball inside Dublin's half. Philly McMahon drove harder. A ferocious tackle with little regard for his own safety. The ball broke to Mayo, Andy Moran fed Mickey Sweeney, who attempted a left-footed point only to be blocked down by the seemingly beaten James McCarthy. Dublin ball. They had taken Mayo's best. And Mayo theirs. Dublin had almost completely fallen apart in 15 barmy minutes. But yet again, they survived. Barely.

The replay was set for the following Saturday. Provided we'd all caught our breath by then.

* * *

Day 370: Saturday, 5 September 2015
All-Ireland semi-final replay, Croke Park (attendance 81,897)
Dublin 3-15 Mayo 1-14

Even a Dub as biased as this one knows that what transpired on this warm Saturday afternoon on the pitch was coloured by that most curious of Irish sporting oddities – the GAA disciplinary process. Where no referee's report is safe, and just about any indiscretion can be made to go away.

Following his late wrestle with Lee Keegan six days earlier, which resulted in a straight red card, Diarmuid Connolly received a dramatic reprieve in the early hours of Saturday morning and duly took up his position at centre-forward in the number 18 jersey that evening. Connolly's red in the first game came for a 'strike' on his arch nemesis, Keegan. What followed was a week of to-ing and fro-ing among the GAA's alphabet soup of disciplinary committees before the Disputes Resolution Authority (DRA) cleared the Dublin star at 2.30am, mere hours before the replay.

In the previous year's All-Ireland semi-final, Keegan had been on the other end of an appeal after his red card in the drawn game with Kerry was overturned, allowing him to suit up for the replay. This time around, Connolly failed in appeals to the – wait for it – Central Hearings Committee (CHC) and Central Appeals Committee (CAC) before finally finding a sympathetic audience with the aforementioned DRA.

Speaking on RTÉ radio, GAA president Aogan Ó Fearghail commented: 'Some people say our systems are fair, some say they are too fair, some say they are unfair. Our system mirrors the justice system. We have a referee that makes the decision on the day. We have what we call a Competitions Control Committee. They look at the evidence and they apportion a penalty based on the rule book.

'Most players and most members accept the penalty at this stage, but if the player seeks a hearing, then they have a hearing. A hearing is actually like it says – it is like a court … In the interests of fairness and being fair to everyone, there is that further level that people can then appeal again. Not many get to that stage, some do, and they have an opportunity to appeal. The Disputes Resolution Authority, which is completely independent of the GAA. It's a legal body and we don't have that many getting to that level.'

When the debris finally cleared and we got back to the merciful comforts of the Croke Park pitch, Mayo picked up where they left off the previous Sunday and looked the better side for large swathes of the opening half. Charging wing-back Paddy Durcan lofted over a fine score in the 53rd minute to give the Connacht men a four-point cushion. But then Mayo blinked. Dublin would outscore them 3-4 to 0-2 in the final 20-odd minutes of play. The cavalry of Alan Brogan, McManamon and Macauley charged from the trenches. Mayo's cough was duly softened.

Here we saw perhaps Paddy Andrews's finest hour in a blue shirt. The St Brigid's forward found five points from play, most of them from acute angles. Bernard Brogan goaled, as did Philly McMahon (who accounted for 1-2 despite the number 4 on his back) before McManamon, the most super of subs, iced the cake with a 1-1 cameo.

Dublin found themselves just one game away from regaining the throne they had abdicated so spectacularly almost a year before. And the team standing in their way? Kerry, of course. Who else …

* * *

Day 385: Sunday, 20 September 2015
All-Ireland final, Croke Park (attendance 82,300)
Dublin 0-12 Kerry 0-9

The dying embers of the decider. Kerry need a goal. On a soaking wet day at Headquarters, they've resorted to the agricultural. Kieran Donaghy has been summoned from the bench. The ball is being sent in early and often. It doesn't quite have snow on it, but it's wetter than an otter's pocket.

This Dublin backline has seen it all before. At this stage of his career, Donaghy – perhaps somewhat unfairly, in hindsight – seems little more than a nuisance for hire. The pantomime villain. Donaghy's career is a study in resourcefulness. He first came to our attention as a member of the TG4 Underdogs squad and enjoyed many fine seasons with the most successful football county in all the land. He arguably swung the previous year's All-Ireland final for the Kingdom, when he gave us one of the greatest post-match lines of all time: 'What d'ya think of that, Joe Brolly?!' Then RTÉ pundit Brolly had been less than complimentary about Donaghy earlier in the season, labelling the Kerryman a 'two-year wonder' and suggesting he should drop his long-time 'Star' nickname. Dear ol' Joe had also claimed early in 2014 that Kerry's famed production line of talent was 'drying up'. The Kingdom would go on to win the next five All-Ireland minor titles, finish runners-up in 2020, and produce in David Clifford a player who was already being compared to the game's all-time greats before he was in his 25th year. Zero out of two for Joe on that count.

Donaghy, of course, is also an excellent basketball player and married his love of hoops alongside his football career throughout his time in the GAA spotlight. When the 6'6" midfielder moved into the edge of the opposition square sometime around the mid-noughties, Gaelic football briefly lost its mind. All of a sudden every football team wanted a giant full-forward. There was only one way to play football now, apparently, and you needed a mammoth target man to pull it off.

For the 2015 Dubs, however, spotting the rangy forward head for the edge of the square no longer prompted panic. If anything, it now appeared more of an admission that the vaunted Kingdom were out of ideas. Donaghy once famously described himself as 'the fiver Kerry keep finding in their arse pocket'. The Dubs kept that pearl diver folded neatly in their fitted chinos on this occasion.

As Dublin repelled a late Kerry attack at the Canal End, leaving Donaghy crumpled on the ground, James McCarthy popped the ball out to substitute Alan Brogan, moving towards the left-half-back position. There may not have been a Dub – past or present – whom you'd want more with ball in hand to see out an All-Ireland final than Bernard's big brother.

It was his first possession since replacing Brian Fenton. He looked up and, spotting a chap he knew well, popped the ball into Bernard's path along the left sideline, halfway up the pitch. Alan, of course, kept moving forward.

Bernard slipped the ball quickly back to his brother, who was now making a beeline for Hill 16, Diarmuid Connolly riding shotgun. Alan eased inside the 45, Connolly slipped to his left. Alan looked to pass to the Vincent's man but didn't. He looked again to offload but didn't. Instead, the 2011 Footballer of the Year steadied himself, remembered to solo after a risky number of steps, dropped his shoulder and bent over the title-clinching score with more or less his final act as a Dublin footballer.

Perfection.

We remembered his tears on the pitch after Donegal the previous year. We feared we'd seen the last of him in blue.

Kingdom marksman Paul Geaney, who made way for Donaghy despite notching two points from play, stated afterwards that the Munster champions' forwards had 'malfunctioned'. Not quite startled earwigs, but this was now a unit whose number Dublin well and truly had.

Éamonn Fitzmaurice, too, admitted his side were 'out-thought, out-worked and outfought'. Fitzmaurice, admirably, was never a man to use 10 words where three will do.

Dublin would command seven spots on that year's All Star selection, among them Rory O'Carroll, who stepped away from the panel that winter at the age of 26 and took off for Auckland. It would be a while before we'd see the Kilmacud Crokes stopper again, but see him again we would. Cian O'Sullivan, in his first season operating within that libero role that helped shore up the Dubs' rearguard, was also named an All Star, as were Philly McMahon, Footballer of the Year Jack McCaffrey, Brian Fenton, Ciarán Kilkenny and Bernard Brogan.

For his part, Jim Gavin was reluctant to draw comparison between this side and the great Dublin teams of the 1970s, Heffo, Hickey, Hanahoe, Keaveney et al. 'Nothing will ever match Kevin Heffernan's team and what he did for Dublin GAA. His spark and genius, we just stand on their shoulders, really. Dublin football wouldn't be where it is today but for those teams. They got the city alive to Gaelic football, so I don't think we'll ever compare to those giants of the game.'

Give it time, Jim. Give it time.

CHAPTER THREE

Mayo Mayhem 2016

From 2011 to 2023, this generation of Dublin players won nine All-Ireland SFC titles in a 13-season span. Of course, the story begins long before then and will continue to run until we're all long gone. But it's fair to say this particular squad were never better for a sustained period than they were for the run covering the 2016 and 2017 seasons. An era within an era.

If it's possible to select the peak of this squad's greatness, we should start looking around the National League campaign of 2016 and maybe draw a line under it sometime around [spoiler alert] Dean Rock's All-Ireland-winning free in the 2017 Championship final. Dublin had found that sweet spot of exhilarating attacking play coupled with a frugality in defence that was positively miserly. Earlier guises of that same squad were arguably weighted too much toward the front foot – hence, Donegal 2014 – and later editions of the Boys in Blue were a far more pragmatic proposition altogether. Masters of the analytics. They chess-moved you into submission. But for about an 18-month period between early 2016 and late 2017, Jim Gavin's Dublin occupied footballing nirvana. A higher plane. A stratosphere where mere mortals had never previously tread.

2016 National League Division 1
Played 9, Won 9, Drew 0, Lost 0
Final position: League winners

Having outlasted Kerry in the rain to close out 2015, Dublin wintered well and hit the ground running at the end of the following January. Kerry were the first opponents in the 2016 National League. It was a decisive win for the Dubs, 2-14 to 0-14, Paddy Andrews and Diarmuid Connolly with the goals.

There was a noticeable absence from the Dublin squad that evening. After a stellar career in blue, Alan Brogan hung up his boots back in the autumn. As he outlined in his *Sunday Independent* column that summer, 'Playing with Dublin gave me a great purpose in life. I gave it everything I had, maybe got obsessive at times, but that is what is required to deliver All-Ireland medals. They don't come easy, they don't come without sacrifice. That's what made it all worthwhile.'

Everything he had – and then some. One of the great Gaelic games careers.

As well as Brogan's departure, Rory O'Carroll, as previously mentioned, was off in New Zealand, and reigning Footballer of the Year Jack McCaffrey was also missing for much of 2016. The flying wingback was pivoting to flying doctor, as his medical training took him around Africa. McCaffrey replaced Davy Byrne against Kerry on League opening night; he replaced the black-carded Philly McMahon (not like you, Philly!) early on against Mayo a week later; and he captained UCD to their first Sigerson Cup title in 20 years when they beat DCU in Belfast. That was largely the extent of his football pursuits in the first half of 2016.

That star-studded UCD team for the Sigerson final included McCaffrey's fellow Dubs David Byrne, Conor Mullally, Michael Fitzsimons, Robbie McDaid, Colm Basquel and Paul Mannion among their starting line-up. Also featured in the forward unit was the eventual Man of the Match, John Heslin of Westmeath. Heslin, who kicked six points in the decider, recounts a telling tale around that famous win. 'We won the Sigerson in 2016, and I'd be good pals with Jack. I'd be good pals with all the lads, as naturally as you would. Jack and I rendezvoused the day after, and I'll never forget, his phone was hopping from the lads he was playing with in Dublin who were training that morning. It was the first time in 20 years UCD had won it, and he was captain!

'But the very next day, he had four or five calls off the Dublin team asking him why the hell wasn't he at training. And this was in February! But that was the drive, and it was the older players, I don't even think management rang. They weren't ringing him having a go. They were saying, "What's the story here? Can we count on you?"'

McCaffrey's football-free plans for 2016 were confirmed on the first week of March, with manager Gavin commenting at the time: 'At the moment, Jack won't be with us for championship. He's a fourth-year medical student in UCD. Jack will be heading off to Africa to get some volunteer work in a hospital there for the summer and then doing some travelling afterwards.

'He's 23 years of age, he's got his life ahead of him. We'd like to have Jack around, but my concentration now is the players that I have and trying to get a performance against Down [in league action] next week. I've worked with Jack since U-21s, so we know each other very well. I understand the type of man that he is. He put a lot of consideration into his decision. We fully respect that and fully support him.'

Despite the loss of the key trio of Brogan Snr, O'Carroll and McCaffrey, the Dublin dynasty was about to embark on its most dominant period yet.

Having opened their league campaign with that six-point win over Kerry in January, Dublin closed it in even more emphatic fashion, decimating the Kingdom by 2-18 to 0-13 in the league final in April. Paul Flynn and Eric Lowndes raised green flags for the Dubs, while the lopsided final score raised a few eyebrows around the country. If Dublin could do this to Kerry …

On the way to that fourth straight league title, their twelfth overall, the Dubs had blitzed all before them, winning seven games out of seven in the group stage, plus the semi-final and final. Nine teams up, nine teams down. The perfect league campaign. They scored 11 goals and 129 points throughout the season, semis and final included, and conceded 4-101 for a staggering difference of +49. They continued to score in bunches while at the same time finding a way to stop you playing. They spread the goals around too. Only Diarmuid Connolly, with three, would account for more than one of those 11; defenders Philly

McMahon, James McCarthy and Eric Lowndes all found the net. You didn't know where the threat was coming from.

In the *Irish Independent* the day after the league final, Colm Keys pinpointed Dublin's plainly superior athleticism. 'When a list of the Dublin backroom team members was circulated in 2013, one title stood out above the rest. The now departed Martin Kennedy was the "athletic" coach. Not strength and conditioning, the label most of his peers go by. Not physical trainer … The emphasis was on "athleticism". You couldn't help drawing on the provision of that title as Dublin ran the clock in this final to the backdrop of cheers each time a player in blue took possession.'

Of the possible challengers to Dublin's supremacy, there were no surprises. Despite recent one-sided form when the two ancient rivals met, Kerry players were still getting dressed every morning thinking only of Celtic crosses. Mickey Harte was reshaping what turned out to be the final incarnation of his Tyrone team to push back towards the top of the mountain as the 2010s faded out. Mayo's joint-management duo of Pat Holmes and Noel Connelly had succumbed to pressure from the very people who had influenced their appointment a year earlier – their own players – and resigned. 'By resigning, we wish to remove any obstacle that the players might perceive as preventing them from winning the All-Ireland,' the departing pair's joint statement read. Replacing them was the eminently likeable Stephen Rochford. The behind-the-scenes goings-on in Mayo may have prompted the odd stifled grin from a smug Dub, but the only thing that really mattered as we stretched toward summer 2016 was the knowledge that Mayo could arrive in Croke Park on any given day aboard a bus with a flat tyre and with no arse in their trousers and still put Jim Gavin's men to the pin of their collar. They knew it. Dublin knew it. Everybody knew it.

* * *

Day 643: Sunday, 4 June 2016
Leinster quarter-final, Nowlan Park (attendance 16,754)
Dublin 2-21 Laois 2-10

And so we found ourselves in the home of hurling (Leinster branch), Nowlan Park, for a Leinster football quarter-final between Dublin and Laois that lasted all of about 15 seconds. Dean Rock rattled the net shortly after throw-in and that, as they say, was that.

Laois had let their feelings be known the previous November when the venue was first suggested. They drew Wicklow in the first round, with the winner going on to meet Dublin somewhere other than GAA Headquarters. Laois felt strongly that it should be their own O'Moore Park, which has 6,200 seats and an 18,000 capacity. The plea fell on deaf ears at GAA fixture committee level, who felt that Nowlan Park, with 17,000 seats and a 25,000 capacity, was more appropriate.

The Laois County Board bridled. 'We were told in 2014 that in the event of Laois drawing with Dublin in the Leinster quarter-final, the replay would be in Portlaoise,' county secretary Niall Handy argued. 'Why should there be any difference if a decision is taken to take Dublin out of Croke Park now?' When the trip to Kilkenny was confirmed, Laois chairman Gerry Kavanagh labelled the decision 'inexplicable' and a 'slap in the face' to his county. 'We're disappointed. We couldn't put into words how we feel about it,' he said.

After the game, Laois boss Mick Lillis also let his feelings be known. 'Yes, it was very heavily weighted towards Dublin, but that's not surprising,' he said, according to Rory Delaney in the *Leinster Express*. 'A lot of Laois people didn't travel, and it was more in protest than anything else, and I can understand why. I'm not going to go down that road again, but the Leinster Council got it seriously wrong, and I just hope they learn from it.'

Rock ended his day's work with 1-10 chalked beside his name. Diarmuid Connolly – fittingly, as the son of a Kilkenny man – took home a goal and four points, and there was a first championship sighting (and first score) of a young forward from Cuala named Con O'Callaghan.

Despite his tender years, O'Callaghan had long been the great white hope of Dublin football. It's not like Dublin had been waiting for O'Callaghan to come along and transform them – after all, the starting forward unit against Laois included Kilkenny, McManamon, Connolly, Mannion, Rock and Brogan; that line-up will generally get it done – but this young dual star from Dalkey promised to be the equal of all of the above. Maybe even better than that.

***

Day 665: Sunday, 26 June 2016
Leinster semi-final, Croke Park (attendance 42,259)
Dublin 0-21 Meath 0-11

On a weekend where the championship competed for headlines with Ireland's Euro 2016 exit at the hands of hosts France, it's fair to say the prospects of an inevitably one-sided Leinster semi-final at Croker did not set pulses racing.

In the end, Dean Rock almost matched Meath by himself. He again reached double figures in the points column, notching 0-10, all but one coming from placed balls. Man of the Match Connolly added four points, Bernard Brogan three. There was also a very late cameo from Con O'Callaghan as he replaced Paul Flynn in the 67th minute. Dubs fans may not have been sure what 'it' was, but we were still seeking confirmation that Con O'Callaghan had 'it'.

DIFFICULT TO BE OPTIMISTIC AFTER DUBLIN DEBACLE ran the headline above Fergal Lynch's match report in the *Meath Chronicle* afterwards. Two weeks later, the struggling Royals would go down by three points to Derry in Dungiven, and that would be that for 2016. As Dublin ascended, their old rivals were in a clear, seemingly irrevocable freefall.

Dublin were, by now, leaving no stone unturned in their quest for an edge. Many members of the squad had for some time been practising yoga, as much to look after the minds as the bodies. Eoghan O'Gara, Templeogue's hardy throwback full-forward, reckoned yoga 'aided me hugely in terms of injury prevention and mobility improvement. I also found the breathing techniques very helpful for concentration and focus before and during training and match days.' Michael Darragh Macauley went as far as to qualify as a yoga instructor. The Dubs were insatiable in their search for that extra one per cent.

Not only did they possess some of the most gifted footballers to ever play the game, Dublin's physicality and fitness levels during this era were as elite as it gets. Suffice to say, it didn't all come from yoga, Pilates and positive reinforcement from the coaching staff. No doubt this group put the work in and suffered plenty on the training pitch. And what they sowed, they duly reaped.

* * *

Day 686: Sunday, 17 July 2016
Leinster final, Croke Park (attendance 38,855)
Dublin 2-19 Westmeath 0-10

The Six in a Row. Well, the first one. Dublin secured another Leinster crown with a dismantling of Westmeath.

Rock – perhaps stung by an off-colour performance in the previous year's All-Ireland semi-final replay against Mayo – began this latest championship season on a tear. He added another eight points here. The greatest freetaker we've ever seen. The inside-forward line of McManamon (1-2), Rock (0-8) and Brogan (1-4) accounted for 2-14. An embarrassment of riches.

That same afternoon, Tyrone and Donegal battered each other almost to a standstill (Tyrone 0-13, Donegal 0-11) in Clones in the

Ulster final. There's little doubt Tyrone were beginning to re-emerge as legitimate contenders for the big prizes. Three-time All-Ireland winning boss Mickey Harte had labelled this latest provincial success as his 'best Ulster title of all' and the county's favourite son, Peter 'the Great' Canavan, was feeling bullish in his Monday morning *Indo* column: 'How far can Tyrone go this year? It's impossible to predict at this stage, but I have no doubt that they are now in the Kerry bracket – in that they are capable of giving the Dubs a run for their money in Croke Park.'

Speaking of Kerry, they had wrapped up Munster by the third day of July, blitzing Tipperary in the provincial final, 3-17 to 2-10. Out west, having accounted for Mayo in the semi-final, Galway were in amongst the goals when they hammered Roscommon in the Connacht final replay, 3-16 to 0-14, at MacHale Park. Roscommon had slipped four goals past Sligo in their own semi, 4-16 to 2-13 the final tally. The first edition of that year's Connacht decider was a cagier affair, with Enda Smith's goal for Roscommon crucial as the sides finished level at 0-13 to 1-10.

Back in Leinster, Dublin had led by just a point at the break in their own decider. Westmeath's plan to get Diarmuid Connolly 'excited', as their manager Tom Cribbin put it, saw a large bout of handbags break out on the half-hour mark.

At half-time, Jim Gavin and crew went to work. Paddy Andrews came in for Eric Lowndes, six forwards became seven, and the Dubs blitzed the Lakemen from the second half's opening ball. Dublin won the second half by 24 points.

'From a Westmeath perspective, in 2015 and 2016, we got the two Leinster finals and that team we had, we were playing our best if you like,' Westmeath forward John Heslin recalled. 'Westmeath have only ever won one Leinster, right? And this team that I was part of got to two Leinster finals back to back. Now nobody celebrates that, but for us and where we came from and even that team, that was something. From a Westmeath perspective, we came up against the Dubs in our province. Any other era, we could have potentially left with one Leinster Championship, you know.

'That Dubs team is probably one of the best teams to ever play the game. But ultimately for us to beat that Dublin team, we would have had to play beyond our absolute best and the Dubs to have an off day. And that off day for that Dublin team didn't really happen too often.'

Round by the back door, Mayo were retooling through the qualifiers, beginning with a 2-14 to 1-12 defeat of Fermanagh in MacHale Park, moving through Kildare by nine points a week later at the same venue before hammering Westmeath 3-15 to 1-14 at Croke Park to set up an All-Ireland quarter-final with the aforementioned Tyrone in early August.

At this point, Dublin faced a familiar problem, one which prompts zero sympathy outside the Pale – and nor should it. On the back of their provincial cakewalk, were the Dubs heading into the knockout stages undercooked? Were they primed for ambush by a Donegal, Tyrone or – heaven forbid – Mayo? The rest of the country wasn't losing sleep. And it's most likely Jim Gavin wasn't either.

* * *

Day 706: Saturday, 6 August 2016
All-Ireland quarter-final, Croke Park (attendance 82,300)
Dublin 1-15 Donegal 1-10

Ah, it's yourselves ... It might have come three weeks too late for Westmeath, but here we certainly did see an 'excited' Diarmuid Connolly – and not in a good way. The St Vincent's man was sent off for two bookable offences, while substitute Eoghan O'Gara was hit with a straight red after a clash with Donegal full-back Neil McGee, who received just a yellow for his part. Brian Fenton also received a late black card.

'They weren't quite "the Dirty Dozen" of 1983. But Dublin won this All-Ireland quarter-final with 12 men on the pitch at the end of it all,' explained John Brennan in his *Sunday World* match report.

We hadn't come across Donegal in championship fare since that infamous semi-final 700-odd days ago. It turned out ambushing Dublin was more or less the final achievement of Jim McGuinness's first stint as Donegal manager. He would leave the post after the 2014 All-Ireland final defeat to Kerry and embark on a coaching odyssey that took him to Glasgow Celtic and Beijing Sinobo Guoan, as well as a stint with Charlotte Independence, who play in USL One, the third tier of American soccerball. In October 2014, McGuinness was replaced by Rory Gallagher, who served under him as selector from 2011 to 2013.

Gallagher's two seasons in the hotseat thus far had resulted in a pair of Ulster final losses, with the 2016 defeat to Tyrone preceded by a reversal at the hands of Monaghan a year earlier. It now also showed two All-Ireland quarter-final defeats to match, having been knocked out by Mayo in Gallagher's first season and now Dublin a year later.

On the pitch, as Dublin survived disciplinary woes to see off the Ulstermen, Dean Rock added to his haul with five points, and Connolly fired over a pair of beauts – one off either foot – from distance in the first half ('You just can't beat class,' purred Marty Morrissey from the RTÉ commentary booth) before his early exit. Ironically, the first meaningful action of the game saw Connolly again thwarted by a Donegal goalkeeper (this time, Mark Anthony McGinley) in a one-on-one goal situation at the Hill 16 end. He'd pull a similar opportunity wide later in the half. There was even another Ryan McHugh goal, if you were feeling particularly nostalgic. Thankfully, it all worked out in the end this time around.

Meanwhile, it was the turn of Paul Mannion to provide the firepower off the bench, grabbing 1-1 having replaced Paddy Andrews with 15 minutes to play. The Kilmacud forward's goal was worth the hefty ticket price alone. His side down to 13, Mannion picked the ball up along the left sideline 60 yards from goal and simply took off, Archie Gemmill-style (ask your da), slaloming past desperate defenders before finally slotting a crisp finish past McGinley. Mustard.

After the match, Gavin complained about the 'special attention' his players received. 'We all knew that would happen,' Gavin stated. 'That some of our players would receive special attention and that was the case and it's up to officials to act on it and if they don't? Eight of them, four umpires and the four men in black ... They're letting the players down on the pitch on both sides, by the way.'

Bernard Brogan was held scoreless and replaced by utility man (and future Dubs selector) Darren Daly after just 48 minutes of play. With mostly the imposing presence of Neil McGee for company, it was as quiet a day in a blue jersey as we had seen in a big championship game for the 2010 Footballer of the Year.

* * *

Day 728: Sunday, 28 August 2016
All-Ireland semi-final, Croke Park (attendance 82,300)
Dublin 0-22 Kerry 2-14

Dublin enjoyed three big wins over Kerry in succession from September 2015 to April 2016. Needless to say, Kerry declined the opportunity to run and find a safe space to hide. Self-pity is not something you'll find on any playing pitch from Killarney to Cahersiveen. Four months after that league final mauling, Dublin and Kerry would play out their latest All-Ireland SFC classic. It would prove a breathtaking match for the ages. Of course it would.

There were few things more terrifying to an opposition fan than the sight of Colm Cooper with a football in his hands and his head looking up. Something beautiful but ultimately heartbreaking usually followed. Remember Semple Stadium in 2001, when Maurice Fitzgerald arced over a piece of art from the sideline to force a replay, even with Dubs boss Tommy Carr marking him tightly? Every game against Cooper felt that way. You were sick of him. But f**king hell, you could watch him all day. For Dub fans, Cooper invoked that strangest of feelings. When you came up against him, you hoped dearly the ball would never come his way – but at the same time, a part of you wanted him in possession just to see what he might do. Much as you tried to hate him, you probably loved him just a little bit.

In 2009, no one startled Dublin's earwigs more than the Gooch. In the odyssey of 2013, Cooper pulled every string he could get his hands on as the old rivals traded blows, *Rocky*-style, until the final bell. At Croke Park this time around, the Kingdom played with guts and desperation, many of them knowing in their bones they were rolling the dice for a final time. Dublin, for their part, operated with the knowledge that nothing can be taken for granted when it comes to the green and gold.

Paul Flynn and a then 32-year-old Bernard Brogan still played the game better than most. But with a decade's miles on their inter-county clock, both men knew the finish line was in sight. Brogan, still as cute as ever, snaffled a pair of vital scores against the Kingdom. But the St Oliver Plunkett Eoghan Ruadh forward's influence on this Dublin attack was lessening with each passing game.

It's the most natural thing in all of sport – nobody can outrun the clock. And the time was arriving when Brogan's place in the full-forward line was no longer signed, sealed and delivered. With older brother Alan's retirement after the previous year's All-Ireland win, we would soon be watching a Brogan-less Dublin team for the first time since forever.

Gooch suffered a serious cruciate ligament injury in the 2014 All-

Ireland Club semi-final. Then the wrong side of 30, we wondered if we'd seen the last of Gaelic football's great jazz artist. The performer who never played the same note twice.

Cooper would call time on his storied inter-county career shortly after this 2016 semi-final. Bernard endured for three more seasons. Two of the greatest to ever own a pair of boots. Magic.

On the pitch, Dean Rock accounted for no less than a dozen points. Diarmuid Connolly bagged a hat-trick of scores, and Kevin McManamon, enjoying an extended run in the starting 15, added a pair along with a rolling-back-the-years Brogan double.

Gooch nicked five points of his own for the Kingdom, Paul Geaney had 1-4, with Darran O'Sullivan also breaching Stephen Cluxton's goal in the most unusual of circumstances. A rare wayward kickout from the Parnells stopper landed right in Geaney's pocket. The Dingle forward fed Donnchadh Walsh, who palmed to O'Sullivan for the Glenbeigh-Glencar man to finish bravely from close range, ending up in a heap in the back of the net for his troubles.

Dublin dodged a late bullet when, leading by a point, Kevin McManamon appeared to foul Kerry's Peter Crowley in scoring position. Referee David Gough allowed play to continue, and Diarmuid Connolly kicked the insurance score for the Boys in Blue just moments later. To his credit, Gough owned up to his miss sometime later, labelling it one of his most difficult experiences as a referee. 'I don't know how many times I have watched it back since. I know I got it wrong. I didn't get it wrong on purpose. I just didn't see it. Michael Fitzsimons, the Dublin corner-back, had come on that day and he had just crossed my line of vision. I knew an impact had happened and the ball spilled. I didn't know whether it was a proper charge or not, but I couldn't call it because I didn't see it.'

That's the thing about Mick Fitz. Impeccable positioning. Always …

We left Mayo having just taken the scenic route to an All-Ireland quarter-final clash with Ulster champions Tyrone. They edged a typically bruising encounter at Croke Park by 13 points to 12, with Man of the Match Lee Keegan producing one of several outstanding performances on his way to a richly deserved Footballer of the Year award. As Dublin and Kerry were chasing each other around Jones's Road on the last weekend of August, Mayo were at home with the feet up, having booked their final spot a week earlier with a comfortable enough defeat of surprise packet Tipperary, 2-13 to 0-14.

Okay. Let's do this …

* * *

Day 749: Sunday, 18 September 2016
All-Ireland final, Croke Park (attendance 82,300)
Dublin 2-9 Mayo 0-15

If you thought, as this writer did, that a quick revisit of the highlights of the 2016 All-Ireland final might help make sense of arguably the most bonkers game of ball this century, you'd be spectacularly wrong.

A half hour into the biggest game of the season, no Dublin player had scored. Yet, bizarrely, the Boys in Blue led by two points. Football, bloody 'ell. Not one but two freakish own goals had Dublin 2-0 to 0-4 ahead by the time Dean Rock tapped over a 14-yard free in the 31st minute to finally get a Dublin name on the scoresheet. Kevin McLoughlin accidentally prodded a scuffed Bernard Brogan effort into his own net for Dublin's first score of the game in the eighth minute. Incredibly, Colm Boyle did the same thing 14 minutes later, toe-poking past David Clarke after Rock mishandled a sublime Diarmuid Connolly kickpass.

'A quite bizarre All-Ireland final in many respects,' Ger Canning offered from the RTÉ gantry. You could say that, Ger. Mayo appeared to have the Dubs all figured out in every corner of the pitch – yet they trailed by five at the break, Dublin 2-4 Mayo 0-5. Was that damned curse real?

Mayo began the second half like a team on a mission. Scoring five points without reply, they had levelled the game after 46 minutes. At last, amid all the dross, a game of football broke out.

Brian Fenton edged the Dubs ahead early in the 51st minute; Rock doubled the lead a minute later. Andy Moran could have had Mayo in front 90 seconds later, but he blazed a goal chance over the bar for just a single point.

Diarmuid Connolly and Lee Keegan renewed acquaintances and wasted some energy by swinging each other around by their respective jerseys before Mayo sub Alan Dillon pulled his side back level, Dublin 2-6 Mayo 0-12, with just over six minutes to play.

Dublin edged ahead again in the 66th minute, John Small this time. Rock put them further clear with a free two minutes later. Dublin overturned the Mayo kickout and Connolly, who else, powered over a gorgeous point. Three in it. The fat lady isn't yet singing, but she's leaning on the side of the piano.

Into the 69th minute, O'Connor angled over a free. There's still life in the Connacht men. Donie Vaughan strode forward for a beauty. The minimum between the sides. Aidan O'Shea, 75 minutes deep and sensing a back-page picture, fanned a horrible effort miles wide. That's surely it? But no, 76 minutes gone, Dublin have a sideline ball and a one-point lead. Connolly palmed the O'Neills underneath the Hogan Stand. 'Just keep it, Dermo!' Hill 16 pleads, but he doesn't listen. The man who always moved to the beat of his own drum fancied putting the exclamation point on the final in his own inimitable fashion. However, his well-struck effort stayed to the right of the post and wide.

In a rare instance of mild on-pitch disharmony between two Dublin players, Connolly and Ciarán Kilkenny briefly argued over the ball before the sideline kick was taken. Maybe Kilkenny wanted to hold possession. Connolly, as he later explained, just wanted to 'put the ball dead. There was what, a minute left in injury time? Just put the ball dead. We could set up for the kickout, which actually didn't happen. We were too slow for the kickout.'

So Mayo had a prayer. They eventually worked a scoring chance from where O'Connor bent over his seventh point – 'the €3m score', as the *Irish Independent* labelled it the following morning, referring to the gate receipts gleaned from yet another Croke Park full house. (On the eve of the 2016 match, the *Indo* claimed the fixture would generate in the region of €15m in turnover for the city on the day. At those prices, may as well do it twice.)

'They ended up getting [the kickout] off short, and they went up and scored a point,' Connolly acknowledged afterwards. 'But I wouldn't say

I regret it. Maybe I should have kept possession of the ball, in hindsight. These things happen in the game. I didn't really think about it. We should have won the game in open play, to be honest. Look, these things happen. We went on and got the job done the second day.'

'I knew the boys would come back,' Mayo boss Stephen Rochford declared, almost convincingly, after a pulsating game. 'You don't go down to see them train in Castlebar and when they go three or four points down thinking "ah we're just going to wave the white flag". That was never in doubt.'

In the other dressing room, Jim Gavin admitted he was 'just delighted to be still in the championship … After that performance, we didn't really deserve to win and we're just happy to be leaving with the opportunity to go at it again.'

Paul Flynn would go further in 2019 in the *Herald*'s 'Decades of the Dubs' series: 'Mayo should have beaten us the first day [in 2016]. There's no denying that. That was the day they should have won their All-Ireland.'

* * *

Day 762: Saturday, 1 October 2016
All-Ireland final replay, Croke Park (attendance 82,249)
Dublin 1-15 Mayo 1-14

It was, in a way, the beginning of the end of an era. Bernard Brogan was not hanging up his boots – or having them hung up for him – but as it turns out, the drawn 2016 All-Ireland final was the last meaningful game the sharpshooting forward would start for Dublin.

Jim Gavin named an unchanged team to play Mayo the second time out, but there were three significant changes when Dublin lined up for the parade: Michael Fitzsimons replaced Davy Byrne, Michael Darragh Macauley made way for Paul Mannion, and Paddy Andrews took the place of Bernard Brogan.

This was unfamiliar territory for Brogan. Here's how he explained it in his autobiography: '[Jim Gavin] told me in 2016 that I wasn't starting for the final replay against Mayo. It was my first time in 10 seasons being dropped for a championship match, but of course Jim didn't frame it in such blunt terms. "I want you to finish the game for us, I want you on at the business end."'

Meanwhile, spooked by how Dublin thwarted their short kickout the first time around, Mayo manager Stephen Rochford gambled – or perhaps overthought the whole bloody thing – and opted to bring in Rob Hennelly in place of David Clarke in goal. Clarke had started every championship game for Mayo since their shock exit to Galway in the Connacht semi-final. Hennelly was between the posts for their championship opener against London and that loss to the Tribesmen. Even by Mayo's standards, it was a bold decision.

Hennelly may have started the game, but Clarke would finish it. Hennelly spilled a speculative Paul Flynn ball into the grateful arms of Paddy Andrews. To compound his error, the keeper then proceeded to pull down the St Brigid's man. Penalty. Black card. All at a time when the sides were level.

Diarmuid Connolly dispatched the penalty past a still-cold Clarke in the 42nd minute, and the Dubs led by three. It was Mayo's second black card of the match. Lee Keegan was also black-carded for a first-half tackle on Connolly, minutes after scoring a goal.

Yet even when everything seemed to go against them, Mayo, of course, were not done. They whittled the deficit down to a single point before Paddy Durcan won a free at the Hill 16 end. One last chance for Cillian O'Connor to tie the game up. His effort was pulled left and wide, however. The Dubs were Two in a Row All-Ireland champions.

In the *Irish Independent*, Vincent Hogan summed up this Shaw-shanked Mayo side, prisoners of the curse, badly in need of redemption, with the headline MAYO BACK WITH A ROCK HAMMER AT THE PRISON WALL. 'There is proclivity for self-harm written into Mayo's modern history and it found expression again here,' Hogan wrote. 'For all of Dublin's greatness – and let there be no ambiguity about their right to that status with an unbeaten run now of 29 competitive games – this also had the feel for Mayo of death by their own folly.'

For the double champs' part, a defiant Bernard Brogan insisted he wasn't going anywhere. 'I'm long enough in the tooth to know what it takes to win an All-Ireland,' he said. 'It's a team game. You look at us over the years and the impact we've had off the bench – the likes of Kev Mac and fellas like that. This year … that was the role I had to take. The way teams are playing against Dublin now, it's hard for an inside forward to have a massive impact … I knew I was going to get a few minutes and I had to try and make an impact when I did.

'A fourth All-Ireland. I never would have dreamed of it when I was a kid. I'm getting a bit older now. You have to cut your cloth to measure.'

An All Star in 2015, the days of Brogan's name being thrown around during similar discussions appeared to be at an end just a year later. A winner of four awards in 2010, 2011, 2013 and 2015, Brogan was Footballer of the Year in 2010 – a season before his big brother Alan. In 2016, Dublin would take home a half dozen All Stars, with Jonny Cooper, Philly McMahon, Brian Fenton, Diarmuid Connolly, Ciarán Kilkenny and Dean Rock named in the end-of-season Team of the Year.

Meanwhile, back at the ranch, had we finally seen the last of Mayo? Don't be daft.

CHAPTER FOUR

The 60-Second Kickout 2017

2017 National League Division 1

Played 8, Won 4, Drew 3, Lost 1

Final position: League runners-up

After losing three out of three the year before, Kerry faced their tormentors twice in the Spring of 2017 and held their ground both times. A draw in Austin Stack Park, Tralee, in Round 5 of the league saw the sides split 26 points evenly on 18 March, Paul Mannion's 74th-minute equaliser being the 26th and final score of the game.

Paul Geaney, long-time thorn in the Dubs' side, accounted for over half of his county's total, with seven points to his name, three coming from play. Dean Rock racked up no less than nine scores, all from placed balls, with a brace from Na Fianna's Conor McHugh and one from Eoghan O'Gara – along with Mannion's kick – completing the scoring for the Boys in Blue on the night.

Mannion's timely intervention ensured the Dubs equalled Kerry's record by going 34 matches unbeaten, league and championship, since losing in Killarney in the third round of the league in March 2015. Dublin would push that number to 36 with a win over Roscommon (2-29 to 0-14) in Croker before beating Monaghan 2-15 to 1-15 in Clones in the final round of league matches. Kerry, naturally, would be the ones to put an end to the streak in the league final.

Kerry came into that group game shorn of their Dr Crokes contingent, who had claimed the All-Ireland Club title the day before in Croke Park with a 1-9 to 1-7 victory over Derry champions Slaughtneil. Leading the Dr Crokes line, our old pal Gooch.

A few weeks after the Dr Crokes win, in April 2017, Gooch announced his retirement from inter-county football at the age of 33. With five All-Irelands and eight All Star awards, Cooper terrorised every team he ever played against, but he saved the best of himself for the Dubs in that 2009 quarter-final and the semi-finals of 2007, 2013 and 2016.

Reflecting on the 2014 cruciate injury that nearly ended his career, Gooch described it as 'an incredibly low point. I didn't know whether I'd ever get back to play with Kerry, never mind win an All-Ireland with Dr Crokes. That's where these guys [clubmates] have hung in and cajoled me along and thankfully I've got back to playing a bit of better football this year and I'm enjoying it. I've pretty much poured everything into this since we lost with Dublin out here in the semi-final last year. I poured everything into Dr Crokes because I knew there wouldn't be too many more opportunities for us again.'

THE 60-SECOND KICKOUT 2017

One of the best to ever do it. Full stop.

Back to the league decider: With Dublin having won four and drawn three of their seven games, the Kingdom scored a psychological blow with a one-point victory at Headquarters: Kerry 0-20 Dublin 1-16. Dublin had won four league titles in a row to give them 12 crowns overall, but Éamonn Fitzmaurice's side were not to be denied their 20th. Paul Geaney slotted over eight points for the Kingdom, while Dean Rock snared a half dozen scores of his own. The Dubs' goal came courtesy of Paul Mannion, who finished with 1-2.

DUBS DELIVERANCE AT LONG LAST FOR KINGDOM ran the headline above Paul Brennan's match report in the *Kerryman*. Make no mistake about it, Kerry wanted this one. They needed it. 'It's only the league,' everyone loves to tell themselves when it hasn't gone their way. With a bit of luck, we wouldn't meet that lot again this term ...

Three weekends after the league final, Dessie Farrell's young Dublin side would win the last All-Ireland U-21 title, beating Galway 2-13 to 2-7 in Tullamore. The competition would be altered slightly from 2018, making it an U-20 grade. It was Dublin's fourth title at the grade in eight seasons following wins in 2010, 2012 and 2014. That 2017 Dublin side included Evan Comerford in goal; Seán McMahon, Cian Murphy and Eoin Murchan in the backline; Brian Howard around midfield with Colm Basquel, Con O'Callaghan and Paddy Small among the forwards. A few months later, one of those eight would be an All Star, while one more would follow suit in 2018. A new Blue Wave was coming.

* * *

UNBEATABLE

Day 1,007: Saturday, 3 June 2017
Leinster quarter-final, O'Moore Park (attendance 13,238)
Dublin 0-19 Carlow 0-7

Jim Gavin was going to need a Plan B. Carlow had earned their crack at the Dubs by defeating Wexford 2-17 to 2-13 in the Leinster preliminary round. It was Carlow's first win in the Leinster Championship since beating Louth in Portlaoise six years earlier, and manager Turlough O'Connor promised his county's fans that 'Carlow will not die softly against Dublin. We'll make it very difficult for them.' To be fair, they did just that at O'Moore Park in Portlaoise a fortnight later. O'Connor's trainer, Steven Poacher, got right to work. A Down man and a PE teacher by trade, Poacher was well known for both his coaching exploits and his endless enthusiasm for football, and he had been welcomed in the tiny Leinster outpost with open arms.

But for a county like Carlow, how do you tackle a job like Dublin? The same way you eat an elephant – one bite at a time. 'We started with the kickouts. I remember reading [Jim] McGuinness's book where he studied hundreds of Cluxton's kickouts,' Poacher explained. 'For example, a small minor detail, we would make sure to mark their right-corner-back, even if we were conceding the kickout, so that Cluxton couldn't just clip one easily to the side with his left foot. We made him turn his body. Just a small thing that helped to slightly slow them down.

'I worked with our goalkeeper on how to kill a full minute on kickouts. We started off with 26 seconds and managed to get it up to 53/54 seconds in the end.'

There's a lot more to playing Dublin than the Xs and Os on the pitch. The travelling roadshow that follows the Boys in Blue brings a certain logistical challenge. Added to that, the Carlow game was to be shown live on Sky Sports. 'Another thing we were not used to at that time was the media circus that follows Dublin. Carlow were absolutely nobody,' Poacher remembers. 'I was getting phone calls from everybody – the *Irish News*, the *Irish Independent* etc. It was weird, but that was all new to us. For Dublin, it's a regular occurrence.

'On the day of our game, I'll never forget the noise for the national anthem. To put it in perspective, when we played London that year, you'd hear a dog barking in the stand. That's the reality, there might have been 35/40 people there. But that day in Portlaoise, with the stand behind you full, the Dubs start "Come on You Boys in Blue" after the first minute or so. The hairs on the back of your neck stand up when you're involved in those occasions.'

Daniel St Ledger captained Carlow that day in Portlaoise and echoed much of what his trainer felt about the task they faced against Jim Gavin's side. 'Skill wise, individual talent wise, but also their pragmatism, their organisation was on a level that no team has hit since and I don't think we'll see again anytime soon. You have conversations with people, you'd be talking about the current state of the All-Ireland, the competitiveness of it or whatever. And that Dublin team set a bar that I don't think another team will hit so you're comparing every team to them, and I just don't think it's fair.'

On the pitch at O'Moore Park, Brendan Murphy lofted over the opening score of the game to give Carlow a very early lead. Captain

Darragh Foley's first-half free from distance, which made the score 0-8 to 0-5 in Dublin's favour at half-time, was as fine a strike as we saw all summer. A second-half red card for Murphy, with the score 0-10 to 0-6 Dublin, turned an already steeply uphill task into an Everest-like quest. Carrying a yellow card, the big midfielder tangled off the ball with the Dublin full-back line's chief pest, Jonny Cooper, and duly went into the referee's book again. After that, the Dubs were relentless.

David held Goliath to the lowest points tally of the season at 19 – one fewer than the 1-17 they would manage against Mayo in the All-Ireland final 15 weeks later. When all was said and done, however, the Dubs finished the job against their well-drilled, determined opponents on the back of Dean Rock's freetaking and Ciarán Kilkenny's ceaseless motor. Bernard Brogan, settling into the final phase of his career in an impact sub role, popped over a pair of scores when he replaced Kevin McManamon after 45 minutes.

'We had never come up against anything like it before, even playing the Kildares, the Meaths, all the rest,' admitted St Ledger. 'There was always a sense with other teams there was a possibility, on a given day, that you could turn them over. In 2018 with Kildare, we always felt that there was a little soft underbelly to some teams, that if we were 100 per cent right, you could pull something off. But with this Dublin team, you were going in and you just hadn't a clue the level they were at. That was the biggest thing for me.'

In all, Carlow played five championship games in 2017, the most since their Leinster-winning campaign of 1944. Having beaten Wexford in Leinster before meeting Dublin, they headed into the qualifiers and beat London by a point in Ruislip and pinged Leitrim at Dr Cullen Park, 2-14 to 0-13. Their adventure would end back in front of the Sky Sports cameras at home to Monaghan in mid-July, where they went down swinging, 1-12 to 1-7. Every debate about improving the lot of the smaller counties involves some talking head insisting that 'they need games'. In 2017, Carlow got games. And they acquitted themselves admirably.

Unfortunately, from a Dubs point of view, the game in O'Moore Park would be best remembered for an incident involving one of Dublin's star performers. Diarmuid Connolly argued with linesman Ciarán Branagan about a sideline ball he felt had been given to Carlow in error, and, unwisely, placed his hands on the match official. It wasn't Connolly's finest moment – it also wasn't the first time that on-pitch rashness had caused him a problem. His sending-off against Mayo in the 2015 semi-final was, of course, turned over by the DRA. Four years before, in the notorious semi-final defeat of Donegal – a game that ended (mercifully) 0-8 to 0-6 in Dublin's favour and nearly finished off dear ol' Pat Spillane – Connolly also saw red after a clash with Marty Boyle. That card was, correctly to be fair, overturned as well.

Gavin had a problem on his hands, and it involved an irreplaceable player. The referee's failure to deal with the incident at the time left Connolly vulnerable to the GAA's convoluted disciplinary process. He had the benefit of that process two years earlier; many felt the other shoe would drop this time around. Yes, we certainly had not heard the last of this one.

*　*　*

Day 1,029: Sunday, 25 June 2017
Leinster semi-final, Croke Park (attendance 33,370)
Dublin 4-29 Westmeath 0-10

Three weeks later, the shoe dropped. Diarmuid Connolly was suspended for 12 weeks. He would be out until the All-Ireland semi-final – should Dublin make it that far.

When it came to Dublin's missing superstar, manager Jim Gavin knew exactly who he felt was to blame. In his interview following this cakewalk over Westmeath, Gavin took aim at RTÉ's *The Sunday Game* and unloaded both barrels. 'We had the national broadcaster in their post-match review, both Pat Spillane and Colm O'Rourke but particularly Pat, read out a pre-determined statement, which was disappointing.

'Particularly because both of them are teachers, you'd hope they'd understand that people do make mistakes and due process should be allowed before we become judge, jury and executioner in one particular incidence.'

Gavin wasn't done. He added: 'I still think [Connolly's] good name was more important and the rights that he has as an individual in the Republic. I think his good name was certainly attacked, that's for sure.'

In his *Irish Independent* column a few days later, Tomás Ó Sé – himself no angel in his playing days, but generally a fair, straight-shooting pundit – described Connolly as 'a special player who can do special things, but he also puts the team in jeopardy at times. At some point, other players in the squad might just be becoming tired of the negative focus another Connolly story brings.'

If that last bit seems a stretch, Ó Sé's suggestion that '*The Sunday Game* does impact on the Central Competitions Committee, even if only in the unconscious' is an interesting idea. 'The greater the TV focus on a game, the greater the scrutiny of their decision-making,' he argued. 'If they can honestly remain immune to the pressure that scrutiny brings, they are remarkable people.'

BLUE MURDER was the *Herald*'s slant the Monday after Dublin's humiliation of Westmeath. It seemed a long time since Tómas's uncle, the late Páidí Ó Sé, had masterminded a Leinster title for the Lakemen in 2004 – hastening the end of the Tommy Lyons era for Dublin in the process.

In the year 2017, Dublin and Westmeath existed in entirely different orbits. Paul Mannion scorched the overmatched pretenders for eight points. Ciarán Kilkenny collected 1-3, while Eoin O'Gara, Shane Carthy, Bernard Brogan and Kevin McManamon all made a mark on the scoreboard off the bench.

Westmeath manager Tom Cribbin wasn't taking the blame for this one. 'My gut feeling beforehand was, my only hope you would have of beating Dublin is to lock down the show completely and stop them scoring goals,' he told reporters afterwards. 'But people didn't want to see that, and players didn't want to see that; they felt we could have a go at them, but we were outclassed.'

It was a painful lesson for Westmeath, a pain keenly felt by their main forward, John Heslin, who recalled the moments after the game without much fondness. 'In 2017, we did a lot of work to say look we've improved on X, Y and Z and we have a chance here against the Dubs. And as a sports person, you need to give yourself that chance, and we genuinely thought there was a chance. I'll never forget, personally, I was the first man on the bus home that day, which I never am. I was gutted because I had myself convinced we had a chance and, actually, we were miles away.'

* * *

Day 1,050: Sunday, 16 July 2017
Leinster final, Croke Park (attendance 66,734)
Dublin 2-23 Kildare 1-17

Otherwise known as Con O'Callaghan's coming-out party. The Cuala star finished his day's work with a dozen points, having taken over free-taking duty from the black-carded Dean Rock and leaving a trail of would-be Kildare defenders in his wake. In just his third championship start, O'Callaghan racked up six from play and six from frees.

Jim Gavin is not one for jumping up and down with excitement when speaking of an individual, but he knew he had something special on his hands with his latest star forward. 'He comes from a really solid background. His club Cuala have done tremendous work in that part of the county for Gaelic games in the last number of years, and Con has been fortunate to be surrounded by some great coaches and great family as well. Within Dublin GAA he's been developed by the development squads and by U-18 and U-21 coaches and managers, so that's been a big influence on him. He played his part. That's probably what we see in training as well.'

Make no mistake, however, this was no cakewalk. Kildare had put it up to their neighbours. Their final score of 1-17 would win you a lot of games of football. Paddy Brophy's late goal might have dressed up the scoreline somewhat, but with Keith Cribbin driving them on from half-back and Kevin Feely finding his range from frees, Cian O'Neill's side made Dublin work hard for their dinner.

MAGNIFICENT SEVEN FOR THE DUBS rang the front page of Monday's *Irish Independent*, adding, 'Dublin claim Leinster record but Kildare expose massive chinks in Gavin's armour.'

Dublin captain Stephen Cluxton equalled the all-time championship appearance record of 88 held by the Ó Sé brothers, Marc and Tomás. By 2017, it was no secret that Cluxton was one of the most influential players in the history of Gaelic football. He had long since changed the way the goalkeeper position was viewed, and how the modern game was played in general. The manager was fulsome in his praise for his goalkeeper extraordinaire. 'His application and how he works at his game continuously is a great example, not only for the younger players in the squad, but for the older members and for the management team as well.'

Gavin and his backroom team had work to do, however. Next up, an All-Ireland quarter-final with Monaghan in three weeks' time.

If Dublin had at least been made break a sweat in Leinster, the same probably couldn't be said of Kerry in Munster. Although Clare ran them to six points, 1-18 to 1-12, in the semi-final, the Kingdom drove over Cork in the provincial final, 1-23 to 0-15. Strangely, it was a similar story for Ulster champions Tyrone, who ran through an unusually lopsided provincial campaign by winning their three games with a combined margin of 28 points. They doubled Derry's 11 points in the quarter-final with 22 of their own; hammered Donegal 1-21 to 1-12 in their last-four meeting; and walloped Down 2-17 to 0-15 in an uncharacteristically high-scoring Ulster final.

In Connacht, it was another year and another false dawn for Mayo – or so it may have seemed to those with short memories. Having beaten Sligo comfortably in the quarter-final, Galway would pop them again in the semis, edging a one-point game, 0-15 to 1-11. To add insult to injury for Mayo, Galway would lose the Connacht final by nine points to Roscommon, 2-15 to 0-12. All of that must mean one thing and one thing only – in a few short weeks, Mayo would push Dublin to the very brink once again. I mean, it's the only thing that would make sense.

* * *

Day 1,070: Saturday, 5 August 2017
All-Ireland quarter-final, Croke Park (attendance 82,300)
Dublin 1-19 Monaghan 0-12

It was the week where the cream of the 2017 football world rose to the top. Kerry hammered Galway; Mayo did likewise to surprise Connacht champions Roscommon, albeit in a replay; Tyrone embarrassed Armagh by 18 points and the Dubs took care of Monaghan with ten points to spare.

Incidentally, pride of place in the weekend sports pages went to Galway hurling sensation Joe Canning, who had the temerity to break the golden rule – in fact, the only rule – of the GAA's long-held in-season code of omertà: Say Nothing. In fact, Say Less Than Nothing. In a fantastic interview with the *Irish Independent*'s Vincent Hogan, printed the day before their All-Ireland SHC semi-final with Tipperary under the headline CANNING UNCOVERED: I REALISE IT'S DIFFERENT STANDARDS I'M JUDGED BY, the Portumna ace spoke plainly about life, love, family, hurling and the chance of an odd pint. And then a strange thing happened. Nothing. Nobody died. The world didn't end. An adult GAA star had an adult conversation – on the record – with a sports journalist, and the earth somehow continued to spin.

The following day, on the same Croke Park pitch where Dublin had accounted for Monaghan 24 hours before, Canning produced a masterclass of stick-play to torch the Premier County for 11 points. His haul accounted for exactly half of the Tribesmen's total (Galway 0-22 Tipperary 1-18) and included a breathtaking injury-time winner from under the Cusack Stand that should send you straight to YouTube this minute for a reminder. (Don't lose your page.)

The Dublin camp of this era largely mirrored the modern GAA approach to the media: Control the Controllables and all that. Most savvy inter-county set-ups had a media manager of some sort. When players were available to speak to reporters, they often said very little.

Ger Loughnane made dummy teamsheets famous during his time in charge of Clare hurlers in the 1990s ('Tell the opposition our team? I wouldn't even tell them the throw-in time!'), and now they were de rigueur throughout the codes. Jim Gavin may be the greatest football manager we've ever seen, but he certainly had his quirks when confronted by a journalist with a microphone and a deadline. The exchanges were not always as cordial as they otherwise could have been.

An uncomfortable press conference after the 2013 All-Ireland semi-final win over Kerry may be a case in point. Having outlasted the Colm Cooper-inspired Kingdom in a good old-fashioned shoot-out, 3-18 to 3-11, Gavin unusually brought captain Stephen Cluxton with him to meet the media after the game. Among the press that day was Vincent Hogan from the *Indo*, he of the abovementioned Canning interview.

'So the press conference goes on and there's about 10 or 11 questions, all to Jim,' Hogan recalled over a decade later, 'and I'm looking at Cluxton who's sitting there beginning to look a little bit uncomfortable, in my opinion, and I decided I'd ask him a question just to include him in the proceedings.

'I asked him if the movement of the Kerry forwards had created problems for them that they hadn't encountered until then. He gave me what I considered a really surly reply, saying, "I don't know, I wasn't marking any of them". There was this kind of silence afterwards. As if, you know, seriously? I looked straight at Jim because I thought out of just pure good manners, Jim would interject, but he just f**king left it there.

'That was that until about three months later. I met Gavin socially.

I let him know exactly what I thought of that moment. And we had it over and back for a short little while. Jim's argument was that he had one job to do with Dublin and that was to win All-Irelands. I told him I thought it was ignorant in that situation that he didn't intervene. Eventually Jim just got up and left.'

Gavin's tunnel-vision approach is far from unique in the GAA world. The modern inter-county manager exerts a level of control over their perceived domain that can at times seem at odds with the ideals of an amateur sports organisation. On his first stint as Donegal boss, Jim McGuinness dropped one of his senior players, Kevin Cassidy, from the squad, citing the player's contribution to a book written by journalist Declan Bogue in 2011 as reason enough to banish the half-back. ('This broke the trust within the group.') McGuinness refused to speak to the media following his county's All-Ireland win a year later as long as Bogue was in the room. Upon his return to the Donegal hotseat in 2024, McGuinness held his grudge against the journalist – and continued the silent treatment.

After a 2018 All-Ireland semi-final victory over Cork, Limerick hurling manager John Kiely famously launched into school principal lecture mode in the post-match press conference, warning a room full of fully grown journalists, in no uncertain terms, that should any of them contact one of his players in the week of the All-Ireland final, he would 'shut the whole thing down'. Vincent Hogan was, naturally, among the assembled hacks that day too. 'Other people have shown poor judgement in certain moments, and I think that's what that was with Kiely,' Hogan surmised. 'But with Jim and Cluxton in 2013, I thought it was outright rudeness.'

Maybe this scepticism about the media can be considered a byproduct of the increasing professionalism of Gaelic games, and the modern, sleek nature of the association has certainly brought advantages. Players are better prepared and better looked after than ever before. Facilities across the country are the envy of other sporting bodies. Croke Park is now a venue to rival any in the world. And only an organisation as committed to coaching development as the GAA could produce a manager like Gavin in the first place. It's all in marked contrast to the 'old days'. Jason Sherlock spoke in his autobiography about missing a training session in the week leading up to Dublin's 1995 All-Ireland win because he was mobbed by fans in the carpark. Back then, anyone could stroll up and demand an autograph, squeeze the cheek or ruffle the hair of their favourite inter-county star. More or less held hostage, Sherlock signed autographs for 90 minutes while his teammates trained.

An 'open' training session in Parnell Park in the run-up to the All-Ireland final in 2013 served as another reminder why county boards feel it prudent to occasionally cocoon their players. Bernard Brogan and Stephen Cluxton were surrounded by fans, young and not-so-young, while a late-arriving Diarmuid Connolly didn't get three feet from his car before being accosted by autograph hunters.

Needless to say, nobody wants a return to the ad-hoc days when players were given no direction whatsoever when it came to dealing with life as an inter-county star – and no journalist expects the times of chatting it up with players in the dressing room while passing around a box of 20 Major to return. But the wall of silence helps no one. Surely it is possible for intelligent adult sport stars to be treated as such and trusted to use their own judgement when it comes to interacting with those 'outside the tent'. Athletes could certainly insist that they don't need the media – and few would disagree – but one might argue that there is a collective responsibility to promote Gaelic sport, and that starts, first and foremost, with our games' most high-profile personalities.

Anyway, we digress. Again. Back to the big white ball. Against the Farney Army, Dead-eye Dean Rock resumed freetaking duties and duly wore out the black spot. Rock would also claim the game's only goal with a cheeky palmed finish five minutes into the second half, ending with 1-7 for his day's work. Rock's fellow inside-forwards, Paul Mannion and Paddy Andrews, would each gather three points from play against an overmatched Monaghan full-back line. Indeed, a trio of late Monaghan scores actually gave the final scoreline a more balanced look than it probably deserved.

Manager Gavin allowed himself to admit that his barnstorming team were rounding into form. 'From a management point of view, you can see that the team is gaining momentum at the right time of year,' he told reporters.

He also quashed any suggestion that the cakewalk his team had enjoyed thus far this season could set them up for a semi-final ambush. The readiness is all. 'There has been a lot of work done away in the shadows,' Gavin assured us. 'You saw when Monaghan did get a bit of a run that they have the capacity and capability to take scores, but our team defence was very strong. We'll have our "A" Game against Tyrone the next day. [Only] 1-11 from play and a lot of wides is something to work on.'

In their final-four clash three weeks later, Mickey Harte's Tyrone were about to find out just what Dublin's 'A' Game looked like. It would prove to be one long afternoon for the Red Hand men.

* * *

Day 1,092: Sunday, 27 August 2017
All-Ireland semi-final, Croke Park (attendance 82,300)
Dublin 2-17 Tyrone 0-11

A semi-final slaughter. The kind of defeat that can send a whole province into a fit of navel-gazing. For once, at least, it wasn't Leinster getting it in the neck.

In the run-up to the game, Dublin had retired to Carton House for one of their weekend training camps and, by all accounts, devised the gameplan that would render Tyrone's notorious blanket defence impotent. At this stage of their development, the Dubs were reportedly solving problems by committee. Gavin was unquestionably the boss, but the group operated very much as a democracy. The players were tasked with the challenge of finding a way around Tyrone. In that Carton House camp, they pored over game film, conferred, reported back, tested, adjusted, tested again. By the time Dublin were ready to leave Maynooth and slip back across the nearby border, nobody from the Red Hand County could have had an inkling of just how much trouble they were in. Full-back Jonny Cooper, a disciple of the data, is said to have told his squad-mates, 'Lads, this completely blows away everything we've done before.'

Dublin would blow Tyrone away too. The game's most magical moment occurred as early as the fifth minute, brought to you by a forward who had quickly become one of his sport's brightest stars. We were still getting comfortable on our Hill 16 perch when Tyrone's Niall Sludden gathered a Niall Morgan kickout and angled his way across midfield before slightly overhitting a handpass towards a teammate which was immediately seized upon by Ciarán Kilkenny. The ball found its way to Con O'Callaghan 60 yards from the Hill 16 goal, and from there, the Cuala forward had only one thing in mind. He ran hard at the Tyrone full-back line, threw a dummy that landed opposing full-back Ronan McNamee closer to the Cusack Stand than the edge of his own square, then strode forward and, just before reaching the 14-yard line, unleashed a hellish right-footed effort that screamed past Morgan. Unstoppable. Unmarkable. Unplayable.

Disciplined as they are, the Dubs' motion-heavy attack appeared in stark contrast to the tactical straitjacket the Tyrone players operated within. 'We're allowed to play with freedom within the system,' O'Callaghan, scorer of 1-2, explained. 'Jim says "Once you get those opportunities, just go for it." Work-rate gets you performance.'

This match also marked the end of an era for Tyrone as their totemic midfielder Sean Cavanagh played his final game. He retired after 16 years with three All-Ireland titles to his name and the unwavering respect of every opponent he faced. Cavanagh and Stephen Cluxton warmly embraced after the game. Two veterans who had seen it all.

'There's obviously huge mutual respect between myself and Stephen.

We have been soldiering against each other since 2002,' recalled Cavanagh. 'He said a few nice words to myself and I told him it was an absolute honour to play against one of the greatest footballers ever. And he is that, he is an inspiration, even to me. He is a fantastic guy off the pitch. I have been lucky enough to get to know him as well. You find in sport, most of the top, top players are really good human beings and good-hearted people.'

The five-time All Star narrowed his attention to the unslayable beast that was running roughshod over Gaelic football. 'Everyone in that group tried their best and we've come up against probably the greatest GAA team I've ever played against, and I've told a few of the Dublin lads [that]. It's tough luck to be part of an era with a team of that magnitude that's dominating the sport in a way that I never thought was possible to dominate.'

ULSTER BUST: 'After a sobering weekend for our provincial champions Tyrone, we ask if Ulster needs a reality check or are things being blown out of proportion?' wondered the front page of *Gaelic Life* the week after the Red Hand's 12-point defeat. In his column, former Donegal ace Kevin Cassidy explained: 'At the start of the year, the four that are left would have been tipped by nearly everyone to be the four semi-finalists so there are no great surprises there. However, I think we are all a little shocked at the gulf in class that now exists between them and the chasing pack. We had four quarter-finals that were over as a contest after 15 minutes as Dublin, Kerry, Tyrone and Mayo simply obliterated their opponents and then sauntered to the final whistle.'

Dublin did that. They broke teams. Broke counties. Broke entire provinces. Ulster seemed in crisis. Tyrone, who had pounded Down in the provincial final and eviscerated Armagh in an All-Ireland quarter-final by 18 points (3-17 to 0-8), were themselves categorically outclassed by a Dublin team that was cresting the highest peak of a seven-year arc. Many former stars of the province were, like Cassidy, wondering where Ulster counties would go from here.

On a day when Dublin could rely on three points from Paul Flynn and 1-1 from Eoghan O'Gara off the bench, there was no run-out for Bernard Brogan or Michael Darragh Macauley, while the returning Diarmuid Connolly made only a very late, brief appearance when the result was well beyond doubt.

Connolly replaced O'Callaghan in the 70th minute although his name, at least, was given a rapturous reception four minutes earlier when Eric Lowndes came on for Paul Mannion but was incorrectly announced as 'Diarmuid Connolly'. The pair may not exactly be 'separated at birth' candidates, but we can see how a mistake could be made. Lowndes, to his credit, saw the funny side of it. 'I thought there was a fight broken out behind me or something,' the St Peregrine's half-back later remembered. 'I didn't know what was going on, to be honest. One of the lads in work [Scoil Bhríde, Blanchardstown, where Lowndes teaches] got me a mug that changes from my face to Dermo's!'

* * *

Day 1,113: Sunday, 17 September 2017
All-Ireland final, Croke Park (attendance 82,300)
Dublin 1-17 Mayo 1-16

Here we go again. When we last left Mayo, they'd been chinned in Connacht by Galway. They would limp into the qualifiers and eventually arrive in Croke Park for an All-Ireland final having circumnavigated the island at least twice, it seemed. Stephen Rochford's side needed extra time to beat Derry in Castlebar on the first day of July, 2-21 to 1-13, on the back of a dozen Cillian O'Connor points. The captain and his brother Diarmuid led them past Clare in Ennis next day out, scoring 1-5 and 1-1 respectively.

Three weeks after the Derry game, they'd require extra innings again to edge past Cork in a shootout in Limerick, 0-27 to 2-20, before needing two bites at Connacht champs Roscommon. Having finished honours even at Croker on 30 July, Roscommon 2-9 Mayo 1-12, Rochford's men made no mistake back at Headquarters a week later, hammering the Rossies 4-19 to 0-9. Their semi-final joust with Kerry also required a replay. The sides finished with 2-14 apiece on 20 August before returning six days later – 24 hours before Dublin saw off Tyrone – where Mayo advanced behind goals from Diarmuid O'Connor and soon-to-be-Footballer of the Year Andy Moran, the final score 2-16 to 0-17. Incidentally, while Mayo were ending the Kerrymen's championship for another year in Croke Park, Mick Bohan's Dublin ladies were whitewashing their Kingdom counterparts in Semple Stadium, 5-10 to 0-11, in their own All-Ireland semi-final. A bad day all round for the green and gold.

By the time they paraded beside the Dubs for a 17 September All-Ireland final, Mayo's men had already played nine championship games that season, two of which went to extra time. In their 10th battle of an endless summer, 90 seconds was all it took for Con O'Callaghan to stamp Dublin's authority on the showpiece game of the year. The Cuala ace gathered possession 45 yards from goal, threw those Shakira hips at Colm Boyle and dashed purposely towards Hill 16 before feathering a delicious finish with the outside tip of his right boot into the bottom corner of the net. Another rabbit pulled from the young magician's hat.

From there, we bore witness to an All-Ireland epic that began with 20 bizarre, error-strewn minutes then played out at a furious pace. After O'Callaghan's early goal, the Dublin forward unit was put in storage by a Mayo backline that had been eating, drinking and sleeping this mission. This Mayo squad had many fans – and probably just as many detractors – but one thing is undeniable: during the almost seven championship campaigns of the Dubs' unbeaten run, absolutely no other team bamboozled the Sky Blues quite like the Connacht men.

Andy Moran led the much-vaunted Dublin rearguard a merry dance, pocketed three tidy scores of his own in the opening 23 minutes, and later slipped Lee Keegan in for a goal that threatened to blow Dublin's Three in a Row plans to smithereens.

If there's a criticism of this Mayo team down through the years, it could be that some of their most high-profile players fail to deliver on the biggest days. That's not a charge anyone anywhere could throw at their peers in blue, and this 2017 decider provided the perfect example. Dean Rock's All-Ireland final got off to a rough start. Anyone who has ever kicked frees at any level will know the importance of that first kick of the game. In Rock's case, rather than a handy routine effort slightly left of the posts for a right-footed kicker (a 'settler'), his first strike at goal on this day came from just under the Cusack Stand. Predictably, the Ballymun man could not find the target.

This miss was followed by a smothered, badly pulled 45 and a weak effort from play that dropped into David Clarke's grateful hands. The crowd murmured. Mayo players were emboldened. The Dubs looked uncomfortable in a manner only Mayo made them. Rock, their nerveless, peerless sniper, seemed to be suffering from the yips. That uncharacteristically poor 16th-minute effort from play was Rock's last miss of the afternoon. He would edge Dublin back into the game just before half-time and eventually finish with seven crucial points. While Rock and his teammates dug in, Mayo, as they are prone to do, worked themselves into a winning position before fumbling for their pistol and shooting themselves in the foot. The 46th minute, Dublin were clinging to a one-point lead but their 'forward line as a unit is not working' according to Dessie Dolan. Mayo pressed towards the Hill 16 end in search of an equaliser. Colm Boyle took a handpass from Aidan O'Shea and turned towards goal only to be met by the full, uncompromising force of John Small. Boyle went down hard. Small, already booked, would surely be sent off. Cillian O'Connor would surely stroke over the levelling free and, with the best part of 25 minutes still to play, Mayo would enjoy a one-man advantage. Surely.

Enter Donie Vaughan. The Mayo full-back arrived on the scene quickly – too quickly – and felt it prudent to put Small lying on the ground beside Boyle. A clear strike. And a clear strike in Gaelic games carries the clear penalty of a straight red card. Small saw yellow followed by red; Vaughan saw just the latter. The free became a throw-up from which Dublin gleaned possession, and those final 25 minutes would be 14-v-14. Co-commentator Dolan summed up what we were all thinking: 'A very careless play in such a high-stakes match.'

From here, the words of Stephen Poacher ring true – Dublin's depth made them almost unbeatable. 'If you watched Mayo playing against them during this era,' the then Carlow trainer points out, 'the best forwards in Dublin, like Connolly or Kilkenny; Mayo had Lee Keegan or Paddy Durcan or Colm Boyle chasing these lads for 50 minutes. Absolutely flagged, starting to wane. But then Dublin spring Kevin McManamon or Bernard Brogan, as they did against Carlow. The strength of their bench was just phenomenal.'

On that day, Dublin sprang Connolly and McManamon by half-time, then Brogan and Paul Flynn five minutes from full-time. Eye-watering strength in depth. Cruel, almost.

In a game that had just about everything, we were treated to a fantastic two-minute snapshot of one of the decade's great man-on-man rivalries. Diarmuid Connolly and Lee Keegan were synonymous with the 10-year odyssey of these two teams. If some of Keegan's more celebrated teammates were indeed often found wanting when the championship heat was at its whitest, that is an accusation which could never be levelled at the Westport winger. He seemed to reserve the best of himself for the Dubs. His battles with Connolly were a major factor in dictating the mood of these games. Joined at the hip, they played each other to a standstill more often than not. Balboa versus Creed. It's up to you which one is which.

Here, in the 54th minute, Keegan broke loose. His team trailing by two points, he cut strong towards goal as the canny Moran eased into possession in the full-forward line. Spotting his hard-running teammate, Moran slipped Keegan through, and his emphatic finish put Mayo in the lead. Not to be outdone, two minutes later, Connolly would level the game with possibly the point of the season. He picked the ball up on the Mayo 45, surrounded by men in red and green shirts including Keegan, Kevin McLoughlin and Tom Parsons. From there, the Vincent's sorcerer ducked, dipped, dived and dodged – paused briefly to gently inquire of referee Joe McQuillan as to the possible whereabouts of a free – before powering over a curling right-footed score that probably deserves a chapter of its own. From there, the teams spat out their gumshields, stood dead centre of the ring and traded blows until they had nothing left. Mayo edged ahead again, two clear. Mannion pulled Dublin to within a point with six minutes to play, 1-15 to 1-14. Bernard Brogan, sprung from the bench a minute later, almost immediately made a score for Man of the Match James McCarthy. All square, 1-15 apiece, five minutes of normal time remained.

In the 67th minute, Connolly's sumptuous pass out wide to Rock was perfectly weighted to sucker Rock's defender into a desperate dive for possession. Rock gathered, his marker flailing in his wake, and, bearing down on goal, kept his nerve to fist the go-ahead point. Dublin 1-16, Mayo 1-15. 'There was a great opportunity for a goal if he wanted to be a hero,' exclaimed Dolan in the RTÉ booth. There was still time, Dessie lad.

Cillian O'Connor equalised for Mayo – the final point of the 3-66 he would amass in that year's championship – making it 1-16 apiece. Then, a Mayo free, 71 minutes on the clock into the Hill 16 end. O'Connor could put them ahead. The Three in a Row could end here. Your mind raced back to 15 years earlier, Dublin–Armagh in the All-Ireland semi-final. The same Croke Park stage, the same time of the game, the same Hill 16 goal. Ray Cosgrove, on his way to an All Star, stood over a potential equaliser that day. The sickening thud of his effort striking the right-hand post still induces a shudder.

In his book *Kings for a Day: The Story of Armagh and their 2002 Journey to Sam Maguire*, Niall McCoy revisited that semi-final with Orchard County manager Joe Kernan. 'My wife Patricia always says the Dublin game was better than the final,' said Kernan. 'After three years, people thought we were doomed and cursed; a load of shite. It was always about what we would do. You never go looking for an excuse. Either we did it or we didn't, it's as simple as that. When the free kick was being taken, I told Paul McGrane to stay in Ray Cosgrove's eye-line. If you watch the video, Paul ran alongside it.'

This time around, 15 years later, as O'Connor's well-struck free cannoned off that same upright, the ping of the post was music to a Dub's ears. Still level. And we have it. We have the ball.

Two and a half minutes into injury time, Kevin McManamon – a half-time sub for Eoghan O'Gara – chased all the way back to intercept a Chris Barrett pass in Dublin's left-half-back position. Mayo players either side of the St Jude's forward could only watch. Desire and selflessness personified.

And then, the day's key moment. There were surely only seconds left. Dublin, patient as ever, worked the ball to the person they would want to have it most. Connolly. He took off right at the heart of the Mayo defence and dared them to stop him. They couldn't. The referee's whistle blew. Connolly's beaming face said it all. A free. A glorious free right in Dean Rock's wheelhouse. Maybe 40 yards from goal, slightly left of the posts. If it was 70 minutes earlier, you would classify it indeed as the perfect 'settler'.

Rock placed the ball, eyed the posts, went through his routine, ignored flying debris from desperate opponents, and kicked himself and his team into immortality. Pandemonium. The camera panned to Jim Gavin. The Round Towers Clondalkin man, the leader of this iconic side, sat motionless. Mayo still had time.

Mayo keeper David Clarke had the ball on his kicking tee and needed to find a teammate. Any teammate. Unfortunately, Clarke could not even find the playing surface. He fanned his kick high and to the right, over the Cusack Stand sideline. Dublin ball. Mayo would never get it back. Dublin survive. The Three in a Row secured. 'The toughest game I've ever played,' admitted Man of the Match McCarthy later.

In a Boylesports-produced conversation in the summer of 2023, Keegan and Connolly remembered 2017 – and Keegan's last-gasp attempt to put off freetaker Rock by flinging his GPS pack at the Ballymun man's feet as he struck the decisive score. 'We were staring down the barrel of another All-Ireland defeat,' Keegan said, plainly. 'I was thinking, what else can I do here?! I went a bit above the threshold, probably. Definitely not one of my best moments, but when you're staring down the barrel of a fifth All-Ireland defeat, desperate times call for desperate measures. The killer for us was how you finished the game after. You just absolutely demoralised us when you got the ball back. That was probably the best game we'd played, collectively. We scored 1-16. And we still lost. That's the sign of how good of a team Dublin were and how much we respected you. It just wasn't enough against ye.'

Connolly, a half-time substitute, had changed the game in a way only the greatest players do. 'In 2017, Lee marked [Ciarán] Kilkenny in the first half,' he recalled. 'Kilkenny came in at half-time and he had been getting, say, 42/43 possessions per game all season. And when he marked Keegan, he came in at half-time and I think he'd seven or eight possessions and he didn't know what hit him. His head was spinning. I remember walking down the tunnel and I said to him, "Just relax. Take a breath and relax." He wasn't used to getting that full press. Lee didn't care anything about the football at all. Kilkenny was his job – him not to get possession. Keegan done an unbelievable job on him in the first half.'

Keegan even allowed time for a 'fond' memory of that heartbreaking day: 'The funniest memory I have is when Connolly came on at half-time in 2017 and we were down at the Cusack stand side [Keegan marking Kilkenny] and he goes, "This is great, you're not coming near me today!"'

Joe Brolly would, six years later in his *Sunday Independent* column, use the final moments of this All-Ireland final as the perfect example of why we needed seismic changes to the playing rules for Gaelic football. Joe suggested a rule for football akin to the 'backcourt' rule in basketball. Once a team takes possession over their own 45, they cannot retreat back. If and when they subsequently pass the opposition's 45, they also cannot retreat back. 'At the moment, a team that is winning can simply work the ball backwards and laterally to the goalkeeper, move upfield, then back downfield, using the keeper as the spare man,' he scribbled in September 2023. 'In the 2017 All-Ireland final, Mayo were a point down and Dublin had a sideline about ten metres outside Mayo's 20-metre line. Bernard Brogan took it short, and Dublin systematically worked the ball the whole way back to Stephen Cluxton. They went back across Mayo's 45, back across the halfway line, back across their own 45, kicked it to Cluxton and played "donkey" with Mayo until the final whistle. With my rule, the Dubs would have had no choice but to go forward. With Mayo hounding them ferociously and no option of playing the ball backwards, it was all they could have done.'

Kieran Shannon, a journalist and sports psychologist with the Mayo panel, spoke on RTÉ's *Morning Ireland* the week after that 2017 final. 'They will go again. It's as simple as that,' he said. 'Mayo are relentless, just as Dublin are. It wouldn't surprise me if the two teams are in next year's final. Dublin are the top team in the country and have the edge over Mayo at the moment. It's about bridging that gap.'

Paul Flynn didn't know it, but having replaced early-injury victim Jack McCaffrey after just seven minutes, he had battled Mayo in championship fare for the final time. McCaffrey, for his part, gave a meme-worthy performance in the background of *The Sunday Game*'s coverage that evening, having come off injured so early in the play.

Flynn was one of the great Dublin warriors and a player who was there from the very start, back when an odd All-Ireland seemed so far away, never mind a clatter of them.

The Fingallians clubman reflected on his battles with the green and red a couple of years later. 'If you look at a game against Mayo from up in the stands, you think "look at all that space! Why aren't they kicking it into the space?"' Flynn told Conor McKeon for the *Herald*'s 'Decades of the Dubs' series in 2019. 'But when you're playing in them, you can't actually see the space because you have a guy literally in your face the whole time. You honestly couldn't see 20 or 30 yards in front of you.

'When you retire, that [rivalry] just dies. It's like "what was I thinking?" You realise they're exactly the same as you are. They were in the same position, doing the same things, trying to win the same cup as you are. You only appreciate afterwards how much in common you had with them.'

Dublin would make up almost half of the footballing All Star selection that year, with Michael Fitzsimons, Cian O'Sullivan, the returning McCaffrey, James McCarthy, Con O'Callaghan, Paul Mannion and Dean Rock all named to the team of the year.

If the Dubs were tempted to sleep contently in their beds that winter, the headlines from the curtain-raising All-Ireland minor final might have induced at least an odd bout of insomnia for the Boys in Blue. Kerry annihilated a Derry team that had had three points to spare over Dublin in their semi-final three weeks earlier. Of the Kingdom's 6-17 in the decider (Derry mustered just 1-8 in reply), their captain David Clifford accounted for no less than four goals and four points. That young man was going to be a problem.

CHAPTER FIVE

Twelve Minutes 2018

The Four in a Row. Chasing immortals. That was what faced Dublin as they embarked on the 2018 inter-county season. Could they match Micko's famous Kingdom side of the late 1970s and early 1980s by winning four straight All-Ireland senior football titles? The reigning champions' year got off to a relaxing start with a team trip to South Africa.

Manager Gavin handed the reins to his selector and fellow hero of 1995 Paul Clarke for the pre-season O'Byrne Cup, which saw Dublin pitched into a three-team group with Offaly and Wexford.

An opening night draw with the Faithful (Dublin 1-13 Offaly 0-16) was achieved largely on the back of Colm Basquel's goal and six points. The Ballyboden forward would serve his time on the relative fringes of the Blues' star-studded squad for several seasons before firmly taking his chance in 2023 with an All Star campaign. Other future notables involved for the Dubs' 'development' unit against Offaly were Seán McMahon at full-back, Brian Howard at centre-back and Killian O'Gara, the left-footed ponytailed brother of Eoghan, in at top of the right.

A one-point Sunday-afternoon loss in Enniscorthy four days later (Wexford 1-12 Dublin 0-14) brought Dublin's involvement in the competition to a close for another year – indeed, Clarke's fledgling squad required a 17-point victory to advance on score difference. A tall order, to be fair. Howard, McMahon and Basquel (0-6) were all in the starting 15 again, as was Paddy Small – another forward who proved a slow burner but was well worth the wait – who finished with a pair of points from play. Our old pals Meath would win the competition this year, beating Westmeath in the final. The Royals had accounted for O'Byrne Cup specialists Longford in the semi-final by virtue of a freetaking competition after the sides were still level following extra time – one for the notebook of any pub quiz enthusiasts amongst us.

Clarker, for his part, quite enjoyed his time in the hotseat. 'I've been lucky to be involved for a long time as a player, as a coach and as a long-time supporter,' the Whitehall Colmcille man said after the Wexford defeat. 'It was great to be asked to be involved by Jim Gavin and to work with a great elite group of players. To say goodbye to it and the campaign being over is disappointing. I enjoyed the time and the conversations and everything I learned. It's a pity that it was only two games and that it has to end now.'

We had a new, improved championship structure to look forward to. Something called the Super 8s was being introduced to replace the traditional quarter-finals. This meant the eventual All-Ireland champions would most likely play at least eight games – not counting replays – if they wanted to get their hands on Sam Maguire. Dublin had needed only six in 2017. All this meant we would have no National League semi-finals this term, meaning the top two in each division would play each other in the final.

2018 National League Division 1
Played 8, Won 6, Drew 1, Lost 1
Final position: League winners

The league opener against Kildare at Croke Park resulted in a seven-point win (2-17 to 2-10) and prompted comparisons between the current Dublin footballers and the Kilkenny hurlers of the noughties. Those comparisons came from beaten Kildare boss Cian O'Neill, who reckoned that, like Brian Cody's prime Cats, Gavin's Dubs 'don't just bang in one [goal], they bang in two – ruthlessly and efficiently, in a very short period of time and put games to bed'.

After that opener, played on Saturday, 27 January, Gavin took the GAA to task for the early start of the league season. 'I don't understand why we play football in January. The players should be with their clubs,' Jim reasoned.

Dublin went up to Omagh a week later and took care of Tyrone by five points, thanks in the main to goals from Ciarán Kilkenny and Eoghan O'Gara and despite a second straight sending off for Scully. The Templeogue Synge Street man received his second yellow card just as Gavin was getting ready to take him off. Dublin returned to Croker for round three of the league and saw off Donegal by the same margin. In the week leading up to the game, however, disaster struck. Bernard

Brogan, who had started the opener against Kildare, was confirmed to have damaged a cruciate ligament in training in the week of the game. He would be out for the foreseeable future. The St Oliver Plunkett Eoghan Ruadh forward had been named in the side to start against Donegal but was replaced by Paddy Andrews.

Round four brought the Dubs down to Castlebar to take on their old pals Mayo in MacHale Park. Scully would remain on the pitch for the duration of this one and even nab one of the goals, as Dublin emerged victorious on a scoreline of 2-10 to 0-12. Paul Mannion nicked the other goal, while Mick Fitzsimons got his marching orders following a straight red card in injury time in a game which saw Stephen Cluxton mark his 100th league appearance for his county with a clean sheet.

This was Dublin's 13th game in a row against Mayo in which they had avoided defeat. Mayo were without their main marksman, Cillian O'Connor, but either way, it was becoming increasingly apparent that Dublin simply had the Connacht men's number. The Dubs, as it happened, were largely without a main marksman of their own – and fans were beginning to ask questions. Diarmuid Connolly made only a brief appearance off the bench in Castlebar. We hadn't seen a whole lot of him since he had captained St Vincent's to a second straight county title the previous October, beating Dean Rock's Ballymun Kickhams 1-8 to 0-8 in the decider. The Marino men, led by true blue icon Brian Mullins, were shocked in the Leinster quarter-final by Wicklow champs Rathnew two weeks later. The Dubliners had been 1/16 favourites before throw-in. Final score in Aughrim: Rathnew 1-13 St Vincent's 1-9. And like that, poof, Dermo was gone …

If it felt like the Dubs had Mayo all figured out, is it possible the same could be true for, dare we say it, Kerry? In round five of the league at Headquarters, Dublin put the Kingdom to the sword in a 2-17 to 0-11 mauling. On the weekend before the Cheltenham Festival, Dublin looked like a Grade One thoroughbred in amongst also-rans. Colm Keys in the following Monday's *Irish Independent* reckoned 'Dublin have never been so far ahead of Kerry'. Bomber Liston, in the same pages, admitted that this 'painful drubbing hurts but the Kingdom are better than this'. Kerry fans were hoping he was right.

On the pitch, Scully goaled for the second game in a row, with Ciarán Kilkenny helping himself to the other one. A miserly backline led by David Byrne and the ruthless Jonny Cooper allowed Kerry only 11 points in a stadium they knew inside out.

A trip to Salthill on St Patrick's weekend was the next port of call. The game saw Dublin drop their first point of the season when the teams split 26 points between them in Pearse Stadium. The action on the western seaboard a day after Paddy's Day was fractious, to say the least. Ciarán Kilkenny would pocket five points from play as the Dubs clawed their way back from three points down on a day when even the mild-mannered Jason Sherlock got into a bit of bother on the sideline. The erstwhile darling of the Hill, Jayo was caught on camera boom-boom-booming Galway freetaker Barry McHugh with a shoulder to the back as the Tribesman tangled with Kilkenny near the Dublin bench. Eoghan O'Gara was sent off for striking Seán Andy Ó Ceallaigh, who himself picked up a black card a couple of minutes later. Gavin, after briefly complaining about the officiating, dusted himself off and surmised: 'Two teams going hard at it. It is March football, and you have two quality teams going head to head.'

Sherlock would receive an eight-week ban for the altercation.

There was still that lingering question for the boss, although he did his utmost to kick it to touch: Where's Dermo? Connolly hadn't been seen in a Dublin shirt since that cameo appearance off the bench against Mayo three weeks earlier. Another panel stalwart, Denis Bastick, had retired the previous November. All of which meant Dublin were shorter on experience and steel than they had been in quite some time (unlikely enforcer Jayo notwithstanding). After Dublin's final league game against Monaghan, Gavin reiterated his claim that Diarmuid Connolly was merely 'resting'. At this stage, there wasn't a GAA fan anywhere – Dub or otherwise – who was buying it.

There may not have been a Connolly sighting against Monaghan, but we did get a first look at Na Fianna bomber Eoin Murchan. The pint-sized defender made his first competitive appearance as a 53rd-minute sub for Darren Daly and would go on to play a key role in Dublin's Four in a Row summer. The conveyor belt continued to spit them out. Round pegs into round holes.

Having presumably received a glowing report from Paul Clarke after his O'Byrne Cup exploits, Raheny's Brian Howard quickly established himself alongside his clubmate Brian Fenton as one of Dublin's main driving forces. Howard started in 14 of Dublin's 16 competitive games in league and championship in 2018, earning the first of two straight All Stars. Throughout the noughties, the northside club had provided Ciarán Whelan and David Henry for the county cause. Henry went on to captain the Dubs in 2010 and was still a squad member a year later when they finally won the big one. Whelan, a barnstorming, point-kicking midfielder, became a crowd favourite who, upon retirement, featured in many a 'Greatest to Never Win it All' argument on high stools the length and breadth of the country. Raheny now again provided a pair of stars to the Boys in Blue as the 2020s approached. Fenton and Howard (Seán McMahon would join them in 2020) could be counted among the very best in the land.

A week after the Monaghan game, on April Fool's Day in Croke Park, Dublin grabbed an unlucky-for-some 13th National League title with an 0-18 to 0-14 win over Galway. The Dubs played the final 20 minutes of that game with just 14 men when Niall Scully was sent off for the third time that league season, having picked up two yellow cards. Paul Mannion, who opened the point-scoring after just 15 seconds, would finish with three from play with Ciarán Kilkenny nabbing a pair of scores, as did substitute Colm Basquel. Murchan came off the bench again, this time replacing John Small 40 minutes in. Shane Walsh scored two points for the Tribesmen. He would win an All-Ireland Club title alongside Mannion for Dublin club Kilmacud Crokes in 2023 after a controversial transfer from his own club, Kilkerrin-Clonberne.

The squad then hunkered down to prepare for the championship. It would be a full two months before we'd see them in (relatively) competitive action again. A few weeks after that league final, the loss of the injured Brogan would be compounded by the revelation that the resting Connolly was off to Boston for the summer. If the Four in a

Row was to be claimed, it would have to be achieved without two of the game's greatest ever forwards.

* * *

Day 1,365: Sunday, 27 May 2018
Leinster quarter-final, O'Moore Park (attendance 11,786)
Dublin 4-25 Wicklow 1-11

'It will take something extraordinary to loosen Gavin's grip on the title' was the strapline above Roy Curtis's match preview in the *Sunday World* the morning of Dublin's 2018 championship opener. The goings-on at O'Moore Park later that afternoon certainly didn't prove him wrong. The following morning, after what the *Indo* described as a 'ruthless Garden rout', it was hard to escape the prevailing wisdom that Sam Maguire was absolutely Dublin's to lose.

Four first-half goals from four different scorers (Fenton, Kilkenny, O'Callaghan and Rock, since you asked) left the Dubs in a position to rack up a record score. It didn't quite come to that, but with Boston-bound Diarmuid Connolly not part of the squad and the veteran presence of Bernard Brogan so cruelly taken away by that knee injury against Kildare, the Dubs' panel still looked as deep and ferocious as ever.

A random, innocuous moment from that game stands out, for some reason. It was the second half and Dublin were enjoying a healthy lead, when Wicklow, having been penned into their own third of the pitch for what seemed like an age, broke up the field with full-back Ross

O'Brien in possession. A faint murmur went up amongst the Wicklow fans. A rare attacking reprieve. O'Brien made it as far as the Dubs' 45, where he was met by the unmovable object that is Jonny Cooper, operating at centre-back that day.

Cooper swarmed the Wicklow man. He was everywhere. O'Brien must have felt surrounded. Referee Ciarán Branagan (Dermo's mate) put the whistle to his lips but didn't blow. Cooper's ferocious tackling was where it always was – right on the edge. Considering this was everything the Dubs fan wants from the number 6, the strangest thought went through the minds of those perched on the uncovered stand side of O'Moore Park: 'Jesus, Jonny … leave him alone!' Eventually, mercifully, Branagan's whistle blew. Relief.

Cooper was furious and remonstrated with the Down referee. It was an insight into not just the Na Fianna veteran but the whole of Jim Gavin's operation. Dublin were cruising. Many miles out of sight. If Ross O'Brien had skipped by Jonny Cooper and clipped over a point, what difference would it have made? To the outcome, none. But that misses the point of what this Dublin panel were about. They were undoubtably the most talented collection of footballers we've ever seen. But more than that, they were quite simply remorseless. They didn't care about you ('the worst thing the Dubs do is ignore you' – Colm Cooper). A footballing terminator. The unkillable machine.

Wicklow manager John Evans's post-match quotes are an insight into the psychology of facing up to the beast on the block when you're outmanned and outgunned. You take your victories where you can. 'There was a lot of good to take out of the game against Dublin. We are the only Division 4 team to score a goal against them, and you look at the likes of Carlow last year, they were only delighted with themselves having only scored seven points against them and we hit them for 1-11. The big thing is we stayed playing and we never came off the bit at all and I was delighted with that.'

* * *

Day 1,379: Sunday, 10 June 2018
Leinster semi-final, Croke Park (attendance 39,028)
Dublin 2-25 Longford 0-12

'Dublin is the big monster that looms over everybody.'
Denis Connerton, Longford manager

In many ways, it was a standard provincial semi-final blowout for the Dubs. But this one came at a price. A James McGivney tackle that was later than your paycheque left Dublin skipper Stephen Cluxton prone on the ground. McGivney was sent off, and Cluxton would be replaced by Evan Comerford, leaving the Blues to duke out a championship game without the Parnells man for the first time in 14 years.

Pub quiz question: Who was the last goalkeeper not named Stephen Cluxton to play a championship game in goal for Dublin? Answer: Brian Murphy, in the (infamous?) 2004 Leinster quarter-final defeat to Westmeath, then of course under the tutelage of Páidí Ó Sé. Cluxton was serving a one-match ban, having been sent off in a

2003 qualifier loss to Armagh.

'We knew what we were facing,' Longford manager Denis Connerton said afterwards, 'one of the greatest teams of this era. I refer to Dublin as the Real Madrid of football. They're an absolutely outstanding team. They're so economical in their shooting and passing, all you can do is admire them ... There were a lot of people in Lourdes and Lough Derg praying for us – obviously prayer that doesn't work.'

Longford forward Robbie Smyth ended his day with five points beside his name. Afterwards, the Abbeylara man acknowledged that 'it's days like this you want. You want to come to Croke Park and play teams like Dublin more often. We just talked about not letting it pass us by, and for everyone to get the best out of themselves and empty the tank.'

On the pitch, Paul Mannion's goal summed up this Dublin team. The Kilmacud Crokes forward dispossessed Liam Connerton before finishing high into the roof of the Longford net. The Dubs' message was clear: We know we're good – but we'll outwork you too. No one epitomised that ideal more than the hard-running, goal-scoring, point-kicking Mannion.

Dean Rock added the second goal, while, as he did against Wicklow, Colm Basquel made a scoring contribution from the bench. Options. Seemingly endless options. Dublin had now won their last six Leinster semi-finals by an aggregate of 111 points. Domination, in the most extreme sense of the word.

Longford would host Kildare a fortnight later in the qualifiers. The Lilywhites escaped Pearse Park with a three-point win, 1-16 to 1-13, ending Longford's championship for another year.

TWELVE MINUTES 2018

* * *

Day 1,393: Sunday, 24 June 2018
Leinster final, Croke Park (attendance 41,728)
Dublin 1-25 Laois 0-10

No Cluxton, no problem, as Dublin wrapped up an eighth Leinster title in a row with plenty to spare over Laois. Not even a 20th-minute penalty miss by Paul Mannion could soften the Dubs' cough. Kerry had won eight Munster titles on the spin on two occasions, but Gavin's side were the first team to achieve the feat in Leinster.

In his *Sunday World* column the following week, after what seemed like weeks of lopsided scores throughout the country, your boy Pat Spillane reckoned SUMMER CAN FINALLY START AFTER DIRE PROVINCIALS.

For those of us feeling nostalgic, a week after Dublin had annexed Leinster, their neighbours Kildare found a new way to beat Mayo that even the Dubs hadn't thought of. The Lilywhites ended Stephen Rochford's men's involvement in this year's championship, beating them by two points at St Conleth's Park – finally bringing to a finish everyone's favourite soap opera of that particular season, the 'Newbridge or Nowhere' saga.

The GAA had initially fixed the round two qualifier as the second half of a double-header in Croke Park, with Cavan–Tyrone serving as the curtain-raiser. This didn't sit right with the Kildare County Board, who stuck to their guns and then threatened to boycott the fixture altogether.

Even Joe Brolly was on their side, the corner-forward-turned-pundit claiming at one point that 'the GAA are acting outside the law of the GAA. It's clear that until it's round four of the qualifiers, the first name out of the hat has a home draw and there's no caveat on that ... So Kildare are entitled [to home advantage] by a matter of right, and a matter of law.'

Kildare duly dug their heels in over the match-day venue, and then backed it up with a performance. Manager Cian O'Neill, to be fair, didn't take all the credit – just most of it. Defeat to Dublin in that classic 2017 final had broken Mayo. They were a shell of themselves the following season. They needed a late Kevin McLoughlin equalising point against Donegal to avoid relegation from Division 1 in the league. They would then fall at the first hurdle in the Connacht Championship when they lost to eventual provincial winners Galway. They beat a poor Limerick side at the Gaelic Grounds in the qualifiers before a last-quarter rally saw them edge past Tipperary at Semple Stadium in a game they had trailed in for long periods. The Kildare defeat put them out of their misery. Rochford would resign as manager shortly afterwards, claiming he 'didn't have the backing of the board'.

The clash of Cavan and Tyrone, incidentally, was moved to Enniskillen, with Mickey Harte's side running out winners, 0-18 to 1-12.

Next up for Jim Gavin and his merry men, the all-new, all-singing, all-dancing Super 8s. Here, the 'Croke Park issue' would come into focus once more. The Super 8s were, in theory, designed to give each county in the two groups of four a home game, an away game and a game at a neutral venue. As Croker was designated as Dublin's 'home' venue and also the most obvious setting for their 'neutral' game, this, some argued, effectively allowed the Boys in Blue two 'home' games. The Dubs' old nemesis Jim McGuinness, then a Sky Sports pundit, framed the situation as 'an opportunity for Dublin and Croke Park to do the right thing and go the same as all the other teams'.

'They're the best team in the country, they're chasing amazing goals season after season,' he went on. 'Just play the game [in Croke Park], play the game away from home and then say, "listen, we don't care where we play the game, play it at a neutral venue". Just do that and everybody will be happy ... The reality is, people from the outside looking in will go "that's a fix, that's set up and Dublin's going to progress again".'

Incidentally, then four years removed from his time as Donegal boss and having flirted with a career in soccer, the Glasgow-based McGuinness would answer 'never say never' when quizzed on the likelihood of him ever returning to inter-county management. More on that (about five years) later ...

The Croker Conundrum had by now become something of a chicken-and-egg issue for the GAA. Dublin's 'home' National League games were moved there by the Leinster Council in 2011 in an attempt to cater for the sizeable Blue Army that follows the county. As Dublin's domination took hold in the following seasons, the arrangement drew the ire of opposing fans, commentators, managers and players alike.

Donegal, who Dublin would meet in their opening Super 8s clash, sought a meeting with the GAA's top brass to ensure what they insisted was 'a level playing field for every team at the All-Ireland quarter-final group stage and to seek clarification on how any county may use a ground as both neutral and home venue'. The intention of the meeting was, they said, 'to ensure that no team has any advantage over any other team'.

Donegal manager Declan Bonner reckoned, 'For all eight teams, I think it's got to be the one playing field, and I don't think it's that level if you have to play two matches away from home and another team has two home games. In terms of fairness, if Donegal were to play Dublin and someone said the game was to be played at a neutral venue, then you would expect somewhere like Cavan or Clones ... Not going into Dublin's back yard to play what is a so-called neutral match.'

* * *

Day 1,413: Saturday, 14 July 2018
Supers 8s Rd1, Croke Park (attendance 53,501)
Dublin 2-15 Donegal 0-16

The headline above Sean McGoldrick's match report in the following morning's *Sunday World* said it all: DIFFERENT FORMAT BUT SAME RESULT FOR THE CHAMPS: RUTHLESS BLUES SET UP CRUNCH CLASH IN OMAGH.

Niall Scully had waited quite a while for his first championship goal for Dublin, and it arrived in the 27th minute. The Templeogue Synge Street man only had to wait another 10 minutes of play for his second. Scully's double gave Dublin five points to spare over the side who had provoked all of this back in 2014.

The Ulstermen were missing one of their most potent weapons, however. Paddy McBrearty, their prolific corner-forward, had suffered a season-ending ACL injury in his side's Ulster final triumph over Fermanagh, robbing Declan Bonner of one of the sweetest left pegs in the land. There's no doubt McBrearty's absence made Donegal a far less dangerous proposition, but no football fan of any persuasion wanted to see the championship series shorn of one of the game's most watchable performers.

From a fallen star to an emerging one: With just two league substitute appearances and one spin off the bench in the Leinster Championship, the aforementioned pocket rocket Eoin Murchan was selected in the starting 15 against Donegal and tasked with keeping tabs on Ryan McHugh. In an otherwise flat Dublin showing, Murchan performed brilliantly, even coming in for special praise from Tomás Ó Sé on that weekend's *Sunday Game*. There was also a first start for Jack McCaffrey since injuring his knee in the previous September's All-Ireland final against Mayo.

Howard would keep his fine summer rolling with a pair of scores from play, while there was the inevitable contribution from the bench as substitutes Cormac Costello and Paul Flynn went home with a brace of points apiece.

By now, that 2017 U-21 All-Ireland Championship win was bearing fruit. Con O'Callaghan was already a star, and by season's end Howard would be as well. Evan Comerford filled in ably for Cluxton when called upon, and Colm Basquel would make four championship appearances that summer, with one for Paddy Small in there as well. But in Eoin

Murchan, Dublin had the kind of weapon that every county manager craved. In the modern game, speed kills – and the diminutive Murchan had pace for days.

* * *

Day 1,420: Saturday, 21 July 2018
Super 8s Rd2, Omagh (attendance 16,205)
Dublin 1-14 Tyrone 0-14

The *Tyrone Herald* offered no fewer than seven pages of coverage on the latest 'Battle of Omagh' with the headline SPIRITED RED HANDS GAIN GROUND ON 'OTHERWORLDLY' DUBS adorning Niall Gartland's match report.

With the persistent narrative that taking Dublin out of Croke Park might put manners on them, so to speak, a gritty victory like this in one of the most difficult away venues in football seems like an important checkmark in the Dubs' 2018 season. If it didn't quite quell the argument over Dublin's Croke Park retainer arrangement, leaving Omagh with all the points on offer at least reminded the naysayers that, when it came to beating this Dublin side, geography was the least of your challenges.

James McCarthy's goal – finished at the second attempt – proved the difference, although Dublin appeared to have matters well in hand before a late surge from the home side.

The loss left Mickey Harte's side needing to beat Donegal to advance to the last four. They didn't know it at the time, but Tyrone would get another chance to stop the seemingly unstoppable Dubs in just a few short weeks' time in the All-Ireland final.

Elsewhere in the wacky world of GAA bureaucracy, Dublin's Croke Park residence was not the only venue arrangement causing unwanted headlines. A request to play a soccer match in tribute to the late former Ireland, Celtic and Manchester United player Liam Miller at Cork's Páirc Uí Chaoimh was initially refused by the association in a move that caused outrage outside the GAA and embarrassment within it. Miller had passed away from pancreatic cancer earlier that year at the age of just 36. The GAA argued that a decision to allow such a fixture – which was being played to raise money for the Corkman's family – could only be made at GAA Congress, which takes place in February. The wheels often turn infuriatingly slowly at GAA board level. Liam Miller's testimonial would, of course, be played at Páirc Uí Chaoimh the following September, with over 43,000 fans turning out for a game that sold out in minutes.

* * *

Day 1,435: Sunday, 5 August 2018
Super 8s Rd3, Croke Park (attendance 33,240)
Dublin 4-24 Roscommon 2-16

'I know. I know. Jim's always keeping an eye on the future. It's a key reason why he's managed to sustain the success. He's friends with Stuart Lancaster in Leinster Rugby who talks about the "performance clock" and how you should avoid letting a

> team grow old together. You don't wait until midnight to make changes. The best managers make changes before it becomes obvious that change is needed. I know that those of us at the back of the bus can't stay on it forever. I know in the near future we'll be getting off it for good.'
>
> Bernard Brogan, *The Hill*

It wasn't supposed to be this way. It wasn't supposed to end like this. To peter out. It was supposed to end with flourish – a wallop, even. Bernard Brogan, one of the greatest to ever do it. He deserved better. We – the fans – deserved better. Even now, some years removed, it's hard to fathom that a six-minute cameo as a blood sub in a largely meaningless Super 8s tie against a beaten Roscommon team would represent the second-to-last action of Bernard Brogan's championship career.

Brother Alan had gotten his swansong three years earlier when he sent that point over into the Hill before moments later holding the Sam Maguire up to that same terrace with one hand and waving goodbye with the other. A Hollywood ending.

There would be no such encore for Bernard, although he would endure for one more year after this and collect two more medals. It wasn't the final chapter the Oliver Plunkett forward desired.

Eoghan O'Gara got his chance here and grabbed it with both hands, bulldozing his way to 2-2 in just 53 minutes, while Cormac Costello made the most of a start, ending with nine points, seven from play. Brogan temporarily replaced Mark Schutte in the 61st minute and traipsed back to the bench in the 67th.

Back to his book: 'I spit in my hands and rub them together. It feels good being back out here. I'm not going to try anything stupid or spectacular. I just want to show Jim and everyone else that I'm moving well and back in the mix … My planting and turning isn't sharp enough yet, and if I tried, I'd only get blocked down and look an eejit … And then I'm making another run, only this time back over to our dugout in the stand. After my little five-minute cameo, Schutte is good to go back on again …

'We make our way back in the dressing room. Lads clasp my hand, pat me on the back, or in Mick's case, throw an arm around my neck and rub me on the head … Then Jim comes over, as he does to everyone. "Great to see you back out there," he smiles. "Thanks a million," I instinctively reply. But within a millisecond in my own head, I'm thinking, Well, no thanks to you! If Schutte hadn't to go off, I wouldn't have got back out there!'

Bernard wouldn't be back out there in any serious way for the rest of the campaign.

***

Day 1,441: Saturday, 11 August 2018
All-Ireland semi-final, Croke Park (attendance 54,715)
Dublin 1-24 Galway 2-12

The Four in a Row was within reach. Ciarán Kilkenny nabbed three points from play against the Tribesmen, while Con O'Callaghan torched their inside line for 1-3. Cormac Costello added 0-3 off the bench, and Kevin McManamon chipped in with a pair of scores of his own. Cluxton saved an Eamonn Brannigan penalty kick. Dublin had booked their place in a sixth All-Ireland final in eight seasons with relatively little fuss.

O'Callaghan, just four months past his 22nd birthday, was becoming football's most devastating attacking force. Howard and Murchan were now knitted seamlessly into the very fabric of the game's most bulletproof side. 'Throughout the year, it's really the new lads that come in every year and keep driving things on a little,' said Jack McCaffrey.

On Monday morning, the *Irish Examiner* was wondering if the decider between Tyrone and Dublin can 'rescue what's been a poor football championship'. Their columnist, former Armagh ace Oisin McConville, declared that 'Gaelic football is becoming very hard to watch'.

Tyrone and Monaghan had played out a forgettable semi-final on the other side of the draw. Niall Sludden's goal would give the Red Hand men the edge – and a one-point victory, 1-13 to 0-15. There were no two ways about it: if you weren't a Dublin fan, the 2018 All-Ireland SFC had not done a whole lot to set your pulse racing. In fact, the 54,716 fans who attended Dublin's routine dismissal of Galway was the lowest turnout at a semi-final involving the Boys in Blue since just 52,606 showed up to see them hammer Leitrim at the same stage in 1994.

'Who, Dubs fans apart, can look forward to 2019 if Jim Gavin's men wipe the floor with the challengers?' Colm Keys asked ominously in the *Irish Independent* the Monday after those two All-Ireland semi-finals.

Day 1,463: Sunday, 2 September 2018
All-Ireland final, Croke Park (attendance 82,300)
Dublin 2-17 Tyrone 1-14

As Dublin eyed up the Four in a Row, 3,000 miles away one of its greatest forwards was winning medals of a different sort. Seven days before the All-Ireland final, Diarmuid Connolly had inspired Donegal Boston to victory in the Boston Senior Championship final in Canton, Massachusetts. Connolly scored 12 points as they saw off Wolfe Tones 0-17 to 0-12. He had slipped over four scores in the semi-final. The kid still had it. No surprise there.

Back on home soil, if the newspapers on the morning of this final were to be believed, it was all over bar the shouting. Could hubris possibly derail the Dubs? In a word, no. SOMETHING SPECIAL IN THE DUBLIN AIR: PILOT GAVIN NEVER DEVIATES FROM THE COURSE was the headline which adorned Roy Curtis's match preview in the *Sunday World*. Beside it, Charlie Redmond assured Blues fans DUBLIN HAVE GOT TOO MUCH.

When Dublin's 26-player squad for the game was revealed, Bernard Brogan's name was not included. Shock or not, and sentiment aside, it was clearly the correct call. This Dublin squad was as stacked as it gets. Brogan had worked night and day to get back in game shape after his early season injury against Kildare, but he had simply run out of time. There were just too many good players ahead of him. In the week leading up to the final, Brogan was beckoned into Jim Gavin's office at their DCU training base. Usually there would be a selector or two for company in moments like this, but this time, it was just player and manager. Man to man. From there, Gavin dropped the bad news. Brogan had not made the cut.

'I can't just take this lying down,' was Brogan's first thought, as described in his autobiography, *The Hill*. He pushed back at his manager: 'Jim, I can't believe you're saying this to me. I'm after breaking my arse to get back …'

Gavin interrupted with, 'I want you to come with us. I want you to travel', throwing Brogan for a loop. It's a most unGavinlike move. Dare we say, an olive branch thrust towards a waning star. A sentimental allowance even, or 'some gesture of respect', as Brogan himself surmised. Gavin continued: 'I want you to warm up with the lads. I want you to be number 27.'

Brogan accepted the offer, as any shrewd chap who realises they're possibly not in the strongest negotiating position would. And why not? Everyone wants to be in the Show. All-conquering sports teams can fool us into believing they exist in a permanent zen-like communal state; a world where ego doesn't exist and where all stakeholders hold equal footing. Players don't have to put differences aside because, apparently, they have no differences. The reality is, people are people. Whether you're Jim Gavin's Dubs, Micko's Kingdom, Brian Cody's Kilkenny, Fergie's United, Belichick's Patriots or Jordan's Bulls, there are those who are artists and those who carry water. For every Eric Cantona, there's a Gary Neville. For every Michael Jordan, there's a Denis Rodman. Egos are not so much checked at the door as managed carefully by a skilled leadership. Here we have Gavin's true genius, arguably the biggest accomplishment of his Dublin coaching career. How do you keep a large group of ultra-talented people, who are competing for playing time, attention and significance, motivated over the course of several trophy-laden seasons? How do you combat what NBA legend Pat Riley terms the 'Disease of More'? Gavin and his backroom team navigated the delicate internal politics of a top inter-county panel as well as anyone ever has. Hey, if it was easy, everyone could do it – and nobody would write books about it …

The Brogans were Dublin footballing royalty. Bernard's father, Bernard Snr, was a star of the immortal 1970s teams that would claim four All-Irelands in a decade and create the Dublin–Kerry rivalry that in many ways continues to define Gaelic football to this day. His legendary surging run and goal ('He's in front of the goal, he can't miss, he hasn't!' – Michael O'Hehir) in the Greatest Game Ever Played, the 1977 All-Ireland semi-final against Kerry, etched his name in Hill 16 folklore. And Bernard Jnr's older brother, Alan, was of course one of the finest forwards to ever wear blue.

Some players arrive on the inter-county scene out of nowhere. Lucky to be there. Thriving against the odds. The plucky upstart. Bernard Brogan Jnr was not one of those guys. He was always going to play for the Dubs. His talent had been earmarked many moons before he ever graced Croke Park. His ascent to the most glamorous senior squad in the land was as inevitable as it was welcome for a Dublin team that wasn't overflowing with star forwards.

Incidentally, Brogan's uncle, Jim Brogan, was also a member of Kevin

Heffernan's Dublin heroes of the 1970s. Unlike his much-celebrated brother and nephews, Jim spent the majority of his inter-county career as a noble squad member. Many years later, in Tom Humphries's book *Dublin v. Kerry*, he described his low-key days with the Boys in Blue as a kind of bonding experience that can only be appreciated by those who live through it. 'You were exposed to this extraordinary gang of people,' he said. 'You were frustrated but there were times when you would say, isn't it great to have such a wonderful experience with such a wonderful group of guys … I played in very few matches. But with perspective I am happy.'

Bernard's situation was obviously not the same. He too had been exposed to an extraordinary gang of people, but he was one of the most extraordinary among them. Now, he may have felt that he was an artist turned water-carrier. To become just another squad member after all those years atop the totem pole would challenge the self-worth of even the most modest player. Brogan, to his credit, handled the crushing blow well – but allowed himself the right to acknowledge the disappointment of essentially missing out on the biggest game of the season. 'In the dressing room after the final, when Jim goes around to shake each of our hands as he always does, he said to me we'll go for one more,' wrote Brogan in his book. 'But that's easy to say in a moment like that.'

Something else that fools us about such high-achieving groups might be the assumption that the Jim Gavins of the world make these life-and-death decisions with a cool hand and a cold heart, when nothing could be further from the truth. Gavin and Brogan had been around the block together. This one stung the boss. In the aftermath of this latest All-Ireland victory, there were some telling quotes from the manager. 'The hardest part of the job is giving the news that a player can't travel,' Gavin said. 'That's the really difficult part because you're breaking a guy's dreams.

'We had 34 on the squad, so to be giving that news to eight players is tough on them. It's testament to Bernard's mental strength to see how well he was moving out there. There's a lot of sacrifice involved. There's such a talented group of players in Dublin. But it's a player's choice. They're volunteering their time.'

Incidentally, this would prove to be the last All-Ireland final of RTÉ broadcaster Michael Lyster's glittering career. 'Everybody's era passes and then there's a new era of different people,' the Galwayman, who first joined the national broadcaster in 1980, told the *Sunday World* in the week leading up to the decider.

On the pitch, the pre-match predictions proved largely accurate as Dublin picked Tyrone apart on their way to a six-point victory. Niall Scully found the net, as did Paul Mannion from the penalty spot. Dean Rock wore out the black spot with seven points, while a backline superbly marshalled by captain Cluxton, Philly McMahon and Jonny Cooper kept the Ulstermen at arm's length.

Some years after the game, Tyrone goalkeeper Niall Morgan reluctantly revealed how quickly Dublin solved their gameplan. 'We went in so underprepared for Dublin in 2018,' he admitted. 'We had three kickouts. The first was "get it away within six seconds". The second was "hit it to an overload under the Hogan Stand" and the third was "hit it to Colm Cavanagh". That was the three kickouts. Within 12 minutes, Ciarán Kilkenny, on the field, had worked out those three kickouts. Dublin had worked them out. Within 12 minutes, they knew exactly what we were going to do. It was mental.'

What was going through Bernard Brogan's mind as he stood on the pitch, another All-Ireland medal in hand but a spotlessly clean pair of boots on his feet and number 27 on his back, having not made it off the bench? Beside him in the dugout, his old running-mate Paul Flynn also hadn't made it into the game, despite the fact he'd played every other game so far that summer, even starting and scoring 1-3 against Roscommon. The torch was being passed before their eyes. The final whistle sounded as these two great servants were busying themselves out along the sideline having a stretch. By then, Gavin had sent Michael Fitzsimons, Cormac Costello, Kevin McManamon, Darren Daly and Michael Darragh Macauley in from the bench. But no Brogan or Flynn.

Eoin Murchan's meteoric rise was complete. Not many realised it but this was actually the Na Fianna clubman's second All-Ireland win as a Dublin squad member. A year earlier, he had failed to make the match-day 26 that took on Mayo. He would serve the team in a different capacity on that occasion. 'I was helping in the stats box for the [Mayo] game,' he told RTÉ Sport after winning in 2018. 'It's good to be out on the pitch! Some of the guys have six medals, a lot of us only have two or three, and that's why we put in so much work during the year. We'll enjoy this one for now, but we'll come back fighting next year.'

There would be seven Dubs named in the All Star team later that year. Defenders Jonny Cooper, James McCarthy and Jack McCaffrey made up half of the back six. Midfielder Brian Fenton landed a first Footballer of the Year award to go with his third All Star. There was also room for Brian Howard, Paul Mannion and Ciarán Kilkenny in the forward line-up.

Philly McMahon's father Phil passed away the month before the final, after a long battle with stomach cancer. He had been diagnosed in the summer of 2017. 'The big word for us this year was "gratitude",' McMahon said after Dublin's fourth straight All-Ireland title. 'There's people in the stadium that probably won't ever see an All-Ireland final again. It's just great to give a bit of happiness to people. These fans travelled all over the country this year so it's nice to give back. We always say it's not going to be around forever, so we'll enjoy it while we have it. These lads gave me a gift last year: my dad could see me win the All-Ireland. He was here in spirit today. There's plenty of people who are probably not here who would love to be here to watch us. So we're grateful for what we have.'

As are we, Philly. The Four in a Row. History. Yet more history.

CHAPTER SIX

So Long, Jim. And Thanks 2019

The Drive for Five. What a long, winding road it would be. In fact, at the end of it, there'd be a surprise change of driver. Dublin headed into the 2019 season short of a man who had in many ways backboned the Gilroy and Gavin eras: Paul Flynn had played his last game for Dublin. 'While my heart says play on, unfortunately my body says it's time to call it a day,' the Fingallians half-forward wrote in announcing his retirement from the inter-county game. A fulcrum of the 2011, 2013, 2015 and 2016 teams, Flynn came off the bench in the 2017 final and had been an unused sub, alongside long-time pal Bernard Brogan, in the 2018 decider. The four-time All Star had also been appointed chief executive of the Gaelic Players Association the previous summer, a position he would hold until late January 2021.

Speaking of the GPA, they were not all that impressed with some of the GAA's latest experimental rules, which were put in place for that year's National Football League. In an effort to curb cautious play, the overuse of the handpass, and negative, spoiling tactics, the brains-trust came up with the following adjustments to the playbook:

- The maximum number of consecutive handpasses is now three.
- A sideline kick must be played forward, except when it is inside the opposing team's 20m line.
- An advanced mark may be taken where the ball is kicked from outside the opposing team's 45, travels 20 metres and is caught clean inside that 45m line.
- A black-card offence would now mean 10 minutes in the sin bin with no replacement.
- Kickouts must be taken from the 20m line.

Three of these rules would be kept and introduced for the start of the following season, namely the advanced mark, sin bin and new kickout directives.

2019 National League Division 1
Played 7, Won 4, Drew 0, Lost 3
Final position: 4th in table

It was finally Mayo's year – in the league, at least. The Connacht men won their 12th National League title, having finished second in the Division 1 table to Kerry. The pair subsequently met in the final, with Mayo running out four-point winners, 3-11 to 2-10.

James Horan was back in the Mayo dugout after replacing Stephen

Rochford, who had stepped aside the previous winter. As is often the case with Mayo, a manager switch was one of the more mundane storylines of the off-season.

An article in *The Mayo News* in late September reported on allegations made by the Mayo International Supporters' Foundation that had resulted in the withholding of €250,000 in funding for their county board. The foundation, it seemed, was not convinced by the manner in which some of their hard-raised funds were being deployed and announced it had 'ceased funding to Mayo County Board until appropriate governance structures are put in place'. The straw that broke the camel's back came after the county board's 'refusal to provide the ten All-Ireland final tickets it had committed to provide for a gala auction [in New York]. These tickets were bought and paid for by a donor on the night of the gala. In the end, the foundation had to pay €5,000 to the county board to secure the ten tickets which had a face value of €950.'

County Board treasurer Kevin O'Toole contested the allegations, which he claimed had 'a huge amount of misinformation' before adding, poetically, 'There are more moving sands in the Mayo Foundation than there are in the Sahara.'

With that backdrop in place, the returning Horan's side would lose just twice in their league campaign. Once, at home to local rivals Galway and once, crucially, to Dublin – their kryptonite – in a one-sided affair at Croke Park. The following week's *Mayo News* headlined that 1-12 to 0-7 late February defeat a REALITY CHECK. Lee Keegan spent some time in the sin bin, while Cormac Costello was chief marksman for a Dublin side that spread the scoring around on the night.

Interestingly, in that same edition of the *Mayo News*, under the headline Mayo Okay with Croker Vote, Ger Flanagan reported that despite their support of the proposal, Mayo County Board chairman Mike Connolly was happy enough to see Donegal's motion that Dublin be kept out of Croke Park for that year's Super 8s rejected at Congress. 'When it was all spelt out at Congress, I could see why it went the way it did,' Connolly said of the proposal that was defeated on a 64-36 percent majority. 'Regardless of this advantage [to Dublin], players wanted to play at Croke Park. Even for ourselves, if we were drawn against Dublin in Parnell Park and only eight thousand people were able to attend the game … we would only get two or three thousand tickets, and it wouldn't be fair to our supporters who are up and down the country. When it came to a game like that, we'd be locking out two-thirds of them.

'A lot of counties want to play in Croke Park too and they want every opportunity. I know it's becoming the home ground for the Dubs, but a lot of counties will say, "Look, if we were to beat them, no better place to beat them than in Croke Park."' Fair play to you, Michael.

After an opening-night loss to Monaghan in Clones (2-13 to 1-13) and a one-point defeat by Kerry at Headquarters in week three (1-18 to 2-14), Dublin would win three of their last four league games to set themselves up nicely for springtime. Tellingly, despite their hot-and-cold record, Gavin's side would goal in all seven league games, finding the net nine times in total.

* * *

Day 1,729: Sunday, 26 May 2019
Leinster quarter-final, O'Moore Park (attendance 14,380)
Dublin 5-21 Louth 0-10

A week before Dublin's championship opener: heartbreak. Anton O'Toole, the Blue Panther, winner of four All-Ireland medals (1974, 1976, 1977 and 1983), passed away at the age of 68. Tributes flowed in from Kevin Moran, Charlie Redmond and Tooler's long-time opponent Pat Spillane – who spoke of the wing-forward's impact on his Kerry side – in the Sunday papers. Dubs and Ireland legend Moran assured us Anton would be dearly missed, while Redmond, former darling of the Hill, described the Templeogue Synge Street man as 'one of a kind'. God speed, Anton. A Dub as thoroughly loved as it gets.

GAVIN STILL OPEN TO CONNOLLY RETURN AS SHOW GETS ON THE ROAD ran the headline beside Donnchadh Boyle's match report in the *Irish Independent* the morning after the Dubs dismantled the Wee County. Remember the theme – we will be returning to it regularly throughout the summer.

Connolly wasn't back – yet – but Rory O'Carroll made a first appearance for Dublin since the All-Ireland final of 2015, a fact which pleased his manager. 'We welcomed him back,' Jim Gavin said. 'He's in based on his performances with Kilmacud Crokes. He's in based on his championship form. It's been a seamless transition for him.'

But what about Dermo, Jim? 'I'd expect to see one or two fellas coming in from clubs who were out there,' he offered, coyly. 'So we've always had an open door policy and if guys are playing well and we ask them and they want to commit to the Dublin football team then we'd be delighted to have them.'

So you're sayin' there's a chance!

On the pitch, Dublin's 26-point win was achieved despite playing the majority of the game a man down following Paul Mannion's dismissal in the 24th minute ('harsh', reckoned Jim, FYI), while Cormac Costello again proved an able deputy for the resting Dean Rock, top-scoring with 1-12, 1-1 of which came from play. Mannion popped over a pair of points before his early bath, while Dublin's other goals came from Brian Fenton, Con O'Callaghan (inevitably), and subs Michael Darragh Macauley and Philly McMahon.

Elsewhere in the *Indo*, Dick Clerkin warned us that MAYO STILL CAN'T BE WRITTEN OFF DESPITE RETURN OF OLD FAILINGS. Another theme we would revisit before all was said and done.

* * *

Day 1,743: Sunday, 9 June 2019
Leinster semi-final, Croke Park (attendance 36,126)
Dublin 0-26 Kildare 0-11

On a day when Stephen Cluxton became the GAA's first ever championship centurion with his 100th All-Ireland appearance in blue, he had to be at his most nimble to celebrate it with a 58th clean sheet.

Dublin took their time moving through the gears against a Kildare side who needed two goes to beat Longford in their provincial semi-final.

Paul Mannion, fresh from his short spin out against Louth, made up for that lost time with a sublime display of forward play.

Beside him, Cormac Costello continued to provide reassurance to Dublin fans everywhere that should we ever lose Dean Rock, we have a fairly decent replacement in the Whitehall Colmcille man.

As Dublin's Leinster dominance continued unabated, manager Gavin went to bat for volunteers throughout the county against claims – which were growing louder – attributing much of Dublin's success to their healthy financial situation. 'We're just fortunate in Dublin that we have some really smart people with their hands on the tiller who have applied to Croke Park [and] got funding,' Gavin argued. 'We're in a fantastic stadium in Croke Park, led by remarkable people [who] have the mortgage paid off.

'If I was in another county, I'd be knocking on their door with a smart business plan to say "we want to use a similar model to what Dublin have". The clubs [in Dublin] fund 50 per cent [of coaching funding]. Croke Park do help, [and] our monies are bridged by the sponsorship we get and gate receipts.

'As to boots on the ground, the teachers who were with these men when they were ten in Croke Park, in the Cumann na mBunscoil games, and the mams and dads – it's probably a bit of an insult to say the funding they got, or rather the coaches got, is what's made them. What has made them is bloody hard work. I can see the pride these guys have in playing for their county, and long may it continue.'

Meath legend Colm O'Rourke, among others, had been calling for Dublin to be split up as far back as 2013. Fair play to him, he even tried to say it was in Dublin's best interests. 'The long-term solution has to be to look at a different model for Dublin – two or three or four different teams,' O'Rourke said on *The Sunday Game* in 2017 when asked to revisit a point he had made four years earlier in a *Sunday Independent* column. 'My idea of the GAA is based on participation, involvement and opportunity. There are thousands of young Dublin footballers, on the Hill and watching on television, who would love the chance to play for the Dubs ... We can't have the population of Dublin being 1.5 or two million going forward and just one team. It just does not make sense.'

Jim Gavin had also addressed the issue when it was first raised. Needless to say, he gave the suggestion short shrift. 'Kerry were dominant in the 2000s in football and Kilkenny and Cork in the hurling, and I didn't hear any talk of splitting those counties in half,' Gavin said in March 2013, before he had won even one trophy with the Dublin senior team. 'The underage structures in Dublin are quite strong and are due to the great vision in the administration quite a number of years ago.'

* * *

Day 1,757: Sunday, 23 June 2019
Leinster final, Croke Park (attendance 47,027)
Dublin 1-17 Meath 0-4

'Some 30 years have passed, a great river of time, a bottomless ocean of days; a wider span of history than Alex Ferguson endured at

Manchester United, almost as deep as the entire expanse of hours gifted to Michael Collins. And yet, for those of us who knew its full pulverising force, the aftershocks of its wild detonation endures, tickling the senses still.'

The words of the inimitable Roy Curtis for independent.ie a couple of years after this game on the 30th anniversary of Dublin and Meath's epic, unforgettable Four in a Row saga of 1991.

I'm reminded of a confused phonecall home a few years ago from my then teenage daughter on her summer excursion to the Gaeltacht. Her confusion was prompted by the playful jeering of a young red-headed buck in Meath colours on County Jersey Night at the céilí ... 'But, Meath never beat Dublin?' she argued, innocently. Of course, she was mercifully too young to remember when beating the dastardly Royals of Fay, McDermott, Geraghty, Giles et al appeared the tallest of tasks. 'Oh, so they used to be good?' comes the surprised follow-up question after I'd made some attempt to explain what Dublin–Meath was like 'back in my day'.

On my earliest days on the Hill, the crowd would bay at Tommy Dowd. Tommy bayed back, then usually kicked the ball over our bar. We all admired the understated and underrated genius of Trevor Giles. (Never out loud, of course.) Much as we'd like to, we can never forget Paul Bealin's late penalty in 1997 – the Canal End posts shook for an age after his infamous miss. Or when a young Peadar Andrews was left to be 'humiliated' (to quote Colm O'Rourke, commentating for RTÉ on the day) by an unstoppable Ollie Murphy in 1999. Or Davy Byrne – who bridged the goalkeeping gap between O'Leary and Cluxton admirably –

spilling the ball into the path of a grateful Graham Geraghty for the most galling of early tap-ins in front of the Hill in the 2001 Leinster final. 'That will be the f***ing difference in the end,' a veteran Hill disciple next to me spat at the time. And it was. It was. Final score on 15 July 2001: Meath 2-11 Dublin 0-14.

Speaking of Ollie Murphy, heartbreaking slayer of Dubs, he at least was responsible for one of the best GAA quotes of all time. Towards the veteran stage of his career, the barrel-like Murphy told a reporter, 'I used to think it was great being a small, nippy corner-forward. But now I know it's better to be a big fat one!'

Andrews, incidentally, recovered fully from his baptism of fire against the Royals and went on to have an excellent inter-county career for many years, collecting an All-Ireland medal of his own with the 2018 Dublin Masters (Over-40s) side.

Jesus, those games used to be great. And dramatic. And stressful. They were none of the above in the year 2019. 'The official position is that this hiccup in Leinster is temporary, and the natural order of competition will be restored,' Colm O'Rourke wrote of the Dubs' dominance of their neighbours in his *Sunday Independent* column before this latest provincial decider. 'I heard that ten years ago, five years ago, and again now. It is a bit like Nero, the Roman Emperor, fiddling while Rome was consumed by fire. Something will turn up to solve the problem. Don't bet on it.'

Colm wasn't finished, and his fatalism proved well founded. 'Like all Meath people, I am slightly afraid of the outcome. Yet there is more to a game than just the bare result. How did players stand up to the test? Did they live up to their responsibilities and perform like men even if things were going badly? Were they brave and honest? Did they never let their heads drop? So there is winning and losing in honour. We must have an honourable performance.'

The following Saturday's front page of the *Meath Chronicle* featured a picture of embattled Meath manager Andy McEntee, under which sat this extended caption: 'The *Meath Chronicle* is asking Meath senior football manager Andy McEntee to apologise after threatening to "take the f***ing head off" one of its sports reporters in the wake of Meath's dispiriting 1-17 to 0-4 defeat to Dublin last Sunday.'

Inside the news pages, editor Gavan Becton (a Dub, long exiled in the Royal County) gave us the full quote – 'I'll take the f***ing head off you if I f***ing see you near the dressing room again' – and his own take on the matter. OUT OF ORDER: 'McEntee launches verbal attack on *Meath Chronicle* reporter who asked a simple question in the wake of Meath's defeat to Dublin in the Leinster final.'

And just for a moment, we felt as though we were back in the fire and brimstone 1990s again. Nostalgia, eh? It's not what it used to be …

* * *

Day 1,777: Saturday, 13 July
Super 8s, Rd1, Croke Park (attendance 30,214)
Dublin 5-18 Cork 1-17

REJUVENATED REBELS CAN GIVE DUBLIN THE CHALLENGE WE'VE ALL BEEN WAITING TO SEE ran the headline above Conor McKeon's match preview on the morning of Dublin's opening Super 8s tussle with Cork. In fairness, Cork had hit Kerry for 3-10 in the Munster final, losing out by three points at Páirc Uí Chaoimh. They looked primed to take a big scalp. That's the thing about Cork GAA teams, they'll make a liar out of you quicker than a racehorse who's been working well at home.

Maybe that's being unkind to the Rebels. After all, the final scoreline does not the full tale tell. The Munster men were in this game for over an hour. Dublin, uncharacteristically, took eight minutes to register a score – a Con O'Callaghan point. Cork, by that stage, had clipped over four of their own. With 62 minutes on the clock, there were just four points between the sides. The Rebels held their shoulder against the door manfully. But eventually the Dubs burst their way in and proceeded to take over the room, the house, the whole property.

'They're an outstanding team,' said Cork manager Ronan McCarthy afterwards. 'First thing, they don't panic. I think their decision-making is really the key thing. They're patient, they'll always wait for the right man to get the shot off – whereas at times we were a bit rushed, a bit hassled, in some of the decisions we made. They're an outstanding team, but I felt we gave as good as we got for a long time.'

On the pitch, Dublin spread the wealth on their way to that final tally of 5-18. After Jack McCaffrey goaled first, Brian Fenton, Michael Darragh Macauley, Niall Scully and Ciarán Kilkenny would also find the back of the net.

The Man of the Match award went to Clontarf comet McCaffrey. It was the flying wing-back who finally broke Cork's resistance a couple of minutes after the hour mark. Driving forward for the umpteenth time, leaving flagging Rebels toiling in his wake, McCaffrey found Con O'Callaghan and he in turn played in Niall Scully, who drove a powerful show past Cork keeper Mark White to give Dublin their third goal and, effectively, the game.

Elsewhere, Mayo, who had lost to Roscommon in the Connacht semi-finals, had been hotly tipped to lay down something of a marker against much-vaunted hosts Kerry. Final score the following day from Fitzgerald Stadium: Kerry 1-22 Mayo 0-15. Expectations and reality. Cork and Mayo, seemingly, had much in common.

Ulster champions Donegal were earmarked as one of the counties with the mettle to halt Dublin's Five in a Row drive. The Ulstermen had beaten Meath 2-19 to 1-13 in their group opener. It would be Donegal's last win of the season. They drew with Kerry in Croke Park and lost a winner-takes-all tie with Mayo in Castlebar. Declan Bonner's men would not get that chance to challenge the Dubs. Fine margins.

Despite there being plenty of on-pitch action around the grounds, it was an interview with Jim Gavin on Dubs TV that stopped the GAA world in its tracks. A manager's chat with his own county's social media channels is usually as by-the-numbers as it gets. Every now and then, however, an Easter egg is dropped. 'Last night's game was tough. There are a lot of tired bodies,' Gavin began. 'The guys will get as much recovery as they can. They all go back to work on Monday morning. We'll try to get a couple of sessions in this week. We had James McCarthy back on the pitch, Eoin Murchan, Jonny Cooper. Diarmuid Connolly is back training with us. Robbie McDaid is back. Darren Gavin is coming back as well this week. There's a whole host of players who are returning to play.'

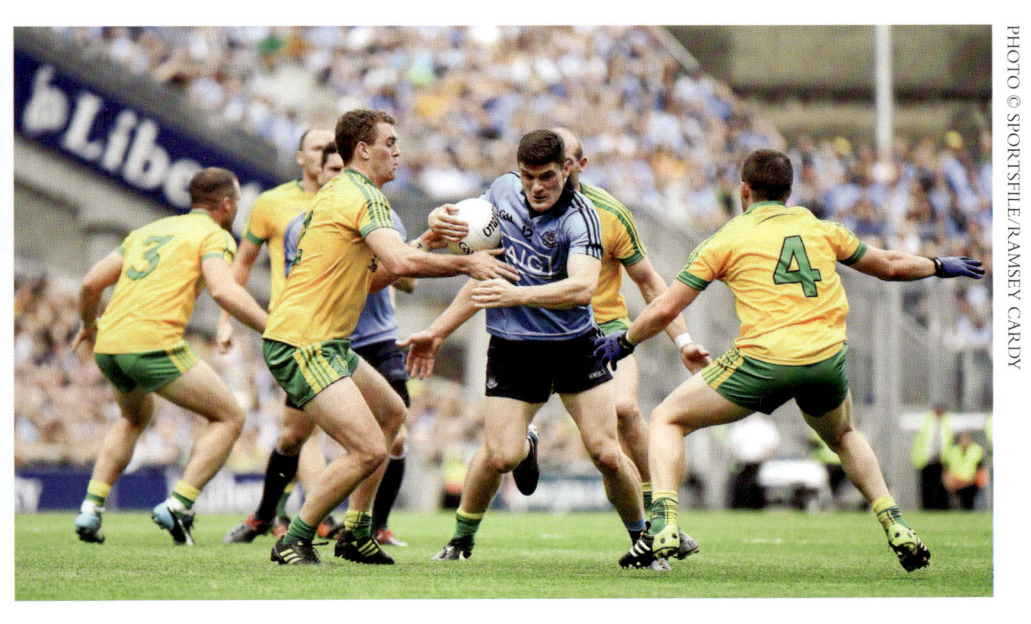

Above: Donegal players swarm Diarmuid Connolly, All-Ireland semi-final, 31 August 2014.
Below: Paul 'Papa' Durcan clears the ball under pressure from Paul Mannion in 2014. Durcan's first-half save from Connolly had kept his side in it – and inadvertently helped create a footballing monster.

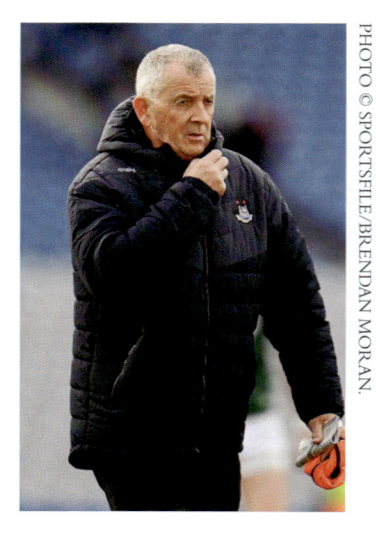

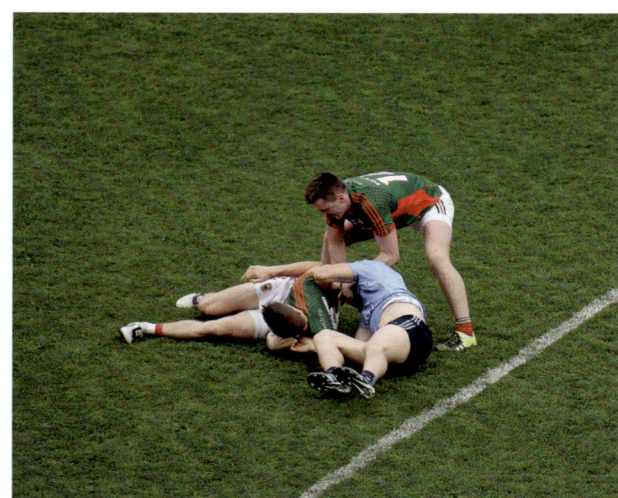

Above left: The man with the plan: The part played by long-time county board secretary John Costello in Dublin's resurgence cannot be overstated.

Above right: Diarmuid Connolly is red-carded after a difference of opinion with Mayo's Lee Keegan in the drawn semi-final in 2015. An eleventh-hour reprieve allowed Connolly start the replay.

Below: Kerry's Darran O'Sullivan ends up in a heap in the back of the net after goalling in the 2016 semi-final. This would mark Colm Cooper's last game against Dublin. As always, he gave us his very best.

PHOTO © SPORTSFILE/DAVID MAHER

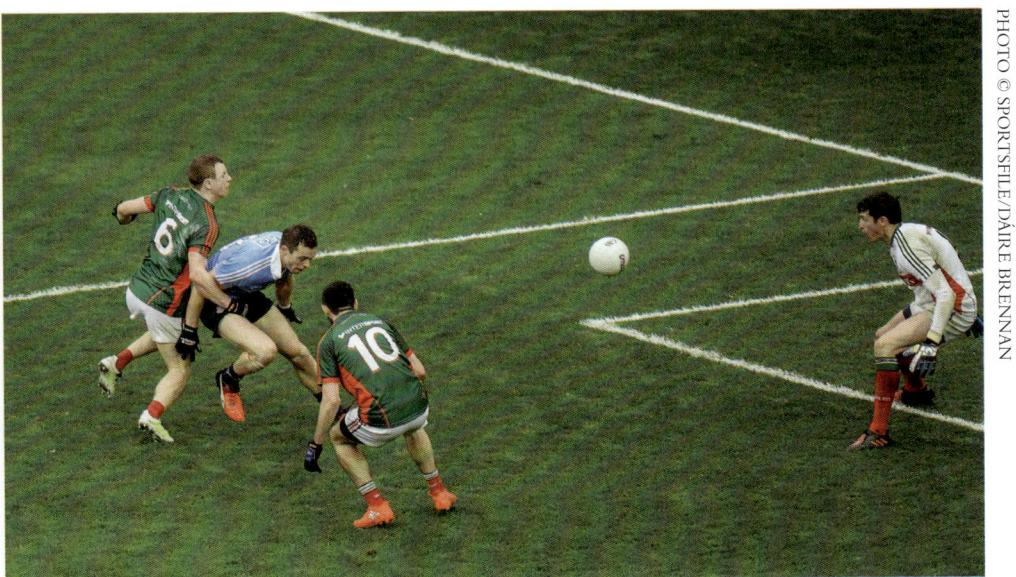

PHOTO © SPORTSFILE/DÁIRE BRENNAN

18 September 2016: When first Kevin McLoughlin (top) and then Colm Boyle (above) put through their own net in the 2016 final, even Dub fans were wondering if that damn Mayo curse was real?

PHOTO © SPORTSFILE/BRENDAN MORAN

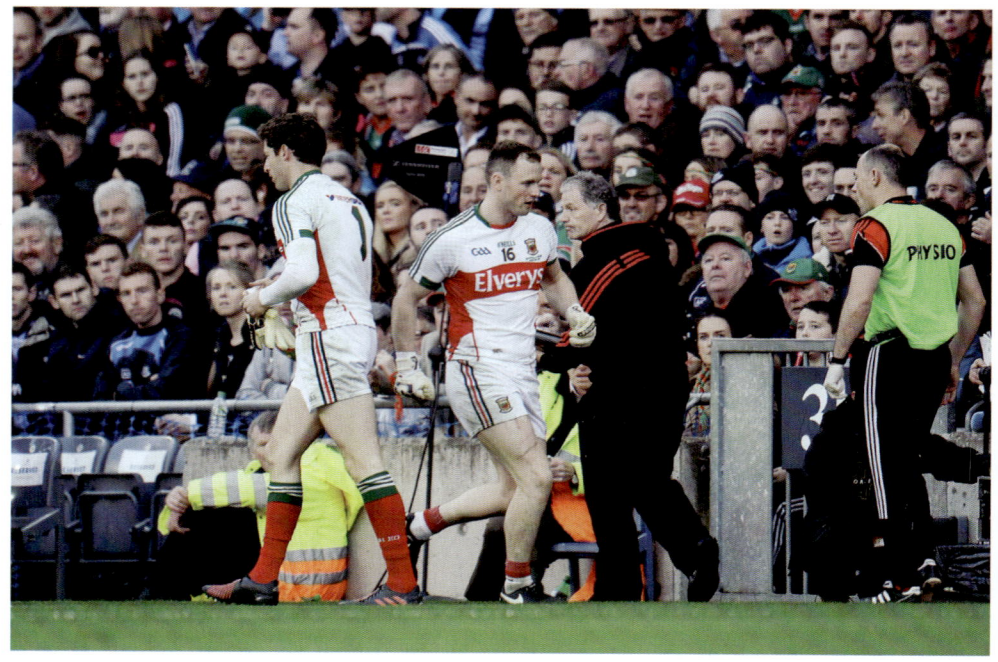

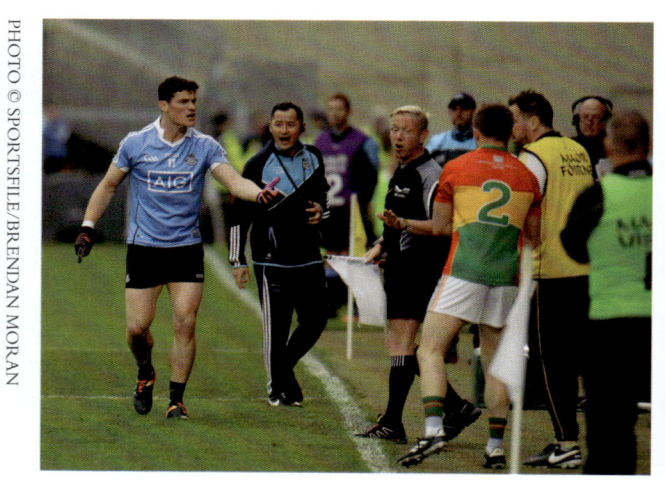

Top: Two ships in a plight. Stephen Rochford may have overthought the whole thing for the 2016 All Ireland final replay on 1 October. David Clarke replaces the black-carded Rob Hennelly in goal for Mayo.

Above left: The beginning of the end. Bernard Brogan was named on the bench for the All-Ireland final replay. in 2016.

Above right: A professional performance against a well-drilled Carlow side would have repercussions for Diarmuid Connolly, 3 June 2017.

27 August 2017: 'A few weeks later, we completely blew away Tyrone.' Eoghan O'Gara goals against the Red Hands in the 2017 semi-final.

17 September 2017: Donie Vaughan was on the scene a bit too quick in the second half of the 2017 final. His intervention let Dublin off the hook.

PHOTO © SPORTSFILE/RAMSEY CARDY

Left: By the time the All-Ireland final rolled around on 17 September 2017, Three in a Row-chasing Dublin were playing football from another planet.

Below, far left: Jonny Cooper's uncompromising approach against Wicklow on 27 May 2018, epitomised the merciless nature of this Dublin generation.

Below left: Diarmuid Connolly in action for Donegal Boston against Wolfetones on 26 August 2018.

Below: 'We felt each other's pain. Maybe that's one of the reasons why we were so successful.' Philly McMahon, wearing a tshirt tribute to his late father, with Cian O'Sullivan after securing the Four in a Row against Tyrone on 2 September 2018.

Above and below: Blitzkreig. Con O'Callaghan pounced twice in a few short minutes in the 2019 semi on 10 August. That was Mayo dealt with for another year.

Above: Eoin Murchan's goal immediately after half-time floored the Kingdom in the 2019 All-Ireland final replay on 14 September in Croke Park.
Below left: All the best, Jim. And thanks.
Below right: Snip, Snip! The disciples of the Hill are always suitably attired.

Bord Gáis Energy
Centra
Centra
GAA.ie
@officialGAA
ERICSSON
ERICSSON
Centra
Centra
35

Above left: Unprecedented times. Dublin and Westmeath met at a deserted O'Moore Park on 7 November 2020 for the Leinster quarter-final.
Left: It was the week before Christmas, and all through the house … Dean Rock's goal in the opening seconds of the 2020 festive final puts the Dubs on the one road.
Above right: Dessie Farrell had completed the Six in a Row and was an All-Ireland-winning manager in his first year in charge. Ciaran Kilkenny had become Dublin's unflappable quarterback.

Above: Daniel Flynn's late Kildare goal in the 2021 Leinster final may have provided a clue that the Dubs were vulnerable.

Below: Diarmuid O'Connor out-Dubs the Dubs. His brilliant intervention swung the mood of the 2021 semi-final on 14 August.

Opposite, top: 'No Dub wants to bow out to Mayo and be haunted.' Dublin went down swinging loudly. Mayo, as always, never took a backward step. Aidan O'Shea (in yellow) had suffered more than most at the hands of this Dubs team.

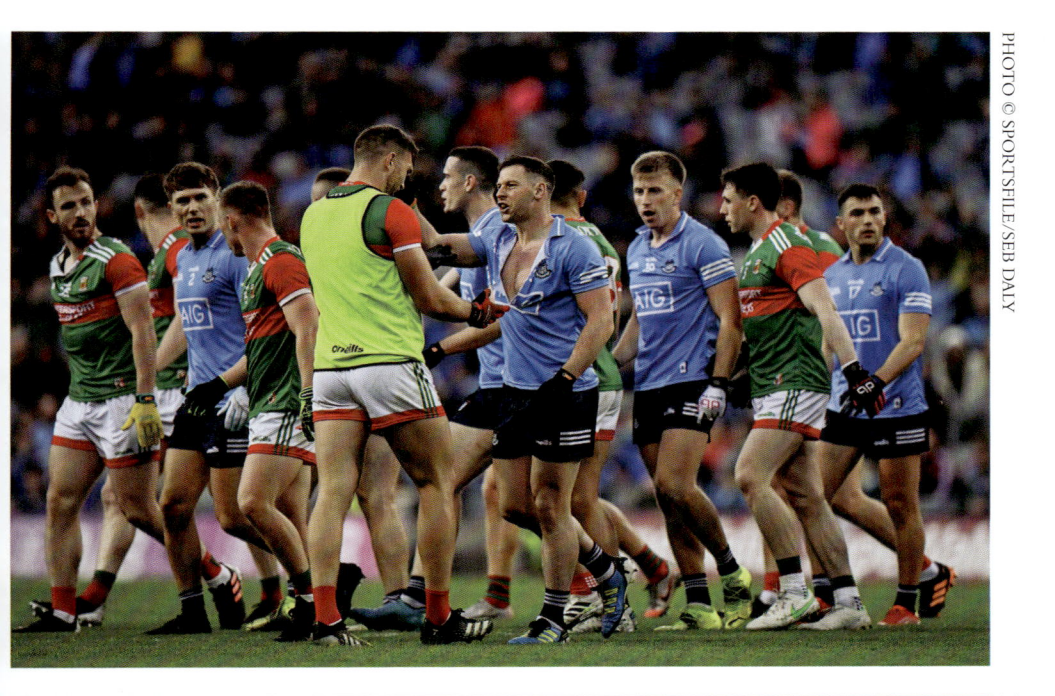

Above: Sean O'Shea's sublime late free sent the Dubs packing on 10 July 2022, after yet another championship classic against the Kingdom.

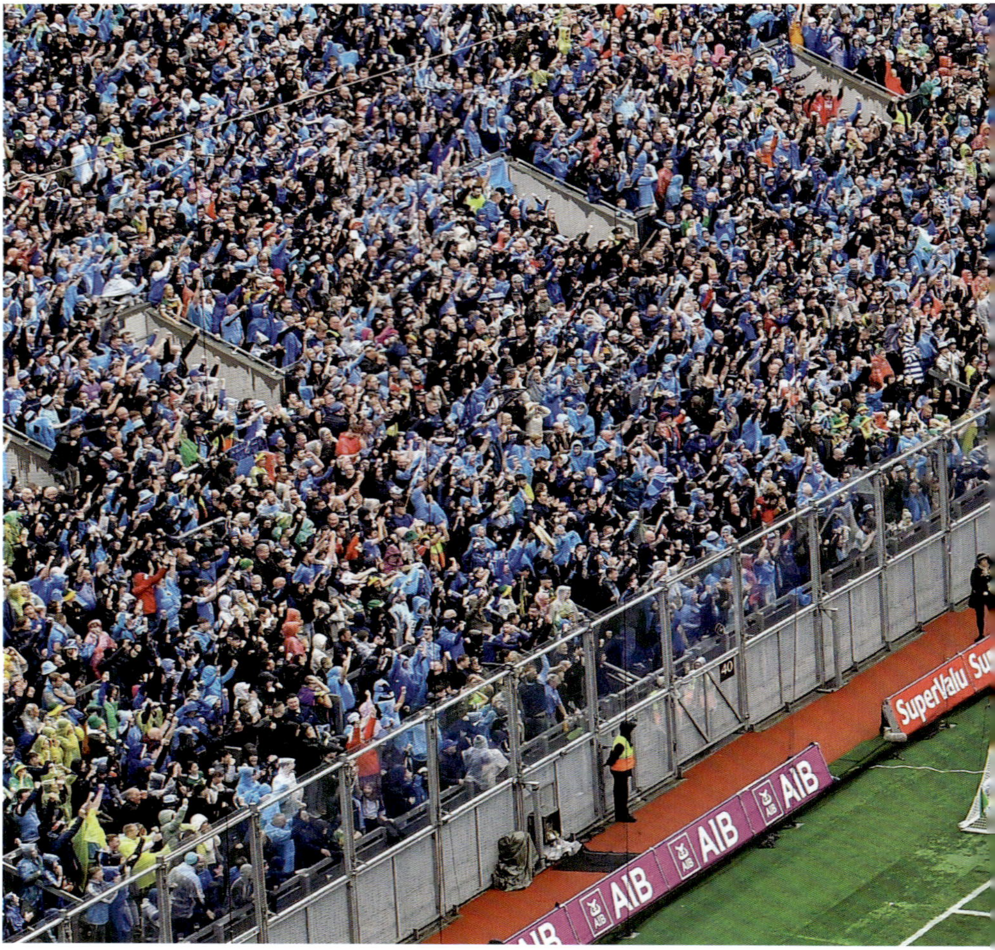
SuperValu
AIB

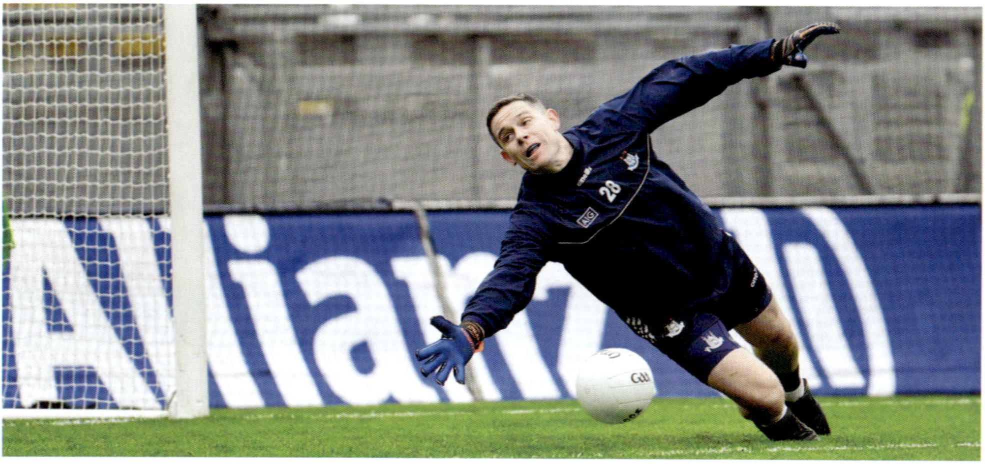

PHOTO © SPORTSFILE/RAMSEY CARDY

PHOTO © SPORTSFILE/PIARAS Ó MÍDHEACH

Far left: Guess who's back? Stephen Cluxton's sensational return signalled Dublin's intent in 2023.

Above: 'You're hardly gonna believe us.' Paddy Small goals. The Hill erupts. All-Ireland final against Kerry, 30 July 2023.

Left: The 999 crew after beating Kerry. Fitzsimons, Cluxton and McCarthy are the first men to win nine All-Ireland football titles.

A quarter-final defeat to Galway on 29 June 2024, felt like the end of football's most glorious era. Had the team that gave us everything finally run out of road? **Above:** Brian Fenton tumbles under a Cein Darcy tackle. **Below:** Pádraic Joyce, as graceful a forward as ever played the game, masterminded a rare early exit for Dessie Farrell's Dubs.

It was classic Gavin. The perfect crime. An announcement to inform the masses that arguably the greatest footballer of his generation was back in harness, dropped casually into the conversation as if rhyming off the items from a grocery list. ('With the demeanour of a fella going into the shop to buy a box of teabags,' as *The Herald*'s Niall Scully perfectly put it.) It was a tactic Gavin's successor, Dessie Farrell, would mirror three years later when announcing the imminent returns of Paul Mannion and Jack McCaffrey. A reminder that, no matter what, the squad comes first. No player is bigger than the collective. And if it ruffles an odd feather or two outside the Pale, even better …

Maybe no one player was bigger than the squad, but it's hard to imagine Jim Gavin bending (if not quite breaking) his own unwritten rules to this extent for any Dublin player other than the inimitable Diarmuid Connolly. The manager, perhaps conscious that this was his final season in charge, was prepared to leave no stone unturned in pursuit of the historic Five in a Row. As it happens, Connolly was all set for another summer Stateside with Donegal Boston when, having made it as far as Dublin Airport, he was reportedly turned back at US Customs pre-clearance owing to a supposed issue with his ESTA application. We were in the third week of June at this stage. There had previously been some excitement around the Dublin GAA scene back in April when Connolly played for St Vincent's (at centre-back, curiously) in the Dublin SFC group stages against first St Brigid's and then Ciarán Kilkenny's Castleknock. The apparent presence of a GPS pack under the half-forward's jersey on the night they met Castleknock at Broomfield was taken by some as a possible sign that Connolly was quite literally being 'monitored' by the county management team.

Then sometime around early July, the night before a weekend training session for the 'non-starting' players, the story goes that a senior playing member of the panel's phone buzzed with a text from Gavin. 'Diarmuid will be there tomorrow. Make sure he's made welcome.' Shortly after that training session, at a team meeting to somewhat explain Connolly's unexpected return to the panel – not that Gavin was in the habit of justifying his every move – a typically unapologetic Connolly is reported to have matter-of-factly reminded his teammates: 'Look, I'm back and I'm here to start. I'm after your jersey ...'

We can discuss the merits of Gavin's move until the cows come home, but the bottom line is, there isn't a manager anywhere who would have rejected the chance to have a player of Connolly's calibre back in harness. Whether we like it or not, the rules of the playground never really leave us. The big kids get the breaks. There wasn't a Dublin fan around – including this one – who wasn't energised by the St Vincent's player's return. Former Dubs boss Paul 'Pillar' Caffrey – who gave Connolly his inter-county debut in 2007 – insisted at the time, 'If you are asking me if I would have brought him back, yes, absolutely – he is that good.' When quizzed if the mercurial playmaker's return could put some noses out of joint among long-time panellists who maybe hadn't, ya know, tried to feck off to America for the summer, Pillar was equally unequivocal. 'It's a good question, but do you know what, they're always upset. And [squad members] 26 to 34 are even more upset. While you have to consider everybody, we're in the business end of things now. Dublin are trying to do something that has never been done by any team in the history of the game. Jim made the decision for the team, and if Diarmuid Connolly can force his way up the pecking order, it will turn out to be a great decision. I definitely think Diarmuid is going to see some game time.'

* * *

Day 1,784: Saturday, 20 July 2019
Super 8s Rd2, Croke Park (attendance 36,530)
Dublin 2-26 Roscommon 0-14

'Dean Rock pierces the posts with the ease of Shane Lowry dispatching a six-inch putt.' Succinctly described by *Sunday World* columnist Roy Curtis as he likened the unerring Ballymun Kickham to the Clara golfer who that morning led the Open Championship at Portrush and would, of course, finish the job that same afternoon.

Roscommon boss Anthony Cunningham has had his share of happy days in Croke Park. This wasn't one of them. 'We'd be a number of years off their physicality,' Cunningham said afterwards. 'They're a seasoned team. They've been training at that level that we've just put a solid year's work into. Gym work and physicality, that you now need to have as part of your armour, is a slow burner. It doesn't come overnight.

'As well as that, they've a huge football brain. They've massive athleticism, speed, a strong midfield. Their goalie is probably the most exceptional goalie on kickouts and has transformed the whole kickout mantra over the last ten years … We can definitely get there, but it will take time.'

The enigmatic Diarmuid Connolly was not in the match-day 23; Dublin also left out Cian O'Sullivan and brought in the returning-from-injury Jonny Cooper and James McCarthy. Dean Rock, who had been eased into the action this term, earned a first start of the summer and duly obliged by going 10/10 from frees and finishing with 1-11 overall.

Next up, a trip to Omagh …

* * *

Day 1,799: Sunday, 4 August 2019
Super 8s, Rd3, Healy Park, Omagh (attendance 15,315)
Dublin 1-16 Tyrone 0-13

Diarmuid Connolly back in a Dublin starting fifteen: who would have believed it? Connolly saw no action in the Roscommon tie at Croker but, having been initially named on the bench, he played from start to end at Healy Park. Well, almost. A 69th-minute black card ended his day slightly early, but it was clear to see the eye for a pass was still there.

'I think Diarmuid loves Dublin, and we love him. Circumstances change for all players,' beamed Gavin afterwards, in what must be described as very non-Gavin language. Gavin's is an existence based around processes and protocols. Usually 'love' does not come into it.

However, Newton's third law of motion insists that every action has an equal and opposite reaction. Diarmuid Connolly took to the field in Omagh that day with number 20 on his back. Gavin made six changes to the originally named team for what was effectively a dead rubber – both sides already safely through to the semi-finals.

Nothing unusual there. These days, punters and pundits are more surprised when an inter-county manager *doesn't* change the named team on match day. Except, in this case, that original team had the names 'B Brogan' and 'E O'Gara' on it. Neither of the men started, and although they were introduced together in the 44th minute – and both would get on the scoreboard – neither would play championship football for Dublin again. They didn't know it this day, but Bernard Brogan and Eoghan O'Gara's Dublin careers were effectively over.

***

Day 1,805: Saturday, 10 August 2019
All-Ireland semi-final, Croke Park (attendance 82,300)
Dublin 3-14 Mayo 1-10

On the front page of the *Irish Independent* on Monday, 12 August, after Dublin had booked their place in yet another All-Ireland final, a pair of blurbs just beneath the title banner referenced two great imponderables of the day. KERRY NEED MORE TO STOP DRIVE FOR FIVE reckoned columnist Eamonn Sweeney. Beside that, a concerned reader had Asked Allison, I WORRY ABOUT MY HUSBAND'S FEMALE FRIEND. Two troubling issues indeed. Neither an easy fix.

In the latest instalment of the quintessential football rivalry of the 2010s, Dublin turned the game on its head in ten devastating second-half minutes, punctuated by the magic of arguably the best forward in the country. Lee Keegan tucked Con O'Callaghan up nicely in the first half at Croke Park. Mayo led 0-8 to 0-6 at the break. The Dubs had even played into their oxygen-giving Hill 16 in that opening period. James Horan's men were right there. This beast that had goaded them for a decade was on the ropes. Could they find the knockout punch?

Speaking of Hill 16, what is it about this ancient (though thoroughly modernised, and not actually all that ancient) terrace that so stirs the blood? As much as, in middle age, one might appreciate a comfortable seat from a decent viewing point in either Hogan or Cusack Stand, there's something primal and 'proper' about standing for sport. Whiff of tobacco, chips and stale beer in the air. Memories – good and bad – haunt those steps like ghosts of championships past. The doomed 1992 All-Ireland final defeat to Donegal. Bealin's penalty. Charlie's penalties. Keith Barr's penalty. Ray Cosgrove's free in 2002. These steps had seen it all. The ancient Romans were legally obliged to stand in the Colosseum, as apparent proof of their nation's virility. Well, few sights in modern sport are more affirmingly virile than a swaying Dub who's had four pints in Meagher's of Ballybough before throw-in. Or an animated culchie who's been supping bottles all the way 'up' to Dublin from the back of the bus. What have the Romans ever done for us?

Back at Headquarters, ten minutes into the second period, the game was over. Mayo, again, looked beaten. Dublin grabbed a quick point from a Dean Rock free which he had won himself, taking his tally from placed balls to four out of four at that point. Mayo won the break off Rob Hennelly's kickout, leading to a long-range shot attempt from

Paddy Durcan. Paddy likes a point against the Dubs. This time, however, his well-struck effort dropped just short and was palmed to safety by Stephen Cluxton with exactly 36:18 on the clock. Less than 30 seconds later, the ball was in the net of the Canal End goal.

Cluxton moved the ball to Jack McCaffrey, who was fouled on his own 21. Dublin worked the free up the left sideline, with the ball eventually popped inside to Mannion, who held off his marker and slipped it to the advancing Ciarán Kilkenny. O'Callaghan, at this point, had walked Keegan into the corner-back position before nudging him aside and cutting hard towards goal. Kilkenny's handpass was on a plate. O'Callaghan's finish was emphatic. Dublin 1-7 Mayo 0-8.

'It was a big half-time for both managers,' said Kevin McStay from the RTÉ commentary box. 'And you have to say, Dublin have come out screaming and fighting.'

Dublin would dominate possession for the next two and a half minutes before Niall Scully drilled a shot over the bar from close range to give them a three-point lead. Mayo were rocked. The Dubs were rocking. From there, Brian Fenton seized a Rob Hennelly kickout that Dublin had begun to dominate. The ball was worked wide-left to Mannion, playing with a bandage on his left elbow, who kicked one of those sublime citeóg points he loves so much to stretch the lead.

Keegan, at this point, was hanging on for dear life – and he was also hanging on to Con O'Callaghan. A free right in front of the posts resulted in a yellow card for Keegan and the easiest of scores for Rock. Dubs by five. Fenton scraped the clouds as he fetched the helpless Hennelly's next restart. From the mark, Fenton found O'Callaghan, who found Mannion and, well, you know the rest. Dubs by six, exactly 42 minutes played.

Mayo finally won a kickout followed by a free just inside the Dublin 45 shortly after that latest Mannion point. Cillian O'Connor could not connect, however, and the Dubs' lead remained six. O'Connor went into the referee's notebook shortly after for persistent fouling (he would eventually go in a second time too) following a face-high tackle on Jonny Cooper about 55 yards from goal. Kilkenny knew exactly where he wanted to send the resulting free. His inch-perfect pass landed in O'Callaghan's lap with just Keegan between the Cuala man and a second goal. O'Callaghan bobbed, weaved, then stepped inside the flailing defender before sliding the ball past Hennelly. Dubs by nine, 2-11 to 0-8. The clock read 45:30. Blitzkrieg.

Fenton and Hennelly, incidentally, would become clubmates in 2023 when the Mayo keeper joined Fenton's home club, Raheny, on Dublin's northside. This prompted one of the great group-chat gags when, as Raheny led reigning All-Ireland champions Kilmacud Crokes towards the business end of a Dubin SFC semi-final and as Fenton claimed another of his goalkeeper's kickouts at Parnell Park to turn the screw further, an unnamed hack – Dub, naturally – quipped, 'Hennelly was always going to be a natural fit for Raheny. Sure he's been kicking the ball to Fenton to years!' Crokes, led by Paul Mannion (and Shane Walsh, s'pose), would prevail on penos, as it happened, before beating Ballyboden St Enda's in the final to secure a third straight county title.

After this latest heartbreaking loss to their long-time nemesis, beleaguered Mayo boss James Horan admitted, 'A team like Dublin are always going to come at you, and we were on the ropes and we didn't deal with it well. They came running at us from a lot of different angles and they really got their tails up so it took us a while to adjust to what was happening, but they were in control of the game by that stage. They had a very strong period, and we just couldn't deal with it.'

Kerry manager Peter Keane, in classic Kingdom fashion, was quick to play the poor mouth regarding their impending date with the reigning champs. '[Kerry keeper] Shane Ryan was on the phone to Gerard Murphy of Vincent Murphy Sports there in Castleisland,' Keane quipped. 'His biggest problem was, would he get two or three pairs of boots because he'd have them worn out kicking the ball out to Dublin … We'll come up in three weeks and we'll do our best. Alright, lads?'

Alright, Peter …

* * *

Day 1,827: Sunday, 1 September 2019
All-Ireland final, Croke Park (attendance 82,300)
Dublin 1-16 Kerry 1-16

Riches aplenty on both sides. The named forward units for the All-Ireland final included enough marquee men to keep the scoreboard ticking over for a half-dozen football teams, never mind just these two. Kerry had an attacking line anchored by Seánie O'Shea at centre-forward, flanked by Stephen O'Brien and captain Gavin White. They would load the bullets for the inside line of David Clifford, Paul

Geaney and Killian Spillane. Tommy Walsh, Shane Enright and Jack Barry were ready to come in from the bench. As it happened, Barry would start in place of Spillane on the day. Dublin, even more star-studded, had Con O'Callaghan at 11, with Niall Scully on one side and Brian Howard on the other. Dean Rock would patrol the edge of the Kingdom's square with Paul Mannion top of the right and Ciarán Kilkenny, nominally at least, in the other corner.

Dublin's bench included household names like Kevin McManamon, the comeback kid Diarmuid Connolly, Cian O'Sullivan, Philly McMahon, Paddy Andrews, Cormac Costello and Eoin Murchan. The bench did not include the name of Bernard Brogan.

'I'm essentially retired as of Friday,' Brogan wrote in his autobiography of his reaction to the news. It was not an altogether unexpected call, but it no doubt stung. There would be no pushback on the part of the player this time around. There would be no number 27 jersey hanging on a dressing-room peg in Croke Park on All-Ireland final day.

'I could tell Jim was genuinely uncomfortable breaking the news,' Brogan remembered. '"Jayo and Declan are here with me," he said, "and we have enormous respect for you. It's very difficult telling you this." I said I understood … And with that phone call, I've played my last game for Dublin. I've worn the jersey for the last time.'

It wasn't supposed to end like this.

If the bould Sean Dempsey from that hauntingly beautiful anthem 'The Rare Ould Times' was indeed 'as Dublin as can be', then some of the narratives floating around in the weeks leading up to the 2019 All-Ireland final could best be described as 'as Kerry as can be'. Dear ol'

Tomas Ó Sé even wheeled out the great Mick O'Dwyer for a Kingdom love-in a couple of Saturdays before the big day in his *Irish Independent* column.

After talking in and around the big game for a few beats, it wasn't long before the two Kerrymen sized up the history-chasing Dubs. 'I suppose what I'm asking you is, will we beat the Dubs?' Tomás asked.

They say you should never go full Yerra. But Micko went full Yerra. 'Jesus, I can't see it, to be honest,' the Kerry legend reckoned. 'But you'd be hoping. I suppose if you were from any other part of the country, maybe you'd like to see the record made. Like I remember when [Roger] Bannister broke the mile record, the whole world was delighted. We won't be delighted if Dublin win the Five in a Row, but they're capable of doing it.'

After that nice set-up, Kingdom attention turned to the appointed referee for the final, David Gough. The *Irish Examiner* carried a story headlined ÉAMONN FITZMAURICE: WHY DAVID GOUGH SHOULDN'T REFEREE DUBLIN–KERRY FINAL. 'I think it's an injustice if he does get the game,' the former Kerry player and manager declared on the *Examiner*'s GAA podcast. 'A final referee has to be a neutral referee. Living and working in Dublin, you are not neutral. If you are living there, you are meeting people in the shop, at work, down the street.'

A schoolteacher in Ballinteer on Dublin's southside and one of the most respected young officials in the game, Gough's mistake back in the 2016 semi-final in missing Kevin McManamon's (alleged) foul on Peter Crowley still hadn't been forgiven down Munster way. This would be Gough's first time refereeing the ancient rivals since that incident. Yes, the Kingdom were pulling out all the stops coming into this one. Even going so far as to suggest a Meathman (Gough is from Slane) might favour the Dubs. That'd be enough to get a man barred from Páirc Tailteann. Either way, the seed was duly planted.

The week before the game, Conor McKeon, writing in the *Irish Independent*, reminded us of the game that prompted it all: Jim Gavin's solitary loss in championship football, that Donegal implosion five years earlier. DONEGAL BLITZ: 'How Gavin's one championship defeat shaped the drive for five. Lessons learned from loss have taken aviation regulator and his team to unprecedented heights.'

'Most of the time it's an organisational issue,' Gavin told McKeon for the piece. 'So if a player isn't executing his skill-set or the game plan … ultimately the root cause of it isn't the player – it's me. The buck stops with me. I'm the manager of the organisation.'

McKeon continued: 'After his public *mea culpa*, Dublin emerged for the 2015 season with greater variation in their defensive play – the most notable tweak being Cian O'Sullivan's presence as a "holding" number six/sweeper. The results for Dublin were immediate. In the 2014 National League, they conceded 8-94, an average concession of 16.8 points per match. That dropped to 2-78 for the 2015 competition, just 12 points per game.

'They conceded only four goals in the 2015 championship and held Kerry to 0-9 in the All-Ireland final. This Saturday will mark five years since Dublin's last championship defeat. Gavin didn't know it when he took sole responsibility for that loss, but it became the starting point for their unprecedented success since.'

At this point, Dublin were 35 championship games into their unbeaten run. They had won 33 of those games and drawn two. They had scored 70 goals and 568 points, used 45 different players and collected 27 All Stars on their way to an average winning margin of 11.7 points, all while being watched live by almost two million paying customers.

When the ball was finally thrown in on the first day of September, the game itself proved a different kind of classic. Tense, bad-tempered at times, and slathered in controversy. Jonny Cooper's first-half red card proved the most talked-about incident of the season – and also inadvertently hastened the end of Joe Brolly's long-running association with RTÉ.

Your opinion on the Na Fianna streetfighter's dismissal probably depends on which side of the Dublin-v-Everybody Else debate you reside. Cooper, marshalling Kerry dangerman David Clifford, went into David Gough's notebook in the 18th minute and, hindsight or not, it would have seemed the prudent move to switch him with, say, Mick Fitzsimons. If Con O'Callaghan was the best forward in the competition in 2019, David Clifford was the closest of runners up. Marking him with a booking already hanging over you was the tallest of orders.

In fact, Cooper's discomfort with the wiry Clifford could be seen as early as the 12th minute when he conceded a penalty for fouling the forward, only for Stephen Cluxton to brilliantly save Paul Geaney's kick. Dear ol' Joe in the RTÉ studio, mind you, felt that the penalty decision was 'a scandal'. And he wasn't finished there.

As half-time approached, Dublin were right where they wanted to be. Four points ahead, thanks in the main to Jack McCaffrey's goal, before disaster struck. A popped handpass from David Moran dropped into Clifford, who nudged/fouled (depending on your persuasion) Cooper and then went crashing to the ground in a tangle with his marker. Cooper had desperately grabbed the Kerryman's arm in a vain attempt to reestablish position. Gough's whistle blew. 'Free out', assumed everyone standing on Hill 16 at the other end of the stadium – even many of those in green and gold! Cooper saw the yellow card for the second time that day, however, followed by red. Somewhere, you can imagine Éamonn Fitzmaurice sending a winky-face emoji into a group chat of Kerry old boys. 'Job done. Yerra.'

Back to the studio with our national broadcaster at half-time. Joanne Cantwell presenting, with Ciarán Whelan, Brolly, and of course Pat Spillane offering their analysis. Eventually, after a bit of shadow-boxing, they got around to the Cooper red.

Brolly, describing the action as we see the replay of Cooper's second yellow: 'This is a free out! Clifford manoeuvres his body around to keep him off him. Cooper tries to get around to get at the ball and instead of it being a free out, it's a free in! It's never in a million years a free.'

Spillane jumps in: 'I think people know over the years I call plays as I see them, and I'm not wearing a Kerry cap. In that incident, what Clifford did was use his body to shield the ball, and what happened was Jonny Cooper grabbed him by the arm and pulled him down. It's a yellow card! Two yellows equal red, he had to go off – they're the facts!'

Whelan: 'No, no, no. A terrible decision.'

After an ad break, Joe effectively inked his own RTÉ P45 with the following: 'The penalty was never a penalty. I think the referee was clearly influenced by the propaganda that's been coming from Kerry. I am so surprised because David's so clear-minded. Clifford knows [Cooper's] on a yellow. He's holding him off, he's blocking him off the play. Hold on, Patrick [Spillane]. We confidently expected that it was a free out, I think you thought that as well. In fact, people were shocked when all of a sudden the yellow card was produced ... [The penalty] was not the first cousin of a penalty.'

It was Brolly's final time in the RTÉ *Sunday Game* studio.

Despite being a player down to start the second half, Dublin would actually edge the first 20 minutes of that period five points to four. When Jack McCaffrey slid over a 55th-minute point to complete his 1-3 total for the day, it appeared the Boys in Blue would complete their historic run in the most impressive fashion. Outmanned but not outgunned. Moments later, however, Killian Spillane had the ball in the Hill 16 net and the Kingdom were humming once more. Tommy Walsh, a 53rd-minute substitute, was instrumental in setting up Spillane's strike. Seán O'Shea levelled the game before Dean Rock's ninth point pushed Dublin back in front, 1-15 to 1-14. O'Shea answered back for the Kingdom. It was substitute Spillane who would then edge Kerry ahead in the 66th minute, leaving Dublin's Five in a Row dreams in mortal danger. Gavin turned to his bench – in came Connolly and Costello. Kerry 1-16, Dublin 1-15. The 70 minutes have been played. We'll have at least seven more, we're told.

We can't move to the replay – and fallout of the first game – without walking ourselves through a score that epitomised this Dublin team, arguably the greatest side of all time. Dean Rock's 74th-minute equaliser, the final score of a breathless game, tells you everything you need to know about this era of Dublin football.

A point down, a man down, three-plus minutes into the seven of injury time signalled. Kerry have possession with their safest pair of hands, David Moran. Just about every player in a blue jersey has a drawer full of All-Ireland medals at home. Every Dub in Croke Park would forgive them if this great run came to an end now. They went out on their shields, we'd say.

But that wasn't how this team operated. They hunted Moran. Tired legs, tired minds, whatever. They swarmed the Kerry midfielder until he coughed up possession. The ball broke to Ciarán Kilkenny near midfield and eventually found its way to the hard-running Eoin Murchan. Murchan drove deep into Kerry territory (he would do so to even greater effect two weeks later, of course) and slipped the ball to a looping Dean Rock. The Ballymun man had nine points to his name by that juncture. He made the 10th look laughably easy. We go again, 13 days from today.

* * *

Day 1,840: Saturday, 14 September 2019
All-Ireland final replay, Croke Park (attendance 82,300)
Dublin 1-18 Kerry 0-15

Relief. History made. But relief, sweet relief.

DOUBLE DUBS, beamed the back page of Monday's *Irish Independent*: 'Ladies make it a hat-trick after historic triumph of Jim Gavin's men as capital enjoy "Eight in a Row" weekend.' Mick Bohan's Jackies had secured their third straight All-Ireland title the day after the men won their first Five in a Row. Any week is a good week to be a Dub, but this one felt extra special.

Much like the semi-final with Mayo, the game itself pivoted around the goings-on immediately after half-time. The first half delivered an exhibition of point-kicking from both sides. Paul Mannion at one end for Dublin, answered quickly by David Clifford at the other for Kerry. Dublin jumped out to an early 0-5 to 0-1 lead. Paul Geaney would drive over a fantastic score off his instep just before the break, leaving the sides level-pegging at 10 points apiece as they withdrew for tea. Twenty scores in one half of football, almost all from play. The two best teams in all the land going at it hammer and tongs. As the great Michael O'Hehir might have said: 'Hallelujah!'

It's easy to say now, but even at the time there was the sense that the game may be over just ten seconds into the second half. Eoin Murchan latched on to the breaking ball from the throw-in and, from the Dublin 65, took off for the Canal End. The Na Fianna man was not for catching. His finish left Shane Ryan no chance in the Kingdom goal. 'I can't remember what happened the goal,' Murchan confessed after the game. 'I just went for it and wanted to see what happened!'

The sides would not be level again for the remainder of the game. Connolly, sprung from the bench at half-time for an injured

Jack McCaffrey, had even Kerry fans off their seats (maybe) with a sumptuous, drilled kick-pass to Ciarán Kilkenny for another Dublin point midway through the half. Stephen Cluxton did his part with a 53rd-minute save from Stephen O'Brien that prevented the Kerrymen drawing level.

In the end, the Dubs would have six points to spare over their oldest enemy. Kilkenny, Mannion and Con O'Callaghan would take home four points each. All but one of Dublin's scores – a Dean Rock 45 – would come from play. It was as comprehensive as it gets, on paper at least.

The last word on this one, however, to Bernard Brogan. Gavin sent six subs into the fray in the replay, with Connolly replacing McCaffrey at half-time, Philly McMahon coming in on 54 minutes and Costello on 57. There were three further subs from 67 minutes on, namely Cian O'Sullivan, Kevin McManamon and lastly Michael Darragh Macauley three minutes into injury time. Dean Rock's 68th-minute score had Dublin comfortably five points in the lead. After the drama of the first day, Brogan had been included on the bench for the replay. Sentiment doesn't come into it, we know, we know, we know. But it might have been fitting to see Brogan finish his career on the pitch. Even in his final minutes in charge, the discipline that helped Gavin bring this group to such unfathomable heights remained to the end.

'It would have been nice to have got on there,' Brogan wrote himself. 'I don't think anyone would have held it against me if I had, but I'm not surprised. And I'm not going to complain or argue. Jim is about to lead his county to a fifth All-Ireland in a row. Something no one in the history of the GAA has ever done before ... Now ... that boy goes back up to the Hill again …

'So he races up to it to get one more blast of electricity from it and waves to acknowledge his gratitude. The Hill responds in style, and it's a wonderful shared moment between us. And then, as it starts chanting BERN-O! BERN-O!, that Boy In Blue high-claps it once more before eventually heading down the tunnel … only this time never to return.'

Ya know. Maybe this is exactly how it was supposed to end.

For the third year in a row, Dublin collected seven All Star awards and, in Stephen Cluxton, they had the Footballer of the Year for a second straight season. As well as the skipper, Michael Fitzsimons, Brian Howard, Jack McCaffrey, Brian Fenton, Paul Mannion and Con O'Callaghan were all named on the Team of the Year.

* * *

And then, just like that, he was gone … As the calendar prepared to flip to December, Jim Gavin announced he was stepping down as manager of the Dublin men's senior football team. Brogan had already announced his inter-county retirement at the end of October, Eoghan O'Gara would follow him a week or so later. In early November, Dublin chairman Seán Stanley had said 'the way [Gavin's] talking about fixtures for the league, I'd say he's definitely staying on.'

On collecting his Footballer of the Year award, Cluxton offered, 'I'll have to talk to Jim and see what part he wants me to play next year.' However, on the final Saturday morning of November, the players were summoned for what was dressed up as a 'team photograph'. Once he had his loyal troops all gathered in the one place, Gavin revealed the real reason they were called together. The architect of the Five in a Row was 'handing back the reins to the county committee'.

Chairman Stanley described the news as a 'bombshell' when it was delivered to him from the county board secretary, John Costello. 'Jim met the team about half twelve [on Saturday] and broke the news to them, and that was it,' he recalled. 'Dublin GAA will forever be grateful to Jim Gavin for his dedication, commitment and contribution as a player and, since 2003, leading the next generation of players at U-21 and senior level.'

Dessie Farrell, who had led Dublin's U-21s to the 2017 All-Ireland title and was currently in charge of the senior side at his home club, Na Fianna, was quickly installed as the outright favourite to take over the top job.

The numbers from Gavin's reign are simply staggering. Six All-Ireland titles in his seven seasons in charge. Gavin's team won 44 out of the 48 championship games that he oversaw – a win rate of almost 92 per cent. They won seven straight Leinster titles and five National Leagues (including four in a row from 2013), giving Gavin 18 major titles out of the 21 his team contested during this era. His team won those 44 championship games by an average margin of 10.6 points. And of course, the number 'one' – for one lone championship defeat in seven seasons. Excellence. On a level we had never seen before in men's Gaelic football.

Former Kerry great Pat Spillane summed Gavin's era up thus: 'His philosophy encompassed all that is positive about Gaelic football.

Dublin played the game the way it should be played.' It was no surprise that, five years later, incoming GAA president Jarlath Burns would seek out Gavin to head up the new Football Review Committee, a group that was tasked with figuring out a way to return the game to a more attractive, crowd-pleasing product.

There is no doubt that Dublin are, at county board level, as well supported as any team has ever been. What a Dublin manager needs, he generally gets. Dublin are not faced with the same logistical or population issues that other counties navigate. Dublin footballers want for very little. Theirs is a career as glamorous as it gets in Gaelic games. But the same can be said of many teams the length and breadth of the country over the years, most of whom went on to win very little, if anything at all. Gavin was the catalyst for it all. His vision for what this Dublin team could be, what they could achieve and the style in which they could achieve it, reveals him as something of a visionary. Sure, in late 2012, he was taking over a team that was barely one year removed from an All-Ireland title and awash with talents named Brogan, Flynn, Cluxton, Cullen and Cooper. Pat Gilroy had indeed laid plenty of groundwork. But nobody saw this coming. Nobody except, perhaps, Jim Gavin. The best to ever do it. Period.

CHAPTER SEVEN

Oh, The Weather Outside Is Frightful 2020

There was a new sheriff in town. Things were going to be different in 2020. 'They will, in time, become known as the halcyon days of Dublin football: The seven years that Jim Gavin spent as the senior football manager, culminating in the only Five in a Row ever achieved in the men's game,' Evanne Ní Chuilinn had reported for RTÉ News on a Saturday evening the previous November. The unparalleled dominance Dublin had enjoyed under Gavin meant the next man had, if you will forgive a massive understatement, particularly big shoes to fill.

The man chosen to try that footwear on for size surprised nobody. A fortnight or so before you tucked into your Christmas dinner in 2019, Dessie Farrell was confirmed as the new manager of the Dublin senior footballers on a three-year term. Farrell had been coaching the senior side at Na Fianna and previously led Dublin underage sides to minor and U21 glory. The current senior panel was filled with players he had managed at underage level. He was, according to his clubmate, former Blues boss Paul 'Pillar' Caffrey, the ideal man for the job. 'Who can follow Jim Gavin, with what he's achieved?' Pillar asked on RTÉ 2FM's *Game On* radio show. 'If you look at the last four Dublin managers, myself included, Jim, Dessie and Pat Gilroy, Dessie is probably more qualified than any of us to step up and continue what has been a great era for Dublin.'

Speaking in early January 2020, Farrell himself declared: 'I've no doubt it's a strong dressing room. This group, as well as being high functioning, they're highly evolved and I'd imagine not inclined to suffer fools gladly. I'm under no illusions there, but my approach is very simple in relation to that – we're all in this together. I've been appointed by the county board now, so for better or worse, I am who they've got, and between us we've got to make this work.'

Yeah, things were going to be very different in the year 2020. But that January, as Farrell took the reins for the first time and used nearly 30 players in an opening-day, one-point O'Byrne Cup loss to Longford at Pearse Park, we had absolutely no inkling whatsoever of just how different they would get …

2020 National League Division 1
Played 7, Won 4, Drew 2, Lost 1
Final position: Runners-up

The 2020 National League began like any other. With the new man in charge, Dublin were denied an opening-night win over Kerry when

David Clifford arced over a fine 80th-minute free to share the spoils at Croke Park on the last weekend of January, 1-19 apiece, in front of over 42,500 punters. Dublin would travel to Castlebar the following week and beat Mayo comfortably (1-11 to 0-8) after Jordan Flynn was sent off with less than a quarter of an hour played, and with Dean Rock nabbing his second goal in as many games.

Farrell had to wait until week four for his first senior managerial win at Croke Park after the Dubs drew with Monaghan 1-15 apiece in their third league game. That win, when it came in late February, saw the Dubs edge Donegal by a point, 1-15 to 1-14, at Headquarters. The following week Dublin lost to Tyrone in Omagh, 1-10 to 1-7. The teams clashed in the tunnel as the players went in at half-time. 'Tyson Fury stuff going on there,' was how Colm O'Rourke put it on *The Sunday Game*. Jack McCaffrey was a half-time substitute in this game and was himself then replaced in the 61st minute, a recurrence of a troublesome hamstring injury thought to have been antagonised by the heavy going at Healy Park.

This seems to have been a key reason for McCaffrey's decision not to rejoin the panel later in the summer for the rescheduled championship, post-Covid shutdown. Indeed, that December, McCaffrey told *The Bernard Brogan Podcast* (hosted, coincidentally, by Bernard Brogan): 'Coming back down from that game, I'd hurt my hamstring, got on the bus, rang a friend in New York, booked a flight to New York the following day, left the country, decided to quit football.'

Thankfully, we hadn't seen the last of the Flying Doctor.

OH, THE WEATHER OUTSIDE IS FRIGHTFUL 2020

* * *

With life as we know it shuddering to a halt in March 2020, sport the world over was shelved within weeks as the Covid pandemic held the globe in a vice-like grip. The Tokyo Olympics were pushed back to 2021. Cancelled altogether were golf's Open Championship and tennis's Wimbledon, while we'd have to wait another year to find out what hilarious method England would find to get knocked out of soccer's Euro 2020 – a competition which neither Ireland side had even qualified for anyway. Fairyhouse and Aintree also fell afoul of the pandemic, although we just about managed to squeeze in Cheltenham before things really went haywire. The Premier League was shut down for a full three months between March and June before returning to depressingly empty stadiums.

As the world – and subsequently sport – began to cautiously emerge, bleary-eyed, from this months-long (and still far from over) nightmare, the GAA season was rejigged, reshaped and rescheduled, but with a classic look. Back to the days of straight knockout we went. Win or go home. In fact, go home either way – because even if you won, the fecking pubs were shut!

The GAA's winter championship would be played in empty stadiums, as would the remainder of the rescheduled National League games. Eerie as it all looked and felt, it is unquestionable that the return to some semblance of normality helped lift the mood of a flagging nation. The decision to 'bring back sport' had its critics in a world still very much in a Covid frenzy, but it's impossible to stress just how much we needed the wonderful distraction of sport as the winter of 2020 loomed.

***

That eventful league evening up in Omagh, on the rare 29th day of February, was to be Dublin's last game of consequence until 17 October, when they finally resumed league action with a four-point win against Meath (1-20 to 0-19) at an empty Parnell Park. And there we had an answer to that oft-asked question, 'How do we get the Dubs out of Croker?' Answer: A global pandemic …

Dublin saw off Galway in Salthill in their final league fixture of the season on 25 October, 2-15 to 0-15. The goals had flowed again for the Dubs throughout the campaign. They found the net in each of their seven fixtures, with the TG4 cameras on hand to see them beat the Tribesmen. Incidentally, Galway manager Pádraic Joyce had called in a favour from an old Tralee IT pal in the weeks leading up to the resumption of GAA activities. Jim McGuinness, the former (and, in 2024, current again) Donegal boss had been taking sessions with the Connacht men in what was described as an 'informal arrangement'. Dublin finished second behind Kerry in the Division 1 table, meaning, with no semi-finals or finals in place for obvious reasons, the Kingdom would claim their 21st National League crown.

***

Day 2,260: Saturday, 7 November 2020
Leinster quarter-final, O'Moore Park, Portlaoise
Dublin 0-22 Westmeath 0-11

There would be no backdoor route through the qualifiers for a Westmeath team who, save for Mayo, had encountered this Dublin team as regularly as anyone during their unprecedented unbeaten run. With hindsight and the healing nature of time, Westmeath's John Heslin can look back at some chastening experiences against the Dubs with detachment and much perspective. He recalled his former college teammate and now the marquee midfielder in the country, Brian Fenton, in his early days within the UCD set-up.

'I was lucky I got to see Brian Fenton in his key development stages. His attention to detail, his willingness to challenge – he was learning off everyone there as well. That's a sign of a great player, if you ask me, that it doesn't matter who's there, he was willing to learn off anyone. Whether that person's starting or not starting or whatever it is, if there's something he could take from them, he was trying to do that. You could always see with those guys that they had the potential, Fenton in particular. The Dubs at the time had maybe James McCarthy and Mike Macauley midfield. Which isn't a bad midfield if you ask me. But Fenton was a different type of baller. And he's come in and just gone from strength to strength.

'When I played against all those Dublin lads I knew from UCD, I didn't treat them as if they were my best friends … Once upon a time I had the mindset of not even talking to opposing players that I knew. Now I can play the game and still stay in the moment … It's life, you have to have a bit of craic as well.'

If ever there was a season when that last statement was pertinent, it was the championship campaign of 2020.

On the O'Moore Park pitch, Dean Rock was as metronomic as ever, slipping over seven points, six from frees, while Ciarán Kilkenny remained at his imperious best. The Castleknock centre-forward found time for five points from play while running the show for Farrell's Boys in Blue. Ballymun Kickhams' Paddy Small, younger brother of half-back John, had by now moved into the starting 15, as had Robbie McDaid of Ballyboden St Enda's and St Jude's midfielder Tom Lahiff. Westmeath's Ray Connellan claimed the score of the game, a wonderful sideline kick just before the half-time break. It was a point that deserved a live audience rather than the deafening silence of the barren Portlaoise terraces. There was no appearance for Paul Mannion in that Leinster opener. An All Star in the previous three seasons, Mannion's influence on Dublin's sixth straight championship would be relatively minor.

When looking for signs of slippage in the early stages of the post-Gavin era, the pedant may have compared Dublin's 11-point winning margin unfavourably with Leinster openers of recent years. The previous five seasons had seen the Dubs open their summer with wins by 27, 11, 12, 23 and 26 points. Incredibly, in this year's shortened, old school, straight knockout championship, Dublin's path to Sam was made a lot easier thanks to a last-minute Mark Keane goal for Cork which ended Kerry's campaign at the Munster semi-final stage. What's that they say about a lucky general?

* * *

Day 2,268: Sunday, 15 November 2020
Leinster semi-final, Croke Park
Dublin 2-23 Laois 0-7

'One of the strangest first years of inter-county management you could have,' said Laois boss Mike Quirke after the game, in what must count as the understatement of a lifetime. Dublin had been 'everything I thought they were going to be' for the former Kerry player.

'You can hear Jonny Cooper at the end of the game when they're up by 19, 20 points or whatever it is, and he's roaring about "let's get another three scores" and it's just leadership and efficiency they have. I said to [selector] Eoin Kearns with 20 minutes to go, "This is really strange, I felt we've done a lot right and yet we're 15 points down." That's Dublin.'

Ciarán Kilkenny had become Dublin's do-it-all, Swiss-army knife quarterback. He clipped Laois for 1-4 here, including a superbly volleyed goal for his second straight Man of the Match performance. In midfield, the regal Brian Fenton dominated and kicked four points from play.

Next up, a Meath team that ran Dublin close in a league encounter at Parnell Park only three weeks before and had just hit Kildare for five goals in their own provincial semi-final.

* * *

Day 2,274: Saturday, 21 November 2020
Leinster final, Croke Park
Dublin 3-21 Meath 0-9

Another Leinster title for Dublin, but even more so than any other year, the Blues' latest provincial cakewalk was the least interesting story of the weekend. Tipperary and Cavan had rocked the GAA world by annexing their respective provincial championships in Munster and Ulster.

We had seen just about every weird and not-so-wonderful thing possible in 2020 – why not throw a walkover in the All-Ireland Championship into the mix? After a towering Dublin display against Meath, Joe Brolly suggested Dublin were 'in danger of rendering Gaelic football redundant' and added that it was 'getting to the point where other teams should refuse to play them'.

Ciarán Kilkenny kept his high scoring pace up with four points from play. Fenton dominated the kickout at either end of the field against the Royals in a majestic Man of the Match display. The Raheny colossus had become the finest midfielder in the game. Was he already the greatest midfielder football had ever seen? What players are in that conversation – O'Shea, Mullins … anyone else? It's a short list either way, and Dublin's number 8 is most certainly on it.

* * *

Day 2,288: Saturday, 5 December 2020
All-Ireland semi-final, Croke Park
Dublin 1-24 Cavan 0-12

And then there were four. An eclectic mix of contenders took their chance in the semi-finals of the All-Ireland Football Championship of 2020. Dublin came out of Leinster; Mayo eked their way through Connacht; and Cavan survived Ulster's alligator swamp. Tipperary, fittingly, were Munster champs.

It was a year that renewed the old-fashioned romance of the provincial championships for many. Poignantly, on the centenary of Bloody Sunday, the four provincial championship winners would mirror the four who had taken the titles in 1920.

In Munster, Cork had possibly left their heart and soul on the Páirc Uí Chaoimh pitch when they chinned Kerry on the line. They could not finish the job back at the same venue for the provincial final a fortnight later against Tipperary, with the Premier County seeing them off 0-17 to 0-14 on the back of seven points from Conor Sweeney and five from Michael Quinlivan. Tipp were crowned Munster kingpins for the first time since 1935, bridging a staggering 85-year gap.

Cavan had not waited 85 years for a return to the top of the Ulster tree, but a dry spell dating back to 1997 was more than long enough for them. They shocked Donegal in the Ulster final to win their first Anglo Celt trophy in 23 years. There were scenes of near mayhem as fans in the Breffni County lined the streets to welcome their triumphant champions home.

UNBEATABLE

There were also legitimate hopes that they could shock Dublin. After all, hadn't inspirational manager Mickey Graham felled Dublin kingpins Kilmacud Crokes during Mullinalaghta's famous run to the club final a year earlier?

Cavan's season had promised so much early in the year before the world stopped. They won three out of their first four games in Division 2 and looked sure to push for promotion. They lost their final two games upon the resumption of play in October, however, first to Kildare in Newbridge and then at home to Roscommon on the last day of the league. All of this meant that Cavan, from looking up at Division 1, were now relegated and destined for the third tier. Despite all of that, they were, seemingly out of absolutely nowhere, Ulster winners and destined for a semi-final date with the reigning All-Ireland champions.

Conor Madden had sprung from the bench with a McManamon-like 1-2 against Donegal as Cavan won that Ulster title. The aura of the all-conquering, Six in a Row-chasing Dubs was not lost on him and his fellow Ulster champs. 'You'd be lying if you said you weren't slightly in awe of coming up against these players who had won five in a row and were probably going to be heralded as the greatest team ever. You'd nearly be saying to yourself that "at least I can say I played against this team". We felt at the time that we had as good a group of players as had been in Cavan in a good number of years, and they were getting to their peak as well.'

Taking on Dublin was far from simple, though. The tallest of orders. That being said, we were some way removed from the off-the-cuff, long-kicking, point-slinging, hard-running Dubs of 2017. Farrell's Boys in Blue were more inclined to pick you apart. Giving the ball away against this functional Dubs outfit was not a good idea – it could be a long time before you saw it again.

Madden explains: 'When we started to study Dublin, the things we realised were how efficient Dublin were going forward, getting shots off in the scoring zone, and in defence they gave away nothing easy at all. They were comfortable in the one-on-one battle. They didn't just play all-out attack or all-out defence, but their transition from defence to attack or attack to defence was something that made us realise, look if we give the ball away, you're going to be punished for it.

'As a team, that was how we viewed the Dubs. Then when you drill down into it, on an individual basis, you start to identify key players. All the teams we played, you would always have your three or four key players. A wing-back or your corner-back who might carry a lot of possession; a midfielder potentially or one or two marquee forwards. With the Dubs, you probably had 10 or 11 lads that really, really need to be watched. You don't know who will be the match-winner on the day.'

As fans, we tend to see only the bells and whistles of the Dubs games: A daring, arcing Diarmuid Connolly pass that lands softly in the hands of a grateful teammate. A booming Paul Flynn point from distance. A soaring Brian Fenton catch with Michael Jordan hangtime. Jack McCaffrey turning on the jets and burning up the sideline, ball in hand and flagging opponent chasing a lost cause some ways behind. Another crafty Bernard Brogan goal finished with nonchalance. But we miss the point. All of those things get you off your seat, but the brilliance of the Dubs was in their mastering of the basics. The devil was in the most minor details.

'The Dubs were coming from such competition within their own squad that they were probably all under the pressure of "if I don't perform, there's two or three players there ready to fill my position". I'd say that led into that,' Madden continued. 'Looking back, it was admirable in the sense that the Dubs didn't really change their tune from minute one to minute 70. Whether they were winning by 10 points or not, they were trying to apply the same things to what they were doing when the game was level earlier on. That's probably a hangover from the number of years when they weren't so successful. They didn't really change, they didn't get carried away with themselves – which probably could be thrown at other teams.'

By the summer – sorry, Christmas – of 2020, the Dubs carried more than just their on-field menace. They now had the aura of a team whom everybody assured you could not be beaten. Jim Gavin. Dessie Farrell. No matter. The Blue juggernaut would run you over. The best thing you could do was just get off the road. With all that rubbish swirling in their heads, the Ulster Champions of 2020 headed down to Headquarters to take their shot. In two separate, socially distanced buses.

Dublin picked Cavan apart at Croke Park, but the Ulster champions had their moments. Had they emptied the barrel in pursuit of a first provincial title in 23 years? Perhaps.

Once the Dubs extended into a gallop, they swallowed up everything in their path. Robbie McDaid, who had replaced the prematurely departed Jack McCaffrey at wing-back, did a more than passable impression of the Clontarf flyer, palming the game's only goal before eventually finishing with a very Jack-like 1-2 from play.

Brian Fenton added four points of his own, as did Ciarán Kilkenny, while the full-forward line of Paddy Small (0-2), Con O'Callaghan (0-4) and Dean Rock (0-6) shared a dozen scores between them.

Looking back on the game and that line-up, Cavan's Madden summarised: 'The thing that made that Dublin team so great was that, even though you didn't feel like you were a million miles off them, they were reflecting that on the scoreboard by putting six, seven, eight points on you and forcing you to have to "go for it". We learned things from playing Dublin. Stuff that you bring back to your own county, even your own club. The stuff they were doing, although they were doing it so perfectly, it wasn't rocket science. It was the fact that they had it so well communicated and so well drilled into them, it became second nature to them.'

Next up for the Dubs, the most familiar of faces on the most familiar of occasions at a most unfamiliar time of year. An All-Ireland final with Mayo, the week before Christmas. James Horan's men would see off Munster champs Tipperary the day after this one on a scoreline of 5-20 to 3-13. A veritable goalfest at the old stadium.

* * *

Day 2,302: Saturday, 19 December 2020
All-Ireland final, Croke Park
Dublin 2-14 Mayo 0-15

CAN HOPE AND HISTORY RHYME? asked the ever-eloquent Vincent Hogan in the *Indo*. 'And so, Horan and his people hope again.

Magnificent Mayo, a spirit still unbroken by the taint of history.' The sports section's front page featured a collage of pictures of losing Mayo teams from All-Ireland finals. Conor Mortimer hunched over, dejected, in 2006. A rueful Ciaran McDonald two years earlier. Aidan O'Shea, face in hands in 2013 after an epic war with Gavin's first-year Dubs. On Christmas week, the ghosts of summers past.

To Hammer the Hammer, Mayo Must Risk Being Nailed warned Tomás Ó Sé in the same pages. That first strike of the hammer came 13 seconds in. O'Shea, wearing number 14, began the game in the middle of the field. It has always seemed a curious tactic of Mayo's against a team with probably the most mobile 'middle-eight' the game has seen. O'Shea has many qualities as a footballer, but he has never had the gears of the Dublin ball-carriers. James McCarthy beat O'Shea to the throw-in before quickly pacing away from the Breaffy man.

A sharp footpass into Niall Scully; McCarthy kept moving, O'Shea kept chasing. The goal opened up, Dean Rock peeled to the back post. McCarthy, back in possession, found the Ballymun man and his palmed finish over David Clarke – the quickest All-Ireland final goal of all time – gave Dublin the perfect start.

Say what you like about Mayo, they aren't afraid of punishment. They've seen it all before. They dusted themselves off after Rock's ridiculously early gut punch and got right back to work. With 2:20 on the clock, the sides were level. In fact, 20 minutes later, Mayo led by two – Dubs 1-3, Mayo 0-8.

And then, another gut punch. Con O'Callaghan gathered possession outside the Mayo 21, head-faked a look at the posts, then stepped inside his man. A quick pass to Niall Scully was returned across the face of Clarke's goal to a cutting O'Callaghan, who boxed Scully's pass on the volley with violence. A right hook that would have wobbled Marvin Hagler. Mayo had largely controlled the previous 20 minutes. And still they trailed.

Cillian O'Connor ended his day with another nine points to add to his tally as Mayo's all-time record scorer. But he had little help. Ryan O'Donoghue was the only other Mayo player to trouble the scoreboard more than once, with both of his points coming in the first half long before his 58th-minute withdrawal. By contrast, Dublin's named full-forward line of O'Callaghan (1-1), Rock (1-4) and Ciarán Kilkenny (0-3) almost matched Mayo by themselves.

The start of the second half proved the crucial stretch of the game. Dublin wing-back Robbie McDaid had been black-carded on the stroke of half-time, leaving the defending champions a man down for the opening ten minutes of the second period. The scoreline at the tea break read Dublin 2-6 Mayo 0-10. The Dubs went into extreme game-managing mode. They simply kept the football. The missing player wasn't missed at all. Midway through the second period, Mayo trailed by just a point, 2-9 to 0-14, and yet, the result felt inevitable. Water breaks were a feature of the games played in the post-Covid world. When Mayo grouped together for some rehydration and one last push with a quarter of the All-Ireland final still to play, you could see it in their demeanour. Or rather, you couldn't. Belief – it just wasn't there. If Dublin were by now conditioned to expect victory, their greatest rivals seemed to be conditioned to expect the opposite.

Darren Coen, a 57th-minute substitute, was the only Mayo forward to score from play in the second half. Brian Howard replaced Seán Bugler at half-time for Dublin and was immense. Mannion, who wouldn't score from play in any of the five championship games, still nailed a difficult free after replacing Paddy Small in the 51st minute of the final.

Con O'Callaghan paid tribute to the vanquished after the game. 'You can review all the tapes that you want and say there are opportunities inside or there are goal opportunities,' the Cuala ace said. 'But when you are in the white heat of battle, and someone is facing you down, putting you under pressure, getting contact on you, it's much different. You are forced to make mistakes and that's something [Mayo] do really well. We struggled to come to grips with that early on.'

In the Sunday papers, the morning after a Saturday-night All-Ireland final, the Dubs had the rare treat of reading about their Six in a Row achievements in the same editions that carried the Christmas TV guides. Not many can say that! What a Sunday it was too, as Mick Bohan's Dublin ladies beat Cork 1-10 to 1-5 to win their fourth All-Ireland title in a row. A weekend to remember in the old town.

The All Star team of 2020 was predictably dominated by Dublin. No fewer than nine of the Boys in Blue made the team of the year. Michael Fitzsimons, James McCarthy, John Small and Eoin Murchan were named among the backs. Brian Fenton was not only an All Star for a fifth time, but he also took home his second Footballer of the Year award. In the forwards, there was room for Niall Scully, Ciarán Kilkenny, Con O'Callaghan and Dean Rock.

OH, THE WEATHER OUTSIDE IS FRIGHTFUL 2020

MAYO WILL BOUNCE BACK NEXT YEAR promised their star David Brady of his countymen in his *Sunday World* column. We wouldn't have to wait long to find out if he was right.

CHAPTER EIGHT

Hell or Connaught: The 2,540th Day 2021

2021 National League Division 1
Played 4, Won 3, Drew 1, Lost 0
Final position: Joint winners

The second season of the Pandemic League began with a furious debate as to just what exactly constituted an 'elite' athlete – the 'amateur' GAA was being kept on hold while our rugby provinces and the semi-professional League of Ireland season were permitted to get up and running. Needless to say, GAA folk took this with all of the grace and humility you would come to expect. Probably.

The front page of the *Irish Independent* on April Fool's Day was no joke, however. DUBLIN GAA STARS HOLD SECRET TRAINING DESPITE COVID RULES shouted the paper's main splash. Dessie Farrell had trouble. It may seem a little bit daft, looking back, to consider just how egregious an error it supposedly was for a group of physically fit young men to go exercising around a wide-open space, but such were the unprecedented times we were all still wading through in the spring of 2021. The 'non-contact session at Innisfails GAA Club' on the Malahide Road had Joe Duffy's disciples up in arms.

From a Dublin point of view, there was no getting away from it – this looked bad for Farrell. 'It wouldn't have happened under Jim Gavin', they'd say. Whoever 'they' are. And perhaps they would be right. The fact that the impromptu session took place about half a day after a Croke Park missive that warned any breach of the collective training ban could place the entire GAA season in jeopardy only made the error of judgement more unforgivable. If you're gonna go, go for a good one. This was not a good one.

Manager Farrell eventually fell on his sword and was hit with a 12-week sideline ban while Dublin forfeited home advantage for one of their league games. This gave us the unusual situation whereby the Boys in Blue played no league match at a 'home' venue (Croke or Parnell parks) in 2021. Again, global medical emergencies seem to be the surest way to solve the Croke Park conundrum.

Needless to say, the cute hoors down in Killarney didn't miss the chance to stick the boot into their old adversaries up in the 'Smoke. Kerry boss Peter Keane felt the Dubs' illegal nine-man training session 'was unfair on society in general'. The week before their league opener, Dublin freetaker Dean Rock addressed Keane's swipe: 'It's certainly not something that I, or the team, would comment on other people's situation like that, but he's very much entitled to his opinion on it ... The GAA did their investigation and they were happy with it ... It was a deeply regrettable incident and never should have happened. It's something we regret.'

When the National League finally got underway, former Dubs ace Ciarán Whelan, writing in his *Herald* column, pronounced the start of the 'phoney war before championship' as a curtailed league campaign saw the divisions split in two, north and south, meaning only three group games for each team, starting in mid-May. In the opener, Cormac Costello matched Roscommon by himself as he smashed 1-13 at Dr Hyde Park, where Dublin ran out 1-22 to 0-16 winners. Mick Galvin filled in on the sideline for the suspended Farrell in a game in which Dublin were awarded no fewer than three penalties. Costello fired the first kick into the net, the second one into the butt of Colm Lavin's post, and the third one over the bar. Dublin had 1-12 on the scoreboard before they registered their first wide. St Vincent's Michael Shiel kept the clean sheet in goal. More on that situation later.

Next up, 20 years after Maurice Fitzgerald kicked the score of the millennium at the home of hurling, Dublin and Kerry would reconvene at Semple Stadium for a bonkers league game that finished all square, as it had in 2001. This time, the final scoreboard flashed Dublin's 4-9 to the Kingdom's more mannerly 1-18. A late David Clifford penalty ensured a share of the spoils for Kerry after a dramatic game. Clifford ended with 1-6, five points coming from play, while Con O'Callaghan bagged all 2-1 of his total from open play. In the *Indo* sport pages, Eamonn Sweeney uttered what we were all thinking: 'Fossa David and Cuala Con are Gaelic's Messi and Ronaldo. They may end up being the two greatest forwards of them all.'

HELL OR CONNAUGHT: THE 2,540TH DAY 2021

A week later, in Tuam, Dublin had four points to spare over a Galway team destined for relegation to Division 2. Cormac Costello got his third goal in as many games, as did O'Callaghan. Final score on match week three: Galway 1-15, Dublin 2-16. At the same time, in Roscommon, Kerry were beating the hosts by six points to set up a 'semi-final' with Tyrone that would lead not to a final but to, well, nowhere!

Dublin took on Donegal in the last four, this time at Breffni Park, Cavan, and handed the Ulstermen a 1-18 to 1-14 defeat. Paddy Small claimed the goal as his left-footed effort past Shaun Patton largely decided a game played under a strange atmosphere. Covid had given our sport many unwanted 'firsts', and a semi-final with no subsequent final was as peculiar as any of them. Stand-in Dubs boss Mick Galvin was, predictably, not a fan. 'You play a game like this, the other semi-final being played on the same night,' the Na Fianna man said. 'We'd look forward to a final but how it came to this, I don't know.'

Evan Comerford had taken over in goal for Dublin after the league opener and acquitted himself ably. But the great unwashed still, naturally, wanted to know where the other fella was. 'We'll be expecting to have Stephen [Cluxton] back as soon as we step back into championship training,' Galvin assured us. Nobody was convinced. Something didn't add up. With that, after Kerry had hammered Tyrone 6-15 to 1-14, we had co-league champions, the Kingdom credited with a 22nd league title, Dublin with their 14th. Of course, Kerry and Tyrone would see each other down the road again in 2021, at a time and place of the Ulstermen's choosing …

In Division 2, Mayo won three games out of three and gained

promotion alongside Kildare – but it came at a cost. Cillian O'Connor, their prolific freetaker, suffered an ACL injury in the Connacht men's league semi-final win over Clare in Ennis. If Mayo were to finally climb the blue mountain, they would have to do it without their all-time record scorer.

* * *

Day 2,499: Sunday, 4 July 2021
Leinster quarter-final, Wexford Park
Dublin 0-15 Wexford 0-7

CLUXTON CONFUSION: DESSIE IN THE DARK AS LEGEND STEPS AWAY BUT HASN'T RETIRED. The *Herald* front page the Monday after Dublin's 2021 championship opener confirmed what we all felt – the scoreline was not the storyline on this occasion. A functional Dublin performance had been more than enough to see off Wexford on the first day of the summer season, but the elephant in the room was the continued absence of six-time All Star goalkeeper Stephen Cluxton. Dublin had now played four competitive games in 2021 and conceded just two goals. But in the modern game, shot-stopping is arguably the least important task in a goalkeeper's day's work.

Cluxton had completely reshaped the model of inter-county goalkeeper. We now preferred to call kickouts 'restarts', and the data analysts told us they were the most influential part of the game. In years past – pre-kicking tee and long before short, clipped passes to the corner-back – many goalkeepers wore rugby-style football boots with ankle support and reinforced insteps to help protect their kicking foot as they endlessly pumped kickouts as high and far as possible week in, week out. The game had changed. Ball retention became paramount. It had largely begun with Cluxton. His absence robbed Dublin of a key weapon in their arsenal. Comerford was certainly able cover, and the fact that, like his predecessor, he was also left-footed gave some fluidity to the transition. But he wasn't Stephen Cluxton. The veteran netminder was sorely missed and would continue to be as the summer developed.

'I don't know, is the honest answer,' said Dessie Farrell when asked about the Parnells man's whereabouts. 'It is not that we are trying to play games here in any way. He's asked for time, and I think he deserves that time. At the end of the day, the service he has given to his county has been immense. When a man asks to step away and take time out, I think a player like Stephen Cluxton deserves that and we will need to respect that.'

At the time – and still a few short years later – it seemed a stunning admission from the manager of the dominant team in the game. One of his most celebrated players had retired. Possibly. And, like us all, Dessie Farrell was none the wiser. We were now in the curious era of inter-county players whom we'd heard very little from during their playing days issuing wordy, rambling, indulgent retirement speeches wherein they thanked everyone from their U-10 manager to the milkman. That wasn't Cluxton's bag. The Parnells man was never going to go out like that. He may not have needed to release a public statement, but there had clearly been a breakdown in communication between captain and manager. Many took it as a sign that the all-conquering Dubs were there for the taking.

On the Wexford Park pitch, the home side were put away mainly on the back of Cormac Costello's freetaking. There was a start in midfield for Peadar Ó Cofaigh-Byrne, while Ryan Basquel began in corner-forward but was replaced by Sean Bugler at half-time. On top of Cluxton's absence, the Paul Mannion-sized hole in the full forward line was looking like a problem. Paddy Andrews had retired after the 2020 win, as had Michael Darragh Macauley.

Sport is funny. You're never quite as far ahead or as far behind as you think you are – or as folk will tell you that you are. A season or two earlier, Dublin appeared to have an endless conveyor belt of scoring forwards at their disposal. Point kicking would never again be a problem. The dark, scoreless days of the noughties were no more. But you lose a Brogan here, a Flynn there, an Andrews, a McManamon, a Mannion … and all of a sudden a relatively threadbare attack was not finding scores so easy to come by.

* * *

Day 2,513: Sunday, 18 July 2021
Leinster semi-final, Croke Park
Dublin 2-16 Meath 1-13

Another day, another Leinster semi-final win, another Where's Wally? question for Dessie Farrell to answer. This time, Kevin McManamon is MIA for this provincial last-four clash with the Royal County.

McManamon, a qualified sports psychologist, was in Tokyo working with the Irish Olympic team but was also, we were told, still very much not retired from inter-county football. He was due back from Japan a few days before a potential All-Ireland semi-final. It was another loose end for Farrell. We had no Cluxton, Mannion or McManamon. Worse still, we had no closure regarding any of the above. 'That's the nature with work commitments,' Farrell reasoned. 'These are amateur players and they're not contracted to play for their county. Work and career is really, really important. It has been all along to Dublin football management teams over the last period and continues to remain that way.'

On the curious case of the missing goalkeeper, Farrell's update was simple: 'No development. It's still as was. As I said at the time, ultimately the decision for what happens next rests with Stephen … We're going to give him the time that he needs to make that decision, and it'll be Stephen that determines what the future holds for him.'

In the lead-up to this semi-final, football analyst Tomás Ó Sé had argued that 'for 15 years, nobody has managed to crack Cluxton – but ironically he could be the one who cracks the Dubs'.

In an empty Croke Park, Meath arguably let the Dubs off the hook. And the rest smelled blood. The Dubs' inside line of Con O'Callaghan (1-3) and Cormac Costello (1-4) did the damage, while Ciarán Kilkenny grabbed five points from play from the centre-forward position. Notably, none of Dublin's four substitutes troubled the scoreboard. That starting 15 was about as strong as it gets, but the reserve cavalry was not what it once was.

In the other semi-final, Jack O'Connor's Kildare (yes, *that* Jack O'Connor) had come through a shootout with Westmeath (2-14 to 0-18) to give themselves another crack at the Six in a Row champs in a fortnight's time.

* * *

Day 2,527: Sunday, 1 August 2021
Leinster final, Croke Park
Dublin 0-20 Kildare 1-9

Hindsight 20:20, etc., but all the signs were there. There was something about Kildare's 62nd-minute goal that left an uneasy feeling in the pit of your stomach. Was it a piece of brilliance from Daniel Flynn? Perhaps. A typically late, last-sting-of-a-dying-wasp flourish from a talented Kildare side that was ultimately meaningless? Maybe. Maybe not.

The score at the time was Dublin 0-16 Kildare 0-8. Just over eight minutes of normal time remained. Dublin had seized control of the game in the few minutes before half-time and never relinquished it. A tight, professional performance. And then came Flynn's goal, a score that arguably revealed a couple of hitherto papered-over cracks in the Dublin structure.

Evan Comerford's kickout found James McCarthy in space along the left sideline. The Ballymun Kickhams star inexplicably – and uncharacteristically – had his pocket picked by Flynn, who took off direct for the Hill 16 goal. No problem, Jonny Cooper was there, planted firm between Flynn and the posts. He would sort this out. But Flynn streamrolled Cooper, leaving the Na Fianna stopper in a most unCooperlike heap on the floor ('Look what he does to Jonny Cooper, leaves him on the ground!' – an incredulous Dessie Dolan in the RTÉ studio). All of a sudden the Kildare forward was within shooting range. And shoot he did, a driven effort that screamed past Comerford into the net.

A spectacular goal, but hardly a score you could countenance Dublin conceding in any of their previous six years' dominance. Nothing about the score sat right. McCarthy dispossessed; Cooper quite literally run over … and might Stephen Cluxton have got a palm to Flynn's powerful strike? We may have been witnessing another sign that the 2021 Dubs were not quite 'at it' as in years before.

Granted, Kildare would score only one more point in the game, and the final gap would be a very comfortable eight points. But, again, the signs were there. Dublin had won six straight All-Ireland finals by an average of just 3.6 points. Twice they had been taken to replays (2016, 2019); twice they had emerged by just a single point (2016, 2017). A lifetime of fine margins.

On the pitch, Kilkenny, Costello and Rock continued to keep their defenders honest – but again, the six subs who came in could offer only a single point from Ryan Basquel when all was said and done.

Rewinding back for a moment to the heady days of 2013, those Dublin games now appear like bohemian, abandon-soaked spectaculars teeming with the insouciance of youthful innocence. The traditions of the catch-and-kick game that football was always meant to be, coupled with the modern brilliance of finely tuned athletes playing on a perfectly engineered dark-green sod. Indulgence personified. Drink it all in. The last days of Rome.

By the summer of 2021, that carefree, all-out-attacking style had mostly been replaced by a mature, pragmatic obsession with 'scoring zones' and possession stats. Indeed, the eight years from 2013 to 2021 provide us with a fantastic study in the analytics-driven evolution of modern Gaelic football. In very simple terms, we just didn't kick the ball as much anymore.

But what of the vanquished? Nobody in Leinster – save, possibly for Meath – had suffered more at the hands of the Dubs over the previous decade than their neighbours in Kildare. If any county should have been equipped to at least keep the Blues honest in Leinster, it would surely be the Lilywhites. Competitive at underage level and geographically close to the capital city, Kildare looked like they should be, at the very least, streets ahead of 'the rest' in their own province.

Kildare's Paul Cribbin had been around for pretty much every step of the 2010s, and he has seen the Dublin revolution at close quarters. It hasn't always been an enjoyable experience for the Johnstownbridge forward. 'My age group of lads in Kildare, we were always competitive or actually on top of Dublin from when I played minor up to U21,' he remembers. 'I always felt then when I made it into the senior panel that that vein would continue on, that it would be nip and tuck between the two teams. It did seem to be a different animal then when we got to senior. Jim Gavin and a lot of managers speak about "the process" and systems, but I believe that their processes and systems were just far superior than any other county's. And then they had the players that were able to seamlessly fit into that. That was the major difference.

'If you match us up, player for player, there wouldn't be as big a difference as those scorelines suggested. Also, anytime we faced Dublin, the issue had been just a period of dominance of goals that we'd concede, one after another. Once they got one or two goals it was very hard, in Croke Park, to get a handle on them.

'They had threats coming from all areas of the pitch so it's very, very hard to defend against and try to implement your own game plan when they seem to be so ruthless in their play. In terms of a pattern of play, they were fairly fluid. You wouldn't necessarily know which forward was going to play in which position, because that's the way the modern game is gone. You can't just be pigeon-holed into one position. You need to know the role of each position, no matter the number on your back, and I think Dublin were probably ahead of the curve in that. A lot of counties do that now, but Dublin were doing that ten years ago.'

* * *

Day 2,540: Saturday, 14 August 2021
All-Ireland semi-final, Croke Park
Dublin 0-14 Mayo 0-17 (AET)

The All-Ireland Champions. Jubilation!
Cream of Leinster Football Is Whipped Cream Now
The Ballina Herald (Saturday, 29 September 1951)

This front-page headline came six days after Mayo won the last of their three All-Irelands, almost 70 years before this semi-final. 'The game won't live as a classic encounter,' wrote the curiously bylined 'Kipper' back in 1951. 'But it will live as a record to Mayomen who completely wiped out a fancied Meath team in a manner which left no doubt as to where the best bunch of footballers in Ireland are today. It will also live in the memories of those metropolitan scribes, who will remember 23rd September 1951 as the day they had to rack their brains to find excuses for a Meath team which existed only in their imagination.'

Ol' Kipper had come in hot. And he wasn't done. 'Mayo did it for the third time – and it won't be the last. One last word – "Well and truly done Mayo".'

Final score on All-Ireland final day at Croke Park on 23 September 1951: Mayo 2-8 Meath 0-9.

Elsewhere on the front page on that fateful day sat the following letter, which, quaint as it is, we freely acknowledge has absolutely nothing to do with football …

'To the Editor, *Ballina Herald*. Dear Sir – You, personally, are not often presented with a bouquet. May I offer you one now – a deep appreciation of your leading article in the *Ballina Herald* of last week extending sympathy to the *Irish Times* upon their colossal loss by fire on September 18th? That a paper from "Hell or Connaught" should send such a generous message of sympathy from a part of Ireland often directly opposed to views expressed by the *Times* makes a singing in the hearts of some of us that in their neighbour's hour of trial great hearts can still rise above creed and politics in this sad, unhappy world of ours, and show us the way to the Kingdom of God. As a constant reader of the *Irish Times* and of your two papers, I am, yours most gratefully. – Octavia Greer, Enniscrone, Sligo.'

In their book *Chasing Sam Maguire*, Dermot Reilly and Colm Keys give us at least part of Meath's side of that 1951 defeat, and it's one that, bizarre GAA season calendar aside, could have just as easily been written in 2021 as in 1951. 'Many attributed Meath's listless performance to the fact their minds were firmly focused on their imminent league final engagement with New York at the Polo Grounds. In preparation for their departure on 25 September, they had been vaccinated in the weeks before the final and questions were asked as to whether this impacted performance. The view expressed in the *Meath Chronicle* was clear: "Training and vaccinations are ill bedfellows".'

STORM MAYO DROWNS DUBLIN:
MAYO LASH SIX IN A ROW LEGENDS DUBLIN BUT IS THIS FINALLY THE END OF THAT OL' CURSE? REIGN OF THE SKY BLUES ENDS AS THE WEST AWAKES TO NEW STRONG SENSE OF BELIEF
Sunday World (Sunday, 15 August 2021)

Seventy years later, and the *Sunday World* went deep on the Dubs' semi-final defeat. 'Like the rampaging Visigoths at the gates of Rome,

Mayo sensed and brilliantly seized their moment. And, after 2,540 days as football's unbeatable, untouchable Caesars, Dublin's empire fell.' Purple prose, as always, from Roy Curtis.

On game day in Croke Park, on the surface at least, all was as rosy as ever in the blue garden at half-time. Dublin led 0-10 to 0-4 at intermission. Ciarán Kilkenny, who would be the only Dub to make the All Star selection in 2021, played as fine a first half of football as he ever had. But we had a familiar feeling in the pit of our stomachs, similar to the one we felt 20 minutes into the infamous Donegal semi-final of 2014 as Dublin slung over long-range score after long-range score. Those of us who see disaster around every corner and pay far too much heed to the law of averages always fear the worst on those days when your team can't seem to miss. You wait with dread for the other shoe to drop. And drop it did. Mayo would outscore Dublin 0-13 to 0-4 over the next 66 minutes of football. James Horan hauled off his captain, Aidan O'Shea, with just 49 minutes played. A brave, dare-we-say-it, Gavin-like call. John Small survived a massive red card scare in the 57th-minute when his heavy challenge on Eoghan McLaughlin sent the Mayo wing-back down the tunnel via motorised stretcher.

Every game has an energy, a personality of its own. Not every bounce of the ball is equal. In the 63rd minute came a moment those of a green and red persuasion might speak of for generations to come. Goalkeeper Rob Hennelly struck a 60-metre free high and to the right of the Canal End goal, which Dublin were defending. Dublin led 0-12 to 0-7. Halfway home. This latest Mayo wide should chip away at whatever remaining fragments of self-belief these old foes of ours had left. Ideal. We got 'em. Again.

But Diarmuid O'Connor still had enough of that belief to chase hard along the endline and beat two Dubs to the dropping ball before volleying it back into play. A bit of extra effort right from the Dubs' own playbook. The ball would arrive in the grateful hands of Kevin McLoughlin, and he in turn arced over a beautiful left-footed score. Few Mayo men had suffered more at the hands of this particular Dublin team than O'Connor and McLoughlin. The Dubs were still in the Mayor's office, four points ahead in an All-Ireland semi-final with time running out. But there was something about that brief passage of play. Some points are worth far more than what they reflect on the scoreboard.

Still, omens or not, the Dubs had Mayo in an Andre the Giant bear-hug and, a la Wrestlemania 3, looked like squeezing them into submission. But Mayo, gluttons for punishment, summoned their inner Hulk Hogan. Whether you consider Dublin the irresistible force or the immovable object is up to you. This time around, finally, Mayo both resisted and removed them.

Hennelly, at the (generously awarded, it must be said) second attempt, drove over a late 45 to force extra time. Conor O'Shea had hounded David Byrne out over his own endline to win the kick in the first place. Beating the champs at their own game. From there, with the Dubs out on their feet and bereft of the usual reinforcements that had gotten them over many a line in years past, the result seemed inevitable. An extraordinary feeling after everything we had seen from this team. A team who always seemed to find a way out of even the stickiest jam.

This time around, you just felt it wasn't there. The team that owed us absolutely nothing, had nothing left. The end, when it comes, is swift and ruthless.

Mayo's sky-blue monkey was off their back. Their players lingered on the playing pitch, soaking in the atmosphere of a job a decade in the making. Mayo had beaten Dublin in championship for the first time since the 2012 All-Ireland semi-final. Keegan, O'Shea and McLoughlin were Mayo leftovers from that tie at the same stage nine years earlier. Throw in back-up keeper David Clarke, unused sub Keith Higgins, and the injured Cillian O'Connor, and Mayo had plenty of personalities around who could reach deep into the memory banks and recall what it was like to actually get one over on this lot. For James McCarthy, Ciarán Kilkenny and substitute Philly McMahon, this was an unfamiliar feeling, but one which they had suffered through before.

Even the hardest of Dub hearts would have struggled not to aim a nod of approval in Mayo stalwart Keegan's direction. More than any one Mayo man, he had thrown everything at Dublin over the last decade. The kitchen sink. His GPS device. Every last breath he had. Finally, he had beaten them. After the game, the Westport ace reflected on a victory he might have been forgiven for thinking he'd never see. 'Just tired, happy,' he laughed. 'When the whistle went, I just wanted to get home! Go home to the family! We just didn't panic as much as we had in the first half. We were kind of dawdling on the ball too much at times. Just started progressing with the ball, we kept moving the ball, we didn't stop. So little things like that. We just kind of ground them down towards the end. The pressure kind of told. Four points [conceded] in

55 minutes against Dublin is no mean feat. We're gonna tick that as a defensive group. As James [Horan] always echoes, "Never panic!"'

The frantic, ill-tempered, scuffle-infused final moments bothered Keegan none. In the 2006 semi-final meeting between the sides, the famous 'Mill at the Hill' had taken place before throw-in, prompted by Mayo 'trespassing' on Dublin territory in staging their warm-up in front of Hill 16. This time around, the row was left until the final seconds of play although, fittingly, it took place in front of the terrace, as players from opposing sides swung each other around by the jersey. 'I don't think I looked at any of it, to be honest,' Keegan shrugged afterwards. 'I think I was looking for someone to carry me off! Something that we've kind of learned is just grind down a game. We were three points up. Dublin had half a goal chance and we just kind of switched on again and really knuckled down. That was kind of the last chance they had. Fair play to the lads. They're comfortable on the ball, a lot more comfortable than I am at times. Our squad depth is huge at the moment. We're not relying on 15 anymore. We've seven or eight guys to come on and do as good a job as the starters. They came on again today, added fresh legs. Did the job and carried us over the line.'

In all, Dublin picked up seven yellow cards and three blacks – many of which came very late on as Mayo saw out the victory. The game's angry denouement might not have bothered Keegan, but it sent some observers into full pearl-clutching mode. The big bad Dubs had not exited in a mannerly enough fashion for some. We do this at times. The very traits we praise successful sportspeople for can often be the same ones we lambast them for once they've finally fallen from grace. Anyone who thought this Dubs' run was ever going to end on a polite note must not have been watching very closely over the preceding decade. You don't achieve sustained excellence on that kind of level without some inherent greed. Dublin didn't want to hand it over. And they certainly didn't want to hand it over to Mayo. Not them. Anyone but them. This was a group who had grown up watching Dublin teams with a soft underbelly crumble when the going was tough. That wasn't going to happen to them. If Mayo wanted it, they were going to have to come here and get it. Pride may be a deadly sin to some who believe in that sort of thing, but it's a prerequisite for winning All-Ireland titles. Dublin raged as the light died. As they should.

In the next day's *Sunday Independent*, now Meath manager Colm O'Rourke's column sat under the headline FEARLESS WARRIORS SEIZE DAY: DUBLIN WERE GREAT CHAMPIONS BUT NOTHING LASTS FOREVER AND IT WAS FITTING THAT MAYO DELIVERED KNOCKOUT BLOW. 'Mayo won because they were able to call on young players who had no fear,' O'Rourke continued. 'When they got a chance they took on their men and kicked some great points. The old order has changed and it will be a while again before Dublin cast such a long shadow.'

Beside O'Rourke in the same pages, his old RTÉ sparring partner Joe Brolly lamented the end of a glorious era – sort of: 'Mayo inspired us and sent us away with hope that this unprecedented period of dominance by one team, this era of oppression, is over. They played with freedom and concentration and manliness and for the first time in seven years Dublin lost in championship, a decade of tyranny over the game that I hope will never be repeated.'

Hey, nobody ever cheered for Goliath ...

Deep in the sports section of the *Irish Independent*, while Colm Keys likened Mayo's redemption to that of Nelson Mandela walking off Robben Island, their 'incarceration over', Vincent Hogan better explained what had happened on the Croke Park sod. '[Mayo's] football had the Dublin copyright stamped all over it by the finish, icy patience and cold militaristic movement directing the champions down one dead-end street after another. But of course, it's never been Mayo's way to travel these roads without melodrama.

'For 50 or so minutes, Dublin looked to be proceeding in sedate and orderly fashion towards another final with just one more casual enunciation of a rivalry that, traditionally, separates Mayo from their humour. Then something changed. Everything changed ... Mayo did something that was an inversion of the logic we, ordinarily, attach to this rivalry. Namely, they broke Dublin with their bench. With young blood untainted by the past.'

In the following week's *Connacht Tribune*, columnist John McIntyre hit the nail on the head. 'When the Dublin football empire finally tumbled, it was only fitting that Mayo were the ones cutting it down to size. No county had been persecuted more during a decade of unprecedented dominance or, conversely, came closest to derailing the Dubs' juggernaut ... Their own people worship them, and the neutrals greatly admire them, but Mayo's search for a first All-Ireland title in 1951 has left our hearts broken for them. Imagine, they have lost every one of their last 12 appearances on football's biggest day, including replays in 1996 and 2016. That appalling record would break most teams, but not Mayo.'

Four weeks later, Mayo's run of All-Ireland final misery would stretch to an unlucky-for-everyone 13. They fell five points short of a surprise-packet Tyrone side who had knocked out Kerry after extra time in their own semi-final a full fortnight after Mayo had finally climbed over Dublin.

It certainly didn't feel that way at the time – for player or fan – but if Dublin had to lose to anyone, it was only right that it was Mayo. They owed us that.

After many end-of-seasons where we pondered if we'd actually seen the last of Mayo, if Dublin had finally shovelled enough mud on their faces, we now readied ourselves for the fast-approaching winter wondering if we'd seen the last of these Dubs. Mayo had reached a dead hand out of the pit and pulled us under the sod. Who knew if Dessie Farrell's group had enough left to drag themselves back out towards daylight.

And so, a full 2,540 blemish-free days since that Donegal trimming, the greatest streak in the history of Gaelic games was over.

CHAPTER NINE

Reflections

They were going to change everything. Change the world. Or at least our tiny, insular part of it. And they did. Just not quite in the way they set out to.

A revisit of the Boys in Blue's Brazil-1970-style sweeping of the 2013 All-Ireland crown now looks fun, quaint, and from a forgotten time. Dublin and Mayo (of course) bounding up and down the pitch at basketball pace, exchanging points, driving the ball long into space (remember space?), risking possession (heaven forbid), losing possession in a game of non-stop, frantic, terrifyingly off-the-cuff, almost naïvely beautiful football.

And yet, when you watch that final now, thrilling as it is, there is that little devil on your shoulder that moans, 'Jaysus, lads, stop kicking it away!' How quickly we become institutionalised by possession stats, scoring zones and risk-averse football.

In the *Herald*'s 'Decades of the Dubs' series in 2019, Paul Flynn, in conversation with Conor McKeon, laments the alteration to that Dublin team's philosophy – necessary and comprehensively successful though that pivot was. 'I always thought that 2013 and 2014 were the best years of my playing career. We were going to change the way football was played – that's what we used to say. The sweeper systems and the defensive football were going to be made redundant if we could get this right in 2014. That's the way we saw it. It was full-on pressing. Risk-reward. And it was such an exciting way to play.'

But then the bould boys from Donegal came along and created a monster. 'The Donegal game in 2014 is one that, even after being involved in the Four in a Row, still hurts,' Flynn reckoned. 'We were so close. But that was definitely the end of something. A very short era. The next few years, even though we were really successful, they weren't as enjoyable. We were playing much more controlled football. We weren't kicking the ball as much. Every turnover was being looked at and analysed. So it was a total change of our whole philosophy. But now, looking back, that was the creation of the "legacy team".'

The Legacy Team. The savants of the Six in a Row. Gavin's Guys. '[The younger players] are moulded into the Jim way of playing and the Jim way of thinking,' according to Flynn. 'There were some of us that Jim inherited that he would have had to work on a bit more because we had our own way of thinking or our own way of playing. Now, this is the full cultivation of his type of player. And they've built a dynamic among themselves. I look back at some games from that period and nearly every time I got the ball, I was passing it to Bernard. We were really close. We were good friends. And we played well together. And I see that a lot with the current crop of players. There's a trust there. It's in your subconscious. So, they're the fellas that are central to all this now. For us and for Jim and for themselves – but especially for Dublin – they just came at the perfect time.'

Timing is everything. Flynn's reflections are completely backed up by the eye test. We'd watched years of Dublin teams whose mood was dictated by their sacred cows. Reputations carried weight and, like it or not, a certain schoolyard politics prevailed. The cool kids got the benefit of the doubt. The benefit of the doubt, sure. But no All-Ireland for 15 years.

Several former players who cut their teeth in the late 1990s have since hinted at the glass ceiling that then existed within a Dublin camp still basking in the glow of the 1995 All-Ireland victory. Senior players guarded their places on the panel jealously. In Neil Cotter's book *Dublin: The Chaos Years,* Ray Cosgrove said of his earliest days on the panel: 'It was a little bit of a closed shop ... It was very competitive, but it was just some senior guys who felt under pressure. I don't think it was anything malicious, just lads who'd been there a long time who feared they were about to be pushed out.'

Indeed, the veteran panel who ended a famine that stretched back to 1983 bridled at some of the 'modern' preparation methods of incoming boss Mickey Whelan after Pat O'Neill had stepped down following their Sam Maguire success. 'I was trying to make them a better team, but they just didn't buy into my innovation,' Whelan later said. 'They didn't see the point of things. Because I had come back from America where I had studied, they probably thought I was arrogant. I was doing strength and weight training in 1995, swimming, lots of different things.'

Future all-conquering manager Jim Gavin, however, was a veteran player whose leadership capability stood out long before his playing days were over. Long-time Dubs defender Eamonn Heery should have won an All-Ireland alongside Gavin & Co in 1995 but, having removed himself from the panel a year earlier, he missed out on football's holy grail. If Ciarán Whelan is the poster child for bad timing, having helped carry Dublin through many lean years between 1995 and 2011 but ending his days in blue without a Celtic cross, Heery deserves a chapter in the same book. The St Vincent's clubman recalled a typically Gavin-esque gesture after Dublin finally claimed Sam in 1995: a simple phone call from Gavin to his former wing-back partner, Heery, that meant the world to the man who missed out. 'I don't know why he did it,' Heery remembered. 'But it was amazing to get it. I have great respect for him for it.' A similar thoughtful attention to detail would serve Gavin well when he stepped into the Dublin big seat nearly 20 years later.

Another of Gavin's former inter-county managers, Tommy Carr, always sensed this leadership potential. Both army men, perhaps they spoke the same language to an extent and saw the world in a similar, somewhat uncompromising way. Carr remembered a Jim Gavin that was then as he appears now: Devoid of bluster. Allergic to bullshit. Character driven. 'Jim was one of those guys you could say, "Jim, you were shite on Sunday." And he'd say "yeah, I know that" and that would be it,' Carr told Cotter in *The Chaos Years*.

Before the Donegal disaster of 2014, there was the infamous 'startled earwigs' of 2009. Much like his successor Gavin, then Dublin manager Pat Gilroy vowed that a defeat like that – against Kerry in an All-Ireland quarter-final that saw the Kingdom romp home, 1-24 to 1-7 – would never happen to his side again.

'If you look at any game, if a guy is on the ball for a minute in the whole game, that's a lot,' Gilroy would say. 'It's the other 69 minutes, what's he doing for that? People who are going to do that, work when they're not on the ball, that's really important to us. If you've got 15 fellas pulling together for that 69 minutes of not being on the ball, that's a crucial part of the game.'

David Hickey, legendary Dublin forward of the 1970s and mentor to dozens of Boys in Blue since, laid out the Gilroy blueprint in the *Herald* 'Decades of the Dubs' supplement: 'He banned all this soccer stuff of kissing the badge and running to the Hill. There was to be no sledging: you respected your opposition, worked hard and cleaned the dressing room when you came in – there were no servants on this team.

'It was a lousy winter that year [2011]. They started training at six in the morning out by Clontarf and the Bull Wall and there was snow on the ground. They worked hard and a lot of guys left but he ended up with a core of fellas who bought into it. It was Corinthian in the maximum sense – you strive, you're honest, you don't cheat and you congratulate the other guy if he beats you.'

Barry Cahill, a half-back turned centre-forward on that 2011 team, went further. 'We started training out in Clanna Gael in November, December, January time, between late 2010 and early 2011,' the St Brigid's man explained. 'I met Pat in the Clayton Hotel before every training session nearly. Six or seven times for an hour and he went through exactly what he wanted me to do.

'It was one-on-one communication and with real honesty. He'd be showing you clips of training matches or other matches and giving you examples of what worked well or what he felt I could bring to it. There was a bit of a journey there. You had to get onboard with it and it wasn't going to happen overnight. But it was all about keeping the communication lines open over a period of time. That was how he got you to buy into his vision.'

Alan Brogan, on his way to a Player of the Year campaign in 2011, rounded out the Gilroy mystique. Simple and unfussed as it was. 'Pat worked really hard on the whole psychological side,' Alan said. 'Pat did a lot of it himself. He obviously studied it. Lads used to buy into that side of things. Pat has a way about him. You knew he was serious, but he was also very fair. He knew how certain lads would react to how he went about addressing an issue or a problem.

'He could do it with a note of sarcasm, just to get his point across. There was no real fear factor there. He wasn't like a dictator. Lads knew that if there was something that they wanted to bring up with him or the group, they could at any stage. It wasn't Pat's way or the highway.'

In his *Indo* column in September 2023, Philly McMahon penned a beautiful piece about his late father, Philip, who passed away from cancer five years before. Within the article, we are brought somewhat behind the curtain of what it is like to have been a member of this once-in-a-lifetime group.

'Ultimately, we had success with Dublin. But it also felt like we had a greater collective purpose, too. We were close. We celebrated each other's triumphs away from football. We felt each other's pain. Maybe that's one of the reasons why we were so successful.

'One night, after a banquet when [my da] was very sick, exhausted and needed medication for pain, he passed through the lobby of the hotel on his way home. Bernard Brogan and Paul Flynn were there mixing with friends and they called him over. Made a big fuss over him. Two minutes earlier he was fit for bed, barely capable of standing up. He was a hunched over, terminally ill man in his sixties, his body screaming for pain relief and sleep. But in that moment, Bernard and Flynner made him ten feet tall.

'We fought battles and won trophies together, but they're the memories that will endure.'

We're reminded of a quote from the late and very great Brian Mullins, the beating heart of those iconic Dublin teams of the 1970s. In a David Walsh piece for *Magill* magazine in 1989, the soaring midfield driving force of Heffo's Army summarised those most glorious of days thus: 'You see that phone. If I had a major problem or an embarrassment in my life, I could pick it up and ring any of the guys I played with at that time. You could not realise how it was unless you lived it. What existed between us went deep. Love? Yes, maybe. Looking back, all I can think is it made my life worth living.'

You could not realise how it was. Unless you lived it. Poetry.

CHAPTER TEN

Where to Now? 2022–2024

In March 2022, six months after having their unbeatable aura removed, Dublin were relegated from Division 1. The unofficial rankings decided by small talk on sidelines, in offices, bars and on building sites around the country no longer read 'Dublin' then 'everyone else' – the 'everyone else' had caught up. The fabled Dubs were wounded. There was blood in the water, and the sharks moved in for the kill.

McCarron's Rescue Act Condemns Dubs to Drop ran the stark headline above Colm Keys's match report on Monaghan's 3-12 to 1-18 National League victory over Dessie Farrell's Dubs in late March. Dublin would be playing in the league's second tier for 2023 after a 2022 campaign in which their attacking unit was described as, among other things, 'stodgy'.

Nobody likes a stodgy forward line. After the Monaghan game, Farrell lamented not so much the relegation, but more the inconsistency of a league campaign that saw Dublin lose five out of seven matches. 'We thought we were at a decent enough trajectory at that point ... It is more disappointing in terms of the quality of the performance. We are looking towards the summer at this point.'

Needless to say, the bould Pat Spillane, in his *Sunday World* column, knew exactly what the poor unfortunate Dubs lacked. 'Their inability to convert their goalscoring chances is proving costly. On average, they have butchered three chances per game during the league, in which they managed to score just two goals from open play ... Brian Fenton is below his best; Brian Howard has been a peripheral figure in some matches; Ciarán Kilkenny has been held scoreless in his last two games ... The message is that Dublin are still breathing but, as I said at the outset, there will be no All-Ireland title for them in 2022.'

Dublin's bona fides as 2022 Sam Maguire contenders were never going to be rubber-stamped during their Leinster Championship campaign, but a quarter-final dismantling of Wexford at Wexford Park at least assured us that the Boys in Blue still had some of that old dog in them. The hosts were put to the sword with a vengeance, and the final score of 1-24 to 0-4 included five points from play for the peerless Brian Fenton at midfield and a pleasing 1-6 for the returning Con O'Callaghan, who had missed the league campaign.

Ciarán Kilkenny finished with five points from play the next day out against Meath in the semi-final, a game Dublin took by 1-27 to 1-14. This led us nicely to a provincial final against Kildare. Here, the Dubs' issues with green flags seemed to correct themselves in one fell swoop. Strikes from John Small, Kilkenny, O'Callaghan (of course) and a Cormac Costello brace gave Dublin a 5-17 to 1-15 win over their neighbours and set up an All-Ireland quarter-final with Cork four weeks later. Were the Dubs back?

There was no Con O'Callaghan and no goals on 25 June against the Rebels, but there were 21 Dublin points on the scoreboard at the final whistle – 11 more than the Munster men managed. It was a victory for the functional, systematic side Dublin had become. Rock wore the black spot out with nine points from frees. Kilkenny added three and Fenton chipped in with a pair. All of this left us with just over a fortnight to wait until a visit with an old friend. The day after Dublin saw off Cork, Kerry would dismantle Mayo in their own quarter-final at Headquarters, 1-18 to 0-13. The loss would spell the end of James Horan's second stint in the Mayo hotseat.

Dublin had a rather large problem, however: the prospect of a Con O'Callaghan-sized hole in their full-forward line. The Cuala ace was in a fitness race to make it for the semi-final. If that wasn't bad enough, the equally important James McCarthy was also struggling to make it on 10 July.

McCarthy *would* make it to face Kerry – and perform sensationally – but O'Callaghan would not. Seanie O'Shea struck a delightful last-minute free from just outside Clucko's 2011 plaque to help Kerry edge it by a point. Yet another classic encounter between football's ancient rivals. In the All-Ireland final, after a shootout for the ages with Galway's Shane Walsh, David Clifford's wait for a Celtic cross would finally end.

Returning Kerry manager Jack O'Connor had done it again. In his third stint in the Kingdom hotseat, O'Connor worked the oracle in much the same way he had in his first two go-rounds. 'Tony Griffin has worked an awful lot with the boys on the mental side of the game,'

O'Connor remarked after the win. 'Staying resilient when you get setbacks, just driving on to the next ball or whatever and it took all that focus and resilience to keep going.'

We like to think that Mannion, McCaffrey and Cluxton – all, at the time, unavailable for selection – watched this game somewhere, separately, and all independently came to the same conclusion: 'Nah, I'm not having this.' In truth, a meeting of minds at James McCarthy's December wedding that year is largely thought to have set the wheels in motion for the talented trio's recommitment to the Dublin cause. Whatever way it happened, all three were back in harness by the time the meat and drink of the 2023 All-Ireland Football Championship rolled around.

You get spoiled as a sports fan. To the overfed Dub, grown fat on sensational summer Sundays, two Sam Maguireless years felt like a famine. How quickly we forgot the starvation of 1996 to 2010. Or those Leinsterless years after 1995 and before Tommy Lyons's lads rocked the province in 2002. Or indeed the trying decade from 1984 to 1994. No, no. For the Metropolitans of the 2020s, two years without winning it all was a tough pill to swallow. It simply wouldn't do. With Cluxton resuming backing vocals, Mannion on bass and McCaffrey back on drums, Dessie Farrell had got the band back together for one last dance. The only question was, could they hotstep it all the way back to the very top of the mountain?

Mannion and McCaffrey were in situ for the Leinster opener against Laois at O'Moore Park, a facile win by 4-30 to 2-9. Cluxton had yet to play after an initial reappearance that was as sensational as it was impressive in its top secrecy. Someday soon, someone is going to tell the story of how Dublin managed to get him in and out of the training ground the week of that National League game against Louth and on and off the team bus without being spotted. A decent yarn it will be, too.

Pat Gilroy was also back. The world's highest paid *maor uisce* joined Farrell's backroom team and, we're told, reintroduced some of his more 'testing' training methods to make sure this Dublin panel was ready for the long days and hard road of the All-Ireland Championship.

If Laois went down without a fight, a Kildare side that were one of the Dubs' Leinster whipping boys for the past decade had no such intentions. They smelled an upset. Kildare came to Croke Park on 30 April and clawed, scratched and bickered for every single inch, then backed it all up with fantastic point-kicking. They brought Dublin to a place the Boys in Blue hadn't had to go to this early in the year for quite some time. The Lilywhites almost – and perhaps should have – pulled it off.

When Jack Robinson's free put Kildare three clear in the 47th minute, a Dublin win of any kind looked unlikely. The scoreline read Kildare 0-11 Dublin 0-8. Glenn Ryan's side had bossed large parts of the game. The Dubs were there for the taking. But Kildare would manage only one more score to Dublin's six in those last 25-plus minutes of play. Farrell's men survived. Just. Was this where we were now? Kildare had recruited a management dream team led by Ryan which included Johnny Doyle, Dermot Earley, Anthony Rainbow and Brian Lacey. Had the men in white made up ground on the regressing Dubs?

For those of us prone to panic, Kildare manager Ryan assuaged our fears at his very first given opportunity. Every advantage Kildare had accrued, every psychological blow they had struck in a hard-fought 70-odd minutes on the pitch was handed back by their manager with a post-match moan that came as music to the ears of fretting Dublin fans. 'It's frustrating from the point of view that – I suppose everyone gives out about the Croke Park thing, but you come up here and you don't get a fair crack of the whip,' Ryan claimed. 'Well, there's fellas walking up and down one side of the official and nobody can do anything down the other end. Fellas standing in my so-called box and my own officials told to get out of it and there's somebody from the other side [in it].

'There's sideline balls not given, a fella tripped up in front of goals, wasn't given. It sounds like sour grapes, but I know I'm reflecting the views of most teams around the country that everything is laid out here [for Dublin], number one, from a familiarity perspective, from a games perspective and, you know, everything else seems to go their way as well. Sure we'll play anywhere, but you want to play anywhere when it's fair. And there wasn't anything glaring, nothing glaring. There were calls went either way, but when you look at stuff that goes on on the sideline and the dressing rooms and all that, you know, it's all wrapped up in it.'

Glenn Ryan was a truly great player for Kildare in the days when the Leinster Championship was wide open. A leader, the ideal on-field general. But the Round Towers clubman committed a cardinal sin as manager of a team at any level this day: he gave his players an excuse to fail. The sides would meet next on the first weekend of June in Nowlan Park, Kildare's nominated home venue in place of the under-renovations

Conleth's Park where, we presume, they got first dibs on the dressing rooms. On this occasion, Ryan's charges would be far more obliging. Final score, Kildare 0-13 Dublin 0-22. A positively resigned look fell across the face of the Lilywhites manager after that defeat compared to his combative tone following the provincial semi-final.

Funnily enough, the day before Kildare's 2023 Leinster semi-final near-miss, Conor McKeon carried a piece in the *Irish Independent* in which he tracked down former Kildare ace Tadhg Fennin, a ghost of Leinster past. In the provincial final replay of 2000, Glenn Ryan – the man now unduly worried about sideline shenanigans and dressing-room downgrades – captained Kildare to glory over a Dublin team who had gone in at the tea break leading by six points. Two goals in 90 seconds after half-time floored Dublin that afternoon. Ryan's modern-day selector, Dermot Earley, got the first, and the nippiest of corner-forwards, Fennin, poached the second. 'We didn't fear Dublin then,' Fennin told McKeon. 'Those Dublin teams, when you asked them a real tough question, we felt they might have a soft centre.' Kildare have not beaten Dublin in championship fare since.

The week after that too-close-for-comfort 2023 semi, in his excellent *Irish Independent* column, Philly McMahon responded to Ryan's assertion that the Dubs have it easy in Croke Park thus: 'I'm curious. When do managers decide this is part of the reason they lost? Do they discuss it with their selectors afterwards? Is it one for the debrief? Or does it come up immediately on the team bus on the way home? What does that conversation sound like?'

McMahon hit the nail on the head. At what point in the Leinster semi-final did the rarified air around Jones's Road suddenly become too much for Kildare to bear? They owned the first 70 per cent of the game. Everything was going for them. On paper, they have a forward unit to trouble any backline. And this day, they carried menace. Their managerial A-Team's plan had come together. However, sometime around the 50-minute mark, the Lilywhites suddenly woke up, mid-flight, Mr T-style, and groggily inquired: 'Hang on, where are we?'

We know what we're talking about. Dublin fans are all too familiar with this story. We lived it. The attractive football team awash with talent who just could never seem to win the big game. From 1996 to 2010, we read this book over and over. Not least in 2000 when Ryan, Earley, Fennin and Co exposed a somewhat exciting Dublin team for exactly what, deep down, it was – all shearing and no wool.

Stephen Cluxton, wearing number 16, finally made his comeback in that tense, frantic Leinster semi-final. Next up was the Leinster final with Mickey Harte's Louth, a team that had pushed Dublin hard in the National League only weeks before. Four years earlier, in the provincial quarter-final, Dublin stripped bare a Louth team who were coming off a good win against Wexford, mauling them for 5-21. In 2023, in the provincial decider this time, the heartless Dubs did it again. Same scoreline, 5-21. Louth at least managed to find 15 points of their own this time around, compared to the 0-10 they replied with in 2019. A testing day for Harte, who received a lot of flak in the aftermath for the Wee County's daring, man-on-man approach.

It was open season for the Dubs' inside forwards. James McCarthy, Paul Mannion and Sean Bugler all goaled, as did substitutes Paddy

Small and Colm Basquel. Cormac Costello had assumed freetaking duties from Dean Rock, who had entered that phase of a player's career which sees them viewed as a '15-minute man'. An overqualified impact sub perhaps, but that seemed to be Rock's lot as the 2023 campaign unfolded. Costello had been patient in his decade on the panel. He had more or less replaced Kevin McManamon as the energy guy off the bench. But by the summer of 2023, he was an undisputed starter and his subsequent scoring return confirmed it.

Four months later, Mickey Harte would send Louth into a tailspin – and Joe Brolly into an epithet-spewing hell – by jumping ship and taking the reins at Derry following Rory Gallagher's acrimonious dismissal. 'The Derry board is a caravan of fools,' began Joe on his podcast *Free State*, which he hosts with the mercifully level-headed Dion Fanning. Brolly signed off with 'F*** them and f*** Mickey Harte.'

Funnily enough, in the studio with Brolly and Fanning that day, trying to get an odd word in, was the man who began it all for Dublin in 2011, Pat Gilroy. And the person who took over the Louth hotseat from Harte? None other than Dublin's number 6 on that heart-stopping day a dozen years earlier, Ger Brennan. Harte would lead Derry to a pre-season McKenna Cup win in January 2024, followed by their first Division 1 National League title for 16 years after an epic, knock-down-drag-out brawl with Dublin that went all the way to penalties at Croke Park. Brennan led Louth to the All-Ireland quarter-finals – the same stage Derry reached. Harte, sensationally, stepped down from the Oak Leaf job after just one season.

WHERE TO NOW? 2022–2024

* * *

It's fair to say that on the afternoon of Sunday, 28 May 2023, Dublin looked about as far from All-Ireland contenders as they had in quite some time. A stuttering, frustrating, joyless draw with a plucky but limited Roscommon side at Croke Park is not the kind of display that usually prompts a glorious run to the Sam Maguire. Dublin looked uninterested and devoid of ideas. Had the most successful group in the history of football had enough? Had their seemingly insatiable desire for All-Ireland titles finally been sated?

At times like this, you're reminded of an interview John Fogarty of the *Irish Examiner* had with former Armagh forward Jamie Clarke back in May of 2016. Under the headline It's a Courageous Thing to Go Away and Do Your Own Thing, the interview quotes were at the same time fascinating, refreshingly honest, bonkers and bizarre. One line in particular stuck out. On playing with his all-conquering club Crossmaglen, almost perennial county champs, the mercurial forward admitted, 'The only reason I am here is because of football. I don't enjoy it as much because of the pressures of having to win all the time and wanting to win just for the sake of winning so nobody else can win. There's a lot more to life than kicking the ball over the bar.'

Dublin looked a bit that way on this afternoon in late May. Had winning for the sake of it become a chore? Were they no longer looking to win it for themselves – but rather just so someone else could not? It felt as if we may be nearing the end of the road. If that was the case, who could complain? This was a group that owed us absolutely nothing.

Final score on the opening matchday of Group 3 in the All-Ireland Series: Dublin 1-11 Roscommon 0-14.

Matchday 2, a week later, brought that back-in-your-box defeat of Kildare in Nowlan Park. The Dubs went into that game without Jack McCaffrey, David Byrne, Ciarán Kilkenny and Paul Mannion, while Costello's ankle injury forced a further late change. It mattered little. Basquel came in and helped himself to five points from play. Dean Rock managed four of his own, as did Con O'Callaghan, and Sean Bugler added three. Kildare may as well have left it all in Croke Park five weeks earlier.

Dublin continued to trend in the direction of All-Ireland contenders with a heartless dismantling of Sligo in Breffni Park, Cavan. The final digits of 3-23 to 0-8 flattered nobody. It may be true that we never judge All-Ireland contenders by how they fare against the Sligos of the world, but there could be no denying it, regardless of how they'd looked against the Rossies, the Dubs were now looking back to something approaching their terrifying best.

O'Callaghan spanked Sligo for 1-5, Basquel followed suit with 1-3, while the lightning pace of Eoin Murchan accounted for the other goal. In all, ten Dublin players scored. The Yeats County simply had no answer. The only cloud on the silver lining was a late injury to Sean Bugler. The Oliver Plunketts man appeared on his way to an All Star nomination. We wouldn't see him again that season.

Meanwhile, having looked bereft of ideas against Dublin, Kildare brilliantly outfought Roscommon in a humdinger of a game in Tullamore: Roscommon 1-15 Kildare 1-16. Mere months after that win and having pushed Dublin to the brink in the Leinster semi, Kildare would lose all seven league games in Division 2 and be relegated to the third tier. After a Leinster semi-final loss to Ger Brennan's Louth at the end of April 2024, they would then drop to the Tailteann Cup for the first time. After three years in charge, Ryan stepped down as Kildare manager immediately following a loss to Laois in Tullamore in the quarter-final of the second-tier competition.

Dublin have won four Leinster minor titles since 2013. Kildare have also won four. Dublin have won six U20/U21 Leinster titles in that time. Kildare have won four. Both counties have twice gone on to win the U21/U20 All-Ireland title during this era – Dublin in 2014 and 2017 (the final year it was played as an U21 grade) and Kildare more recently in 2018 and 2023. Naas CBS went to two straight Hogan Cup finals in 2019 and 2022 (the competition was not contested in 2020 or 2021), winning it at the second attempt. Kildare are a county that produces footballers. Lots of them. Footballers who arrive on their senior panel with medals in their pocket. The on-pitch gulf between Dublin and Kildare at senior level is a Leinster headscratcher. The frustrating life of the Lilywhite football fan continues unabated.

* * *

Despite our concerns, Dublin had timed their run at the 2023 Sam Maguire perfectly, it seemed. Modern sports teams talk less of 'seasons', pre- or off-, but more of 'peaks'. You want to do your best work when it matters most. A Dublin team that looked one-paced and uninterested at the end of May against Roscommon were beginning to look in top order five weeks later for an All-Ireland quarter-final with Mayo.

Philly McMahon always gave it to you straight when he played – and he was just as direct in his Saturday morning *Irish Independent* column. The day before this clash, he assured us that this wasn't, in fact, just another game. Trust Me. No Dublin Veteran Wants to Bow Out to Mayo and Be Haunted was the headline above the Ballymun man's weekly words of wisdom. Beside McMahon's prose, Frank Roche recalled the Mayo 'breakthrough' two years before. 'In one unravelling hour, the Dubs turned from champs into chumps. Now Farrell's old guard returns, seeking to banish their Mayo demons.' Game on.

In a sense, we'd watched this movie before. A first half that suggested there was little between the teams. A third quarter that seemed to confirm that, in fact, there was a Grand Canyon-sized gap between them. Colm Basquel's first goal midway through the opening half helped Dublin into a one-point lead at the tea break. His second goal, in the 40th minute, arguably ended the game with over half an hour still to play.

Basquel's second provides us with another snapshot of what makes this Dublin team great. An overhit James McCarthy pass intended for Cormac Costello slips by him and his marker towards the endline. Mayo's Sam Callinan attempts to shepherd the ball over the line for a kickout, but Paul Mannion cleverly nips in to dispossess the Ballina man and the ball finally finds Costello. Costello races hard at Colm Reape's goal and, at the last possible moment, slips a pass to Basquel, who palms home from point-blank range.

Paul Mannion is about as talented a forward as you will find. One of the best in the country. He doesn't need to chase lost causes over the endline in order to gain a place on even the best panel in the country. But he does it anyway. Cormac Costello strikes you as the kind of forward who absolutely loves a goal. A shoot-on-sight hitman. Tunnel-visioned, even. He could well have slipped the ball under Reape himself and run, arms aloft, to the Hill. He most likely would have scored. And, sure, hadn't Basquel already got his goal! But Costello knew the percentage play. He played his teammate in and ensured his side had one foot in an All-Ireland final. Their first in three years.

First-year Mayo manager Kevin McStay had swapped the comfort of the RTÉ studio for the often uncomfortable GAA inter-county sideline. And he seemed to be enjoying it for the most part – right up until the second half of this quarter-final. 'Up to half-time we had plenty of energy, we were flying it, we were in great form and shape at half-time,' McStay told his old RTÉ pals after the loss. 'Just small things went against us in terms of the chances, and then Dublin went on a really hot streak and never let up. They really executed some great scores. They're a very fine team, no question.'

Monaghan were put away smartly in a semi-final that reminded us why Brian Fenton is about as good as it gets when it comes to midfield play. The following day, Kerry were made to work hard to overcome the most stubborn Derry side who ever lived. Against the gallant Farney men, Fenton lofted over a pair of late scores when it mattered most, while Costello continued his high-scoring year with seven points. Super-sub Dean Rock iced the cake with a late goal, and we were in business. In truth, Rock's strike had juiced the numbers. Monaghan were the real deal.

We like to tell ourselves Dublin–Kerry is 'the final everybody wants'. Easy to say that, mind, when you're from Dublin. Or Kerry.

* * *

In a sense, this might have been Dublin's most impressive All-Ireland title of the nine they collected from 2011 to 2023. Big statement, maybe, but hear us out. None of Dublin's other winning seasons, with the possible exception of 2011, began with more teams who – privately or publicly – had legitimate aspirations of winning the Sam Maguire. The top table seemed to have more seats than ever before. The Dubs were vulnerable; two semi-final exits in two years were apparent proof of that. Mayo had McStay at the helm and, as usual, had a lot to say for themselves. Derry were the coming team and could boast 'the System'. Tyrone still had fresh memories of 2021 to draw on. Galway had style, coupled with the knowledge that they were so close the year before. And Kerry were, well, Kerry.

But when all was said and done, Dublin were last men standing. This author had the pleasure of taking in the All-Ireland final from a jam-packed Gilhooley's bar in Brisbane the night before Ireland's women's soccer team met Nigeria in their final World Cup fixture. A season that began in a Baltinglass January, as Killian O'Gara led Dublin with 1-4 in an O'Byrne Cup win over Wicklow, ended in the somewhat warmer climes of a Brisbane winter. Despite the very early Monday morning throw-in, Australia time, you couldn't have slipped a copy of the *Herald* in the front door by the time the All-Ireland final got underway – even if you took out the Lidl catalogue in the middle. Standing room only. There were punters from every corner of this island, plenty wearing Kerry colours who didn't exactly sound like they'd grown up in Dingle. As one Killarney man – with more than a passing resemblance to prime Bomber Liston – quipped in the gents at half-time, 'Sure half the f***ers I'm talking to out there in Kerry jerseys aren't from Kerry a'tall!'

Paddy Small broke the final open in the second half with a deflected strike that levelled the score. Kerry had snuck 1-8 to 0-8 ahead thanks, in no small part, to Paul Geaney's excellent goal shortly before half-time. Michael Fitzsimons did about as good a job marking David Clifford as anyone is ever likely to do. The fact that Clifford scored 0-3 from full-forward in an All-Ireland final while helping set up Geaney's goal and still got criticism for not getting enough done is testament to the level we expect from the Fossa sorcerer. The young man was being discussed as the best of all time by the time he was 24.

For the Dubs, Brian Fenton thrived in midfield with a pair of scores, while James McCarthy reminded us why a growing number of fans in the capital seriously consider him the greatest Dublin footballer of all time. McCarthy, Fitzsimons and Stephen Cluxton rewrote the record books by becoming the first three men to accumulate nine All-Ireland titles. It really was a day of days in the old stadium.

Kerry manager Jack O'Connor offered afterwards: 'It's a tough one because I thought there were stages in that second half where we were, I won't say in control, but that we were playing within ourselves. The

[Small] goal was a huge turning point. It gave massive energy to Dublin playing into the Hill. While our boys reacted fairly well to the goal, the effort it took to come back from it and go back up three, that possibly took it out of our fellas in the last five-ten minutes.'

The two counties would meet again in the ladies' All-Ireland final two weeks later, where Dublin would again prevail behind a tour de force from Hannah Tyrrell and captain Carla Rowe. As in the men's decider, an uncompromising Dublin full-back kept a star Kingdom forward in check, as Leah Caffrey shadowed the freescoring Louise Ní Mhuircheartaigh smartly. Final score between the mná on Sunday, 13 August 2023: Dublin 0-18 Kerry 1-10.

David Clifford was crowned 2023 Player of the Year at the All Stars banquet the following November. Louise Ní Mhuircheartaigh took the ladies' award in a clean sweep for the Kingdom. Michael Fitzsimons and Leah Caffrey both won All Star awards to place neatly beside their Celtic crosses. A fair trade-off.

Fitzsimons's former college teammate at UCD, Westmeath's John Heslin, remembered a player who got every last drop out of himself. 'He captained UCD, and you see lads' development at that stage of life and they put muscle on and they change their physique, and Mick Fitz really did that on top of all his studies. He was a physio, came back and did medicine then as well. What a great individual. Jack Mac, as well, they're just examples of great athletes, but who developed themselves. They didn't just have talent, they worked exceptionally hard. Mick Fitz has nine All-Ireland medals. If you asked me that in 2011, I would have said no way.'

WHERE TO NOW? 2022–2024

The day after that 2023 men's final, the *Irish Independent* featured a picture of the joyous trio of Fitzsimons, Cluxton and McCarthy beneath the caption 'The 999 Squad'. The back page showed a crouching Fenton empathising with the beaten but brilliant David Clifford, sitting on the Croke Park turf, after the final whistle. Game recognising game.

The Jacks. They were indeed all the way Back …

A mere twelve months later, however, the entire landscape of the football world had changed. Changed utterly, it seemed. Dublin had brought back everybody: Farrell, Cluxton, McCarthy, Fitzsimons, Mannion and McCaffrey were all on board as the Dubs sought to go back-to-back in 2024. But a quarter-final defeat to a ravenous Galway side who were bereft of All-Ireland success since 2001 saw the Boys in Blue sent home for the summer before we had reached July.

With 60 minutes on the clock at Croke Park on 29 June, Dublin led the Tribesmen by three points. But Galway were not done. Tomo Culhane came off the bench for the Connacht men to kick what proved to be the winning score. When the final whistle sounded – as the West awakened in the most delirious fashion – it confirmed that Dublin had failed to progress past the All-Ireland quarter-final stage for the first time since the infamous 'startled earwigs' episode against Kerry in 2009.

Pádraic Joyce – a two-time Celtic Cross winner as one of the game's most gifted forwards in 1998 and 2001 – had masterminded a wonderful run to the final for his county despite his squad being without several star performers throughout the campaign. Indeed, against Dublin, midfielder Seán Kelly was hauled ashore, hobbled, midway through the opening half. Damien Comer still seemed shorn of his usual power and devilment in the full-forward line and Shane Walsh spent much of the second half limping his way through the play. Yet, all grit, spit and vinegar, Galway prevailed.

Along with Dublin's early exit, Mayo had lost on penalties to Derry in the preliminary quarter-final, and Kerry – who had by then knocked out Derry in a forgettable last-eight clash – were chinned by Armagh after extra-time in the semi-final. All of this meant that, for the first time since Cork and Down contested the 2010 decider, the All-Ireland football final would not include at least one of Dublin, Kerry or Mayo. Galway and Armagh cared not a jot, however. The pair played out a pulsating decider on the last Sunday of July as the Orchard County pinched their second ever All-Ireland title in a one-point nailbiter at Headquarters: final score Armagh 1-11, Galway 0-13.

It was a curious football year altogether. The 'split season' – designed to improve the GAA calendar and give some valuable time back to the clubs – though admirable in intent, had not proved universally popular, to say the least. The condensed nature of the inter-county season had led to much public outcry. Added to that, the increasingly pedestrian style of the modern game was simply making matches less of a spectacle – and fans voted with their feet. The 2024 championship saw many games played at a worryingly slow pace in front of sparse crowds of muted fans. The sport appeared stuck in a quagmire, and the new GAA president, Armagh's Jarlath Burns, was determined to tackle the issue head-on.

The instantly maligned round-robin group system before the quarter-finals had led to several games that were effectively dead rubbers. In short, it was harder to get knocked out of the competition at that stage than it was to stay in it! That summer, Derry, Monaghan and Roscommon all made the last eight despite each winning only one of their four group matches. 'We're doing consultations at the moment with the provinces,' Burns said in June of 2024, while the championship was in full flow (or what little flow there was). 'One of the themes coming through really is the lack of jeopardy. I share this view ... The championship should have jeopardy, it should be more of a blunt instrument. The clue is in the title of the competition. The championship is there to get champions ... I would imagine next year there is going to be change.'

For their part, Dublin – having ransacked Leinster for the 14th year in a row by beating Meath (3-19 to 0-12), Offaly (3-22 to 0-11) and Louth (1-19 to 2-12) – won two and drew one of their subsequent group games. They began with a handy win over Roscommon, 2-19 to 0-13, at Croke Park at the end of May before dismantling Cavan, 5-17 to 0-13, in Breffni Park on the first day of June. They ended with a crucial 17-points apiece draw with Mayo in Dr Hyde Park when Cormac Costello's last-second equaliser rubber-stamped Dublin's quarter-final slot and sent Mayo into that doomed preliminary tie with Derry.

After vanquishing the reigning champs in what turned out to be quite a thrilling quarter-final, Galway manager Joyce paid tribute to the departing title holders. 'A fantastic team, Dublin,' he remarked. 'They are the standard-bearers and if we could get half the success they had we'd be happy enough.'

His counterpart, Dessie Farrell, had turned to his bench in the hope that it could get Dublin out of a jam, as it had countless times before. But when he got there, the cupboard was bare. 'We looked to the bench for impact and it was a bit of a mixed bag,' he said. 'Some of those games it is very difficult to come in when momentum is going against you and it is difficult to arrest that, no matter who you are. It didn't work out, you make the calls, you make the plays and you take your chances but unfortunately today we just couldn't get there.'

'It could be an end of an era for some of those Dublin players,' Farrell added after the game. 'I'm not going to pre-empt anything, but if it is, they have been wonderful servants and they died with their boots on.'

They died with their boots on. Went down swinging. Left it all on the field. Dress it up whatever way suits you. If ever a panel of players had nothing left to prove – and perhaps nothing left to give – it was the Dublin senior footballers who had graced this most recent glorious, imperious decade.

Bring on the Dubs …

CHAPTER ELEVEN

Best of the Best: Dubs v Rest of World

We've made it this far – why not wrap things up with a row? Or at least a good old fashioned 'greatest' debate. We've had a go at picking the best 15 who represented Dublin during the 2,540 days they went unbeaten in the championship. The cream of the Six in a Row crop. Cards on the table – this wasn't as easy as we thought it would be. But we're confident we have come up with more or less the right answer.

As the fella says, we'll start at the beginning, with a few easy ones. There were eight 'non-negotiables' in our selection, those being Stephen Cluxton, Jonny Cooper, Brian Fenton, James McCarthy, Diarmuid Connolly, Ciarán Kilkenny, Con O'Callaghan and Dean Rock. That part was easy. After that octet, we were always unlikely to overlook Michael Fitzsimons, Philly McMahon and Jack McCaffrey. Fair to say, it got a bit tougher after that. Not because of the players we wanted to include, but rather the ones we were forced to leave out.

Hard to believe we couldn't find a starting spot for Paul Flynn, but

Flynn did most of his best work pre-2017, so it's a place on the bench for the Fingallians stalwart. If we extended the selection period back to 2011, Flynn would be one of the non-negotiables. You could argue that Bernard Brogan's trajectory was similar, but for our money he just shaded a starting spot ahead of Kevin McManamon and his old pal Paul. I mean, it's Bernard feckin' Brogan! If we insist on promoting Flynn into the starting 15, don't ask us to pick who to drop between Connolly, Brogan or Mannion. For our money, the full-back line of Fitzsimons, Cooper and McMahon picks itself – although Naomh Olaf fans might argue the vastly underrated David Byrne deserves a look in the number 4 jersey. They could have a point too.

Along half-back, Cian O'Sullivan took on the most notable role of all from 2015 onwards when he was tasked with ensuring Jim Gavin's Dubs never 'had a Donegal' again. John Small has manned the number 6 shirt ably, and you're not going to do much better at wing-back than Jack McCaffrey. For those of us too young to have seen Jack O'Shea and Brian Mullins play midfield but old enough to have enjoyed Darragh Ó Sé, Ciaran Whelan, Anthony Tohill and Sean Cavanagh, we would argue that Brian Fenton tops the lot í lár na páirce. A supreme talent who would enhance any 'best of' team you care to put together. Perhaps the best number 8 the game has seen. Beside him, James McCarthy has legitimate claims to the mantle of greatest Dublin footballer of all time. Although the goalkeeper might have a shout for that title too.

We've picked our team in a traditional set-up, from 1-15. But in the modern game, the 'middle eight' in particular are often interchangeable.

This is especially true of the ultra-fluid, total football squad that Jim Gavin unleashed on the GAA in the middle part of the last decade. McCaffrey is as dangerous as any scoring forward. McCarthy can operate all across half-back, while all six forwards could rotate in whatever direction they like without this team missing a beat.

It's a team that includes the greatest goalkeeper we've ever seen in Cluxton; two of the toughest man-markers in Cooper and Fitzsimons; the ultimate wing-back in McCaffrey; a midfield pairing that could have been created in a lab; the genius of Diarmuid Connolly alongside the suave playmaking of Ciarán Kilkenny and the game's finest freetaker in Dean Rock. Meanwhile, we could put our feet up and enjoy scores on tap from Mannion, Brogan and O'Callaghan. Yeah, that might work.

Probably fair to say that the effectiveness of McManamon, Macauley and Costello from the bench during their careers made it easy to leave them as reserves in this case. It wouldn't be the first time we cracked and took the easy way out.

A quick scan through the team sheets from the 2015–2021 championship games might offer some vindication of our selection. The nearest this 'team' ever came to actually playing together in championship action was the 2017 All-Ireland final against Mayo, when 13 of the 15 shown below all started, with Eoghan O'Gara and Paddy Andrews rounding out the starting side on that occasion. Added to that, all six subs who came on that day against Mayo as the Dubs won their third All-Ireland in a row happen to be included in our fictional squad, namely Flynn, Connolly, McManamon, Brogan, Scully and Costello.

As we opined elsewhere in this book, Dublin were probably never better than they were at the end of the 2017 season. When you look at the names below and consider a couple more that we left out, it's easy to see why.

1. Stephen Cluxton

2. Michael Fitzsimons   3. Jonny Cooper   4. Philly McMahon

5. Cian O'Sullivan   6. John Small   7. Jack McCaffrey

8. Brian Fenton   9. James McCarthy

10. Diarmuid Connolly   11. Ciarán Kilkenny   12. Paul Mannion

13. Bernard Brogan   14. Con O'Callaghan   15. Dean Rock

Bench:
16. Paul Flynn, 17. Brian Howard, 18. Kevin McManamon,
19. Michael Darragh Macauley, 20. Niall Scully,
21. Cormac Costello.

***

Opposition Fantasy Fifteen

And, sure, won't they need someone to play! Gluttons for punishment that we are, we've gone back through the archives to pick the best 15 Dublin faced during their unbeaten streak at the very top of the football pyramid. Again, there were some non-negotiables involved, namely Lee Keegan, Colm Boyle and Cillian O'Connor of Mayo along with Kerry pair Seanie O'Shea and David Clifford.

After that, it was quite a task. While we endeavoured to pick the best active 15 from that seven-season stretch, we chose only players who actually played against Dublin during that time and tried our best to favour those who had showed well in their battles with the Boys in Blue. There are plenty who may be considered unlucky not to make the cut and several worthy honourable mentions. Chief among them, the Gooch, who had some of his best days against the Dubs during his prime, but he met this particular Dublin team only twice, in 2015 and 2016, when he was in the veteran stage of his illustrious career. Philly McMahon shut him down in the 2015 final, but Gooch was at his brilliant best a year later in a semi-final cracker that the Dubs just edged.

Paddy Durcan of Mayo may seem a glaring omission, and you could slot him in there somewhere, possibly at the expense of his county-mate Chris Barrett – but that's a decent argument for another day. Paudie Clifford is a fine foil to his brother's outrageous skillset, and Cathal McShane of Tyrone kept the Dublin full-back firmly on their toes whenever he was in town. Roscommon's Diarmuid Murtagh is another who troubled the Dubs without, perhaps, enough back-up to give them real issues, as did Conor McManus of Monaghan – although he gave every defence fits from the edge of the square over a glorious 18-year career.

The Dubs were rarely made uncomfortable in Leinster during this spell, but Longford's Robbie Smyth found time to collect five points against them at Croke Park in 2018. Dublin met Westmeath four times in provincial competition during the streak, and it was Darren Quinn in goal for three of those in 2015, 2016 and 2017. Needless to say, the Dublin attack kept the tidy Tyrrellspass stopper plenty busy. Quinn's teammate John Heslin never took a backward step when the Dubs were in town – he scored in all four games between Westmeath and Dublin in this era. In a 2019 All-Ireland Group Stage clash with Cork, which Dublin won with a bit to spare, the Rebel duo of Luke Connolly and Brian Hurley went home with 1-3 and four points respectively. If not Rory Beggan of Monaghan between the sticks, Tyrone number 1 Niall Morgan would prove a more than able last line of defence.

That craic between the 'Rest of World' half-back line and Dublin's half-forwards would be worth tuning in for by itself. The Dublin full-back unit would have to be at their imperious best to quieten Geaney, Clifford and Moran. The Dubs should hold the edge in midfield, but who might prevail in a fictional clash between these make-believe sides? We'll take Dublin by two points, 2-18 to 1-19. *'You're hardly gonna believe us …'*

BEST OF THE BEST: DUBS V REST OF WORLD

1. Rory Beggan
(Monaghan)

2. Oisin Mullin   3. Ronan McNamee   4. Chris Barrett
(Mayo)   (Tyrone)   (Mayo)

5. Lee Keegan   6. Colm Boyle   7. Peter Harte
(Mayo)   (Mayo)   (Tyrone)

8. David Moran   9. Matty Ruane
(Kerry)   (Mayo)

10. Michael Murphy   11. Sean O'Shea   12. Cillian O'Connor
(Donegal)   (Kerry)   (Mayo)

13. Paul Geaney   14. David Clifford   15. Andy Moran
(Kerry)   (Kerry)   (Mayo)

CHAPTER TWELVE

Lies, Damned Lies, And ...

In seven seasons from 2015 to 2021, the Dublin senior footballers etched their image onto the Mount Rushmore of the greatest teams our sport has ever seen. We'll let you argue amongst yourselves over which teams occupy the other three spaces. Dublin's six All-Ireland titles in a row from 2015 to 2020 is a feat that may never be matched and saw them set new standards in footballing excellence.

This Dublin team may have been the first to win five men's football titles in a row in 2019 – and subsequently the first, of course, to win six when they broke their own mark in Dessie Farrell's first season – but they do not own the record for most consecutive All-Ireland titles. That distinction belongs to the Kerry ladies' football squad, who won nine straight titles from 1982 to 1990 when the women's inter-county game was, admittedly, still somewhat in its infancy. Cork ladies would, incredibly, win 11 All-Ireland titles in 12 seasons from 2005 to 2016. Dublin's Jackies interrupted the Rebelettes' hegemony with their 2010 triumph under Donegal man Gerry McGill.

On the camogie field, it might surprise you to learn that Dublin were the standard bearers of the post-WWII game, winning eight in a row from 1948–1955 and then notching an even ten straight from 1957–1966. Unfortunately, Dublin have won only one All-Ireland camogie title since, in 1984.

Kerry, still the winningest team in men's football in terms of All-Irelands, were famously a late Seamus Darby goal away from managing the then mythical Five in a Row against Offaly back in 1982, having won the Sam Maguire in 1978, 1979, 1980 and 1981. In hurling, Brian Cody's remorseless Kilkenny side won four in a row from 2006 to 2009, while more recently John Kiely's Limerick bulldozed their way to four straight All-Ireland titles from 2020 to 2023.

Delving into the data of the Dubs' streak throws up plenty that you would expect to find as well as a few nuggets that might surprise you – or at the very least jog your memory. From 2015 to 2021, Dublin played 46 championship games, winning 42, drawing three and losing, of course, just the one. They enjoyed a scoring difference of +499 during that time. In terms of appearances, two men led the way: Brian Fenton and Ciarán Kilkenny played in 44 of those 46 games and were in the starting 15 each time. Dean Rock started 38 of 46, coming off the bench in three other games, while Stephen Cluxton and Jonny Cooper both played in 40, although one of Cooper's appearances came as a substitute. Remarkably, Michael Fitzsimons played in 43 of the 46 games – but a surprising 14 of those came in a substitute's role. The Cuala defender was already an experienced member of the Dublin panel – and a two-time All-Ireland winner – when the 2015 season began. But herein may lie a pub quiz question. Fitzsimons's first 11 appearances in the championship during this Dubs run all came off the bench. His first start of this streak was a big one, however – the 2016 All-Ireland final replay against Mayo.

Four players made exactly one appearance for Dublin between 2015 and 2021. After an impressive league campaign, Darren Gavin of Lucan Sarsfields started the 2019 Leinster quarter-final clash with Louth in Portlaoise. Cuala's Conor Mullally, more familiar to Boys in Blue hurling aficionados, made one footballing appearance off the bench against Roscommon in the 2018 Super 8s. Kilmacud Crokes' Cian O'Connor made a substitute appearance in Healy Park in a Super 8s clash with Tyrone in 2019, while Cian Murphy of Thomas Davis came in off the bench against Meath in the 2021 Leinster semi-final. Murphy would later firmly establish himself as a match-day regular from 2022 onwards. Another Lucan man, Emmett Ó Conghaile, a highly rated midfielder in both codes when emerging from the minor ranks, made just two substitute appearances during the streak. Curiously, both came in Leinster competition against Kildare – yet they came seven seasons apart, the first in 2015 and the other in 2021.

On the scoreboard, Dean Rock, unsurprisingly, was the marksman-in-chief of a panel that outscored, outbattled and out-thought just about all before them. By our calculations, Rock accounted for 11 goals and 232 points during this seven-year stretch, with 161 of those points coming from frees and a further 16 from 45s. Con O'Callaghan tormented full-back lines with nine goals in championship competition during this spell. The Cuala ace gave fans some of the most memorable moments of the streak. Ciarán Kilkenny and the underrated Niall Scully accounted for five goals apiece. Bernard Brogan collected seven goals; Diarmuid Connolly added six and Eoghan O'Gara five. Brian Fenton, Michael Darragh Macauley and Kevin McManamon all raised four green flags apiece.

Dublin squads of this era were, of course, backboned by superstar operators like Brogan, Fenton, McCarthy, Cluxton, Kilkenny and O'Callaghan. But they were also supported admirably by role players who rarely put a foot wrong. Kevin McManamon will be remembered as the quintessential impact substitute, the man who turned big games on their head, generally in Dublin's favour. Indeed, of McManamon's 34 appearances during the unbeaten streak, 21 of them would come from the bench – but perhaps it might surprise you to be reminded that the St Jude's forward started all seven of Dublin's 2016 championship games and scored 1-9 from play while he was at it. Darren Daly had moved into the veteran stage of his playing career as this Dublin team were peaking. Of his 22 appearances during this era, the Fingal Ravens player came off the bench for all but three of them. His diving one-handed block in the 78th minute of the 2016 All-Ireland final replay – the very last act of a one-point game – remains a warm, abiding memory of Daly's days in blue.

Eric Lowndes was something of a Swiss army knife utility man during his Dublin career, but the St Peregrine's man started no fewer than 10 championship games during this streak and came off the bench in 11 more – a handful more than even the most statistically aware fan might have guessed. Michael Darragh Macauley played in 32 of the

46 games, starting 18 of them, while Paddy Andrews started 16 and came in from the bench in 11 more. Speaking of Macauley, along with Cormac Costello he held the distinction of logging more appearances than games played. Both men 'appeared' twice in the one game when they started, were replaced, and were later brought back on. Macauley double-jobbed against Laois in 2016, and Costello did likewise against Mayo in 2021. Philly McMahon always fancied himself as one of those defenders who could play a bit and he was often proven right, notching 2-16 during this run while usually marking one of the opposition's best forwards. Jack McCaffrey, the Clontarf wing-back who struck fear in opposing defences, helped himself to 3-14 in 28 appearances during the run. Eoghan O'Gara may have only started two games during this spell, with eight more appearances coming from the bench, but he made hay while the sun shone on him. The Templeogue Synge Street forward nabbed 5-6 in his limited time on the pitch.

But the true beauty of this era of Dublin football cannot really be found in the numbers. To paraphrase that great philosopher Homer J. Simpson, we 'can come up with statistics to prove anything – 14 per cent of people know that'. The Dublin team that initially moved through the 2013 Gaelic football season like a comet shook the game at its foundations and, whether some would admit it or not, struck an element of fear into the established big guns of the day. In the early 2010s, Donegal, Tyrone, Mayo, Kerry and, yes, Dublin were simply not playing football in this throw-back, fearless manner. Jim Gavin's side began games on the front foot – and from there pressed forward. Of course, as we know, the shortcomings exposed by Donegal in 2014 threw a spanner in the works but eventually helped deliver the unbeatable, almost flawless football factory that held the game hostage for, well, 2,540 glorious days.

'We were going to change the way football was played,' offered Paul Flynn back in that 2019 *Herald* interview.

And they did. They did.

CHAPTER THIRTEEN

The Games: (About) A Decade of the Dubs

Dublin in Championship, 2013–2024

2013

Leinster quarter-final
Saturday, 1 June 2013, Croke Park (attendance 33,008)
Dublin 1-22 Westmeath 0-9
Dublin: S Cluxton; D Daly, R O'Carroll, J Cooper; J McCarthy, G Brennan, J McCaffrey 0-1; MD Macauley, C O'Sullivan 0-1; P Flynn 0-3, C Kilkenny 0-1, D Connolly 0-3; P Mannion 0-1, P Andrews 1-3, B Brogan 0-7 (5f). **Subs:** K O'Brien for Daly, N Devereux for McCarthy, D Rock 0-2 (1f) for Mannion, D Bastick for Macauley, C Costello for Brogan.
Westmeath: G Connaughton; M McCallon, K Gavin, K Maguire; D Harte, P Sharry, J Gaffey; D Duffy, J Heslin 0-5f; K Martin 0-1, C McCormack, J Dolan; G Egan, D Glennon 0-2, C Curley. **Subs:** Damian Dolan for Curley, D Daly for Duffy, D Corroon 0-1 for J Dolan, P Bannon for Egan, A Purcell for McCallon.
Referee: Eddie Kinsella (Laois).

Leinster semi-final
Sunday, 30 June 2013, Croke Park (attendance 53,204)
Dublin 4-16 Kildare 1-9
Dublin: S Cluxton 0-4 (3 45, 1f); D Daly, R O'Carroll, J Cooper; J McCarthy, G Brennan 0-1, J McCaffrey; MD Macauley, C O'Sullivan; P Flynn, C Kilkenny 0-4, D Connolly 1-0; P Mannion 1-1, P Andrews 0-1, B Brogan 1-1. **Subs:** E O'Gara 1-2 for Andrews, K McManamon for Brogan, K Nolan for Brennan (bs), K O'Brien for Daly, D Rock 0-2f for Connolly, N Devereux for O'Sullivan.
Kildare: S Connolly; P Kelly, D Hyland, H McGrillen; E O'Callaghan, M Foley, E Bolton; D Flynn, S Hurley 0-1; P Cribbin 0-2, N Kelly, E O'Flaherty 0-3 (1f); J Doyle 0-2 (1f), D Flynn, P Brophy 1-1. **Subs:** S Johnston for Daniel Flynn, A Smith for N Kelly, P O'Neill for D Flynn, M O'Flaherty for O'Callaghan, F Dowling for Doyle.
Referee: J McQuillan (Cavan).

Leinster final
Sunday, 14 July 2013, Croke Park (attendance 54,485)
Dublin 2-15 Meath 0-14
Dublin: S Cluxton 0-3 (2 45, 1f); P O'Brien, R O'Carroll, J Cooper; J McCarthy, G Brennan, J McCaffrey; MD Macauley, C O'Sullivan; P Flynn 1-1, C Kilkenny 0-3, D Connolly 0-1; P Mannion 1-4 (0-2f), E O'Gara, B Brogan 0-1f. **Subs:** K McManamon for O'Gara, D Bastick for O'Sullivan, D Daly for Brennan, D Rock 0-2 (1f) for Brogan, B Cullen for Connolly.
Meath: P O'Rourke; D Keoghan, K Reilly, B Menton; P Harnan, M Burke; S Kenny, B Meade 0-1, C Gillespie; P Byrne, D Carroll, G Reilly; E Wallace 0-2, S Bray 0-2, M Newman 0-8 (5f). **Subs:** P Gilsenan for Byrne, C Lenihan for Kenny, J Sheridan 0-1 for Carroll, A Tormey for Meade, D McDonagh for Wallace.
Referee: E Kinsella (Laois).

All-Ireland quarter-final
Saturday, 3 August 2013, Croke Park (attendance 70,018)
Dublin 1-16 Cork 0-14
Dublin: S Cluxton 0-6 (2f, 4 45); J Cooper, R O'Carroll, K O'Brien; J McCarthy, G Brennan, J McCaffrey 1-0; MD Macauley 0-1, C O'Sullivan; P Flynn 0-2, C Kilkenny 0-2, D Connolly; P Mannion, B Cullen, B Brogan 0-1f. **Subs:** D Rock 0-2 for Cullen, P McMahon for Cooper, K McManamon 0-1 for Mannion, D Bastick 0-1 for Macauley, E O'Gara for Kilkenny.
Cork: A Quirke; E Cadogan, M Shields, T Clancy; D Cahalane 1 45, G Canty, J Loughrey 0-1; A O'Connor, P O'Neill; M Collins 0-2 (1f), A Walsh, J O'Rourke 0-1; D Goulding 0-5 (2f, 1 45), C Sheehan 0-1, B Hurley 0-3. **Subs:** P Kissane for Cadogan, P Kerrigan for O'Rourke, J O'Sullivan for Clancy, D O'Connor for O'Connor, T Clancy for Canty.
Referee: D Coldrick (Meath).

All-Ireland semi-final
Sunday, 1 September 2013, Croke Park (attendance 81,553)
Dublin 3-18 Kerry 3-11
Dublin: S Cluxton 0-1f; K O'Brien, R O'Carroll, J Cooper; J McCarthy, G Brennan, J McCaffrey; MD Macauley 0-1, C O'Sullivan 0-1; P Flynn, C Kilkenny 0-2, D Connolly 0-4 (1f); P Mannion 1-0, P Andrews 0-1, B Brogan 0-6 (2f). **Subs:** P McMahon for O'Brien, D Bastick for Brennan, D Rock 0-2 for Kilkenny, E O'Gara 1-0 for Mannion, K McManamon 1-0 for Brogan.
Kerry: B Kealy; M Ó Sé, M Griffin, S Enright; T Ó Sé, P Crowley, F Fitzgerald; A Maher, J Buckley; P Galvin 0-2, C Cooper 0-4 (2f), D Walsh 1-0; Darran O'Sullivan 0-1, Declan O'Sullivan 0-1, J O'Donoghue 2-3. **Subs:** D Moran for Buckley, E Brosnan for Enright, K Donaghy for Galvin, A O'Mahony for Griffin, K Sherwood for Crowley.
Referee: C Reilly (Meath).

THE GAMES: (ABOUT) A DECADE OF THE DUBS

All-Ireland final
Sunday, 22 September 2013, Croke Park (attendance 82,724)
Dublin 2-12 Mayo 1-14
Dublin: S Cluxton 0-2 (1 45, 1f); P McMahon, R O'Carroll, J Cooper; J McCarthy, G Brennan 0-1, J McCaffrey; MD Macauley, C O'Sullivan 0-1; P Flynn 0-1, C Kilkenny, D Connolly 0-1; P Mannion, P Andrews 0-1, B Brogan 2-3 (0-1f). **Subs:** E O'Gara 0-2 for Mannion, Darren Daly for McCaffrey, Dean Rock for Kilkenny, K McManamon for Andrews, D Bastick for Cooper.
Mayo: R Hennelly; T Cunniffe, G Cafferkey, C Barrett; L Keegan 0-2, D Vaughan, C Boyle; A O'Shea, S O'Shea 0-1; K McLoughlin, K Higgins 0-1, A Dillon; C O'Connor 0-8f, A Freeman, A Moran 1-2. **Subs:** M Conroy for Freeman, E Varley for Dillon, B Moran for S O'Shea, J Doherty for Moran.
Referee: J McQuillan (Cavan).

2014

Leinster quarter-final
Sunday, 8 June 2014, Croke Park (attendance 40,960)
Dublin 2-12 Laois 0-16
Dublin: S Cluxton 0-2 (1f, 1 45); P McMahon, R O'Carroll, D Daly; J Cooper, N Devereux, J McCarthy 0-1; MD Macauley 1-0, C O'Sullivan 0-1; P Flynn 0-2, A Brogan 0-2, D Connolly 1-1; P Andrews 0-1, E O'Gara 0-1, B Brogan 0-1f. **Subs:** K McManamon 0-2 for B Brogan, J McCaffrey for Daly, B Cullen 0-1 for O'Gara, C Costello 0-3 for A Brogan, D Rock 0-3f for O'Sullivan, P Mannion for Andrews.
Laois: G Brody; P McMahon, P Begley, P O'Leary; D Strong 0-2, S Attride, C Begley; K Meaney, J O'Loughlin 0-1; J Finn 0-1, C Meredith, B Sheehan; R Munnelly 0-7 (2f), D Kingston 0-3 (2f), D Conway 0-1. **Subs:** N Donoher 0-1 for Sheehan, E Lowry for Meaney, R Kehoe for Attride, E O'Carroll for Conway, J Finn for Kingston.
Referee: P Hughes (Armagh).

Leinster semi-final
Sunday, 29 June 2014, Croke Park (attendance 46,279)
Dublin 2-25 Wexford 1-12
Dublin: S Cluxton 0-1 (1 45), P McMahon 0-1, J Cooper, R O'Carroll, J McCarthy, K Nolan, N Devereux 0-1, MD Macauley 0-1, C O'Sullivan, P Flynn 1-2, D Rock 0-4f, D Connolly 0-2 (1f), P Mannion 0-3, A Brogan 0-1, K McManamon. **Subs:** C Costello 1-5 (0-2f) for Rock, E O'Gara 0-2 for Brogan, J McCaffrey for McManamon, T Brady 0-2 for O'Sullivan, M Fitzsimons for Devereux, B Cullen for Macauley.
Wexford: S Roche, C Carty, G Molloy, R Tierney, M Furlong, B Malone, A Flynn, D Waters 1-0, P Byrne, K O'Grady 0-1, PJ Banville 0-3, T Rossiter, C Lyng 0-1f, B Brosnan 0-6 (3f), J Holmes 0-1. **Subs:** Cillian Kehoe for Holmes, M O'Regan for Flynn, E Nolan for Byrne, D Dunne for Rossiter, Colm Kehoe for O'Grady, G Cullen for Banville.
Referee: C Branagan (Down).

Leinster final
Sunday, 20 July 2014, Croke Park (attendance 62,620)
Dublin 3-20 Meath 1-10
Dublin: S Cluxton 0-1 45; P McMahon, R O'Carroll, M Fitzsimons; J McCarthy, N Devereux, J McCaffrey 0-1; MD Macauley, C O'Sullivan 0-1; P Flynn 0-1, A Brogan 0-1, D Connolly 0-1; K McManamon 1-5, P Mannion, B Brogan 1-6 (0-3f). **Subs:** C Costello 0-1 for Mannion, D Rock 0-1 for Connolly, E O'Gara 1-1 for A Brogan, D Daly for Devereux, D Bastick for Macauley, T Brady for O'Sullivan.
Meath: P O'Rourke; E Harrington, K O'Reilly, B Menton; P Hernan, D Keogan, D Tobin; G Reilly, S O'Rourke 0-2f; D Carroll 0-1, B McMahon, A Tormey 0-2; D McDonagh, S Bray 0-2, M Newman 1-2 (0-1f). **Subs:** J Wallace for Reilly, M Burke for Carroll, D Bray 0-1 for McDonagh, B Meade for S O'Rourke, J McEntee for McMahon, P Gilsenan for Tobin.
Referee: P Hughes (Armagh).

All-Ireland quarter-final
Saturday, 9 August 2014, Croke Park (attendance 72,440)
Dublin 2-11 Monaghan 0-11
Dublin: S Cluxton 0-1 45; M Fitzsimons, R O'Carroll, P McMahon; J McCarthy, J Cooper 0-1, N Devereux; MD Macauley, C O'Sullivan; P Flynn 0-2, K McManamon 0-1, D Connolly 1-2 (0-1f); A Brogan 0-3, E O'Gara 0-2, B Brogan 1-7 (0-6f). **Subs:** C Costello 0-1 for McManamon, D Rock 0-2 for O'Sullivan, J McCaffrey for Cooper, P Andrews for O'Gara, D Daly for McMahon, P Mannion for A Brogan.
Monaghan: R Beggan 0-1 45; C Walshe, D Wylie, R Wylie; V Corey, D Mone, F Kelly; D Clerkin 0-2, D Hughes 0-2f; P Donaghy, K Duffy, S Gollogly; K Hughes, C McGuinness, C McManus 0-6 (4f). **Subs:** P Finlay for Donaghy, J McCarron for McGuinness, G Doogan for Gollogly, O Duffy for Clerkin, C Boyle for Duffy, C Galligan for Kelly.
Referee: M Duffy (Sligo).

All-Ireland semi-final
Sunday, 31 August 2014, Croke Park (attendance 82,300)
Dublin 0-17 Donegal 3-14
Dublin: S Cluxton; M Fitzsimons, R O'Carroll, P McMahon 0-1; J McCarthy, J Cooper, J McCaffrey; MD Macauley, C O'Sullivan; P Flynn 0-4, C Costello, D Connolly 0-5 (1f); A Brogan 0-2, E O'Gara, B Brogan 0-3 (1f). **Subs:** N Devereux for McCaffrey, K McManamon for Costello, D Rock for O'Gara, P Andrews 0-2 for A Brogan, D Daly for Cooper, P Mannion for O'Sullivan.
Donegal: P Durcan; E McGee, N McGee, P McGrath; A Thompson, K Lacey 0-1, F McGlynn 0-1; N Gallagher, O MacNiallais 0-1; R Kavanagh 0-1, L McLoone, R McHugh 2-2; David Walsh, M Murphy 0-3 (2f), C McFadden 1-3 (0-2f). **Subs:** C Toye for Walsh, P McBrearty 0-2 for McLoone, Declan Walsh for N McGee (bc), M McElhinney for Kavanagh, D O'Connor for McFadden, M O'Reilly for MacNiallais.
Referee: J McQuillan (Cavan).

2015

Leinster quarter-final
Sunday, 31 May 2015, Croke Park (attendance 33,544)
Dublin 4-25 Longford 0-10
Dublin: S Cluxton; J Cooper, David Byrne, P McMahon 0-1; J Small, D Daly, J McCaffrey; B Fenton 0-1, D Bastick; P Flynn 1-3, C Kilkenny 0-3, D Connolly 1-0; K McManamon 0-2, D Rock 1-6 (0-2f, 0-2 45), B Brogan 1-6. **Subs:** M Fitzsimons for McMahon, T Brady 0-1 for Connolly, MD Macauley for Bastick, P Andrews 0-1 for Flynn, E Lowndes 0-1 for Cooper, A Brogan for B Brogan.
Longford: P Collum 0-1 45; D Brady, B Gilleran, C Farrelly; D Masterson, B O'Farrell, CP Smyth; M Quinn, K Diffley; P Foy, R McEntire, R McNerney; R Connor 0-3, B Kavanagh 0-5 (4f), B McKeon. **Subs:** L Connerton 0-1 for McKeon, D Reynolds for Diffley (bc), A Rowan for Smyth, P Gill for Connor, F Battrim for Masterson, E Williams for McNerney.
Referee: C Lane (Cork).

Leinster semi-final
Sunday, 28 June 2015, Croke Park (attendance 50,324)
Dublin 5-18 Kildare 0-14
Dublin: S Cluxton; P McMahon 0-1, J Cooper, R O'Carroll; J Small, C O'Sullivan, J McCaffrey; B Fenton, MD Macauley; P Flynn, K McManamon, C Kilkenny 0-4; D Rock 1-4 (0-4f) D Connolly 2-3, B Brogan 2-3. **Subs:** J McCarthy for Small, A Brogan 0-3 for McManamon, P Andrews for Flynn, M Fitzsimons for O'Carroll, E O Conghaile for Fenton, D Daly for O'Sullivan.
Kildare: Donnellan; O Lyons, M O'Grady, C Fitzpatrick; K Murnaghan, E Doyle, E Bolton 0-1; G White, P Cribbin 0-1; P O'Neill 0-2, E O'Flaherty 0-4 (2f), C McNally 0-1; A Smith 0-1, P Fogarty 0-3, E Callaghan. **Subs:** N Kelly 0-1 for Callaghan, T Moolick for White, H Lynch for McNally, C Heeney for Donnellan (bc), F Dowling for Bolton.
Referee: D Coldrick (Meath).

THE GAMES: (ABOUT) A DECADE OF THE DUBS

Leinster final
Sunday, 12 July 2015, Croke Park (attendance 49,840)
Dublin 2-13 Westmeath 0-6
Dublin: S Cluxton; J Cooper, R O'Carroll, P McMahon 0-1; J McCarthy 0-1, C O'Sullivan, J McCaffrey 1-0; B Fenton, MD Macauley 0-1; P Flynn, C Kilkenny 0-3, D Connolly 0-3; D Rock 0-2f, K McManamon, B Brogan 1-1. **Subs:** M Fitzsimons for Cooper, P Andrews for McManamon, D Bastick for Macauley, A Brogan 0-1 for Rock, J Small for McMahon, T Brady for Connolly.
Westmeath: D Quinn; K Daly, K Maguire, J Gilligan; P Holloway, K Martin 0-2, J Dolan; D Corroon, F Boyle 0-1; G Egan, P Sharry, R Connellan; D Lynch, J Heslin 0-3 (2f), S Dempsey. **Subs:** K Gavin for Dempsey, C McCormack for Connellan, D Glennon for Holloway, J Egan for Heslin, J Gonoud for McCormack.
Referee: J McQuillan (Cavan).

All-Ireland quarter-final
Sunday, 2 August 2015, Croke Park (attendance 56,680)
Dublin 2-23 Fermanagh 2-15
Dublin: S Cluxton; J Cooper, R O'Carroll, P McMahon; J McCarthy, C O'Sullivan, J McCaffrey; B Fenton 0-1, D Bastick; P Flynn 1-1, C Kilkenny 0-3, D Connolly 0-2; D Rock 0-7 (2f, 1 45), P Andrews 0-3, B Brogan 1-6. **Subs:** MD Macauley for Bastick, K McManamon for Kilkenny, A Brogan for Connolly, M Fitzsimons for Cooper, J Small for McCarthy, C Costello for Andrews.
Fermanagh: T Treacy; M Jones, M O'Brien, N Cassidy; D McCusker, R McCluskey, J McMahon; E Donnelly, R O'Callaghan; B Mulrone 0-3, R Jones, R Corrigan; P McCusker, S Quigley 1-8 (0-4f), T Corrigan 1-2 (0-1f). **Subs:** D Kelly for P McCusker, T Daly for M Jones, C Jones 0-2 for D McCusker, D Kille for R Corrigan.
Referee: P O'Sullivan (Kerry).

All-Ireland semi-final
Sunday, 30 August 2015, Croke Park (attendance 82,300)
Dublin 2-12 Mayo 1-15
Dublin: S Cluxton; R O'Carroll, P McMahon, J Cooper; J McCarthy, C O'Sullivan, J McCaffrey 0-1; B Fenton, MD Macauley; P Flynn, P Andrews 0-2, C Kilkenny 0-3; D Rock, D Connolly 1-2 (1-0 pen, 0-1f), B Brogan 0-2. **Subs:** M Fitzsimons for O'Carroll (bs), K McManamon 1-1 for Rock, J Small for Cooper, D Bastick for Macauley (bc), A Brogan 0-1 for Andrews, T Brady for Fenton, E Lowndes for Bastick (bc).
Mayo: D Clarke; C Barrett, G Cafferkey, K Higgins 0-1; D Vaughan, L Keegan 0-1, C Boyle; T Parsons, S O'Shea; D Drake, J Doherty, D O'Connor 0-1; K McLoughlin, A O'Shea, C O'Connor 1-9 (0-8f, 1-0 pen, 0-1 45). **Subs:** P Durcan for Vaughan, A Moran 0-2 for Drake, A Freeman 0-1 for Doherty, B Moran for S O'Shea, M Sweeney for D O'Connor.
Referee: J McQuillan (Cavan).

All-Ireland semi-final replay
Saturday, 5 September 2015, Croke Park (attendance 81,897)
Dublin 3-15 Mayo 1-14
Dublin: S Cluxton; P McMahon 1-2, R O'Carroll, J Cooper; J McCarthy 0-1, C O'Sullivan, J McCaffrey; B Fenton 0-1, D Bastick; P Flynn, D Connolly, C Kilkenny 0-2; B Brogan 1-1, P Andrews 0-5, D Rock 0-2f. **Subs:** MD Macauley for Bastick, M Fitzsimons for Cooper, A Brogan for Flynn, K McManamon 1-1 for Rock, E Lowndes for Connolly, J Small for B Brogan.
Mayo: R Hennelly; K Higgins, G Cafferkey, C Barrett; D Vaughan, L Keegan 0-1, C Boyle; T Parsons, B Moran 0-1; D O'Connor 0-2, S O'Shea, K McLoughlin 0-1; J Doherty, C O'Connor 1-6 (0-5f), A O'Shea 0-1. **Subs:** P Durcan 0-1 for Vaughan, A Moran 0-1f for S O'Shea (bc), D Drake for Boyle, S Coen for Parsons, M Ronaldson for McLoughlin.
Referee: E Kinsella (Laois).

THE GAMES: (ABOUT) A DECADE OF THE DUBS

All-Ireland final
Sunday, 20 September 2015, Croke Park (attendance 82,300)
Dublin 0-12 Kerry 0-9
Dublin: S Cluxton 0-1f; J Cooper, R O'Carroll, P McMahon 0-1; J McCarthy, C O'Sullivan, J McCaffrey 0-1; B Fenton 0-1, D Bastick; P Flynn 0-2, D Connolly, C Kilkenny; B Brogan 0-2 (1f), D Rock 0-2f, P Andrews 0-1. **Subs:** K McManamon for Rock, MD Macauley for Bastick, M Fitzsimons for Cooper, J Small for McCaffrey, D Daly for O'Sullivan, A Brogan 0-1 for Fenton.
Kerry: B Kealy; F Fitzgerald, A O'Mahony, S Enright; J Lyne 0-1, P Crowley, K Young; A Maher, D Moran; S O'Brien, J Buckley, D Walsh; C Cooper, P Geaney 0-2, J O'Donoghue 0-3. **Subs:** D O'Sullivan 0-2 for O'Brien, B Sheehan 0-1f for Buckley, K Donaghy for Geaney, P Galvin for Moran, P Murphy for O'Mahony (bc), BJ Keane for O'Donoghue.
Referee: D Coldrick (Meath).

2016

Leinster quarter-final
Sunday, 4 June 2016, Nowlan Park (attendance 16,754)
Dublin 2-21 Laois 2-10
Dublin: S Cluxton; D Byrne 0-1, J Cooper, P McMahon; J McCarthy, C O'Sullivan, J Small; B Fenton, MD Macauley; C Kilkenny 0-4, K McManamon 0-1, D Connolly 1-4; P Mannion, D Rock 1-10 (0-6f), B Brogan. **Subs:** D Bastick for Macauley, Macauley for Bastick, C Costello for Brogan, C O'Callaghan 0-1 for Mannion, D Daly for O'Sullivan, E Lowndes for Cooper, E O'Gara for Rock.
Laois: G Brody; M Timmons, P Cotter, S Attride 1-0; D O'Connor 0-1, D Strong 0-1, G Dillon; J O'Loughlin 0-1, B Quigley; C Begley, P Cahillane 1-2 (1-0 pen, 0-2f), E O'Carroll; D Kingston 0-2 (1f), C Meredith, G Walsh 0-1. **Subs:** K Meaney 0-1 for O'Carroll, N Donoher for Walsh, R Munnelly 0-1 for Dillon, A Farrell for Cahillane, R O'Connor for Meredith, G Hanrahan for Cotter.
Referee: C Branagan (Down).

Leinster semi-final
Sunday, 26 June 2016, Croke Park (attendance 42,259)
Dublin 0-21 Meath 0-11
Dublin: S Cluxton; David Byrne, J Cooper, P McMahon; J Small, C O'Sullivan, J McCarthy; B Fenton 0-1, D Bastick; P Flynn 0-2, C Kilkenny, D Connolly 0-4; K McManamon, D Rock 0-10 (9f), B Brogan 0-3.
Subs: MD Macauley for Bastick, P Mannion 0-1 for Brogan, P Andrews for McManamon, E Lowndes for Small, M Fitzsimons for O'Sullivan, C O'Callaghan for Flynn.
Meath: P O'Rourke; D Keogan, M Burke, D Smyth; A Douglas, D Tobin, C O'Brien; H Rooney, A Tormey; E Wallace 0-1, G Reilly 0-3, P Harnan; M Newman 0-4 (3f), C O'Sullivan 0-2 (1f), D McDonagh. **Subs:** R Jones 0-1 for Tormey, S Lavin for Wallace, S Tobin for McDonagh, J Wallace for Reilly, C Finn for Douglas, B McMahon for O'Sullivan. J Wallace (bc).
Referee: R Hickey (Clare).

Leinster final
Sunday, 17 July 2016, Croke Park (attendance 38,855)
Dublin 2-19 Westmeath 0-10
Dublin: S Cluxton; J Cooper, P McMahon, D Byrne; J Small 0-1, C O'Sullivan, E Lowndes; B Fenton, MD Macauley; P Flynn 0-1, C Kilkenny, D Connolly 0-1; K McManamon 1-2, D Rock 0-8 (7f), B Brogan 1-4.
Subs: P Andrews 0-2 for Lowndes, C O'Callaghan for Macauley, D Bastick for Connolly, D Daly for Small, M Fitzsimons for O'Sullivan, P Mannion for Rock.
Westmeath: D Quinn; K Daly, A Stone, J Gonoud; K Maguire, J Dolan, D Lynch; D Corroon 0-1, G Egan 0-2; F Boyle, P Sharry, R Connellan; K Martin, J Heslin 0-6 (5f), C McCormack 0-1. **Subs:** D Daly for Connellan, S Corcoran for Lynch, S Duncan for Daly, J Connellan for Martin, R Gorman for Maguire, D McNicholas for Sharry.
Referee: F Kelly (Longford).

THE GAMES: (ABOUT) A DECADE OF THE DUBS

All-Ireland quarter-final
Saturday, 6 August 2016, Croke Park (attendance 82,300)
Dublin 1-15 Donegal 1-10
Dublin: S Cluxton; P McMahon 0-1, J Cooper 0-1, D Byrne; C Kilkenny 0-1, C O'Sullivan, J Small; B Fenton, MD Macauley; P Flynn, K McManamon 0-3, P Andrews 0-1; D Rock 0-5f, D Connolly 0-2, B Brogan. **Subs:** D Daly for Brogan, D Bastick for Macauley, P Mannion 1-1 for Andrews, E O'Gara for McManamon, Eric Lowndes for Rock.
Donegal: MA McGinley; P McGrath, N McGee, E McGee; R McHugh 1-0, K Lacey, F McGlynn; R Kavanagh, O MacNiallais; A Thompson 0-1, M McElhinney, E McHugh; P McBrearty 0-3 (2f), M Murphy 0-6 (5f, 1 45), M O'Reilly. **Subs:** C Gillespie for MacNiallais, L McLoone for Kavanagh, C Toye for Thompson, M McHugh for E McGee, C Thompson for McElhinney, C McFadden for Lacey.
Referee: C Branagan (Down).

All-Ireland semi-final
Sunday, 28 August 2016, Croke Park (attendance 82,300)
Dublin 0-22 Kerry 2-14
Dublin: S Cluxton; D Byrne, P McMahon 0-1, J Cooper; J Small, C O'Sullivan, J McCarthy; B Fenton 0-1, MD Macauley; P Flynn, D Connolly 0-3, C Kilkenny; K McManamon 0-2, D Rock 0-12 (8f, 2 45), B Brogan 0-2. **Subs:** P Andrews for Flynn, P Mannion for Small, E O'Gara 0-1 for Macauley, M Fitzsimons for Cooper, C Costello for Brogan.
Kerry: B Kelly; S Enright, M Griffin, K Young; A O'Mahony, P Crowley, T Morley; A Maher, D Moran 0-1; D Walsh, D O'Sullivan 1-0, P Murphy 0-1; C Cooper 0-5 (4f), K Donaghy, P Geaney 1-4. **Subs:** S O'Brien 0-1 for O'Sullivan, J O'Donoghue 0-1 for Donaghy, BJ Keane 0-1 for Walsh, B Ó Beaglaoich for Morley, B Sheehan for Maher, M Ó Sé for Geaney.
Referee: D Gough (Meath).

All-Ireland final
Sunday, 18 September 2016, Croke Park (attendance 82,300)
Dublin 2-9 Mayo 0-15
Dublin: S Cluxton; P McMahon, J Cooper, D Byrne; J McCarthy, C O'Sullivan, J Small 0-1; B Fenton 0-1 MD Macauley; P Flynn, K McManamon, C Kilkenny; D Rock 0-4 (3f), D Connolly 0-1, B Brogan. **Subs:** P Andrews 0-2 for McCarthy (bc), P Mannion for McManamon, M Fitzsimons for Macauley, E O'Gara for Brogan, D Daly for Byrne, D Bastick for Flynn.
Mayo: D Clarke; B Harrison, D Vaughan 0-2, K Higgins; L Keegan, C Boyle, P Durcan 0-1; S O'Shea, T Parsons 0-1; K McLoughlin, A O'Shea, D O'Connor; J Doherty 0-1, A Moran 0-2, C O'Connor 0-7 (5f). **Subs:** A Dillon 0-1 for S O'Shea, C Barrett for Boyle, B Moran for Dillon, S Coen for D O'Connor, E Regan for A Moran, C Loftus for Regan.
Referee: C Lane (Cork).

All-Ireland final replay
Saturday, 1 October 2016, Croke Park (attendance 82,249)
Dublin 1-15 Mayo 1-14
Dublin: S Cluxton; P McMahon, J Cooper, M Fitzsimons; J McCarthy, C O'Sullivan, J Small; B Fenton, P Flynn; P Andrews, K McManamon 0-1, C Kilkenny; D Rock 0-9 (7f), D Connolly 1-1 (1-0 pen), P Mannion. **Subs:** D Byrne for Cooper (bc), B Brogan 0-1 for Andrews, MD Macauley for Mannion, C Costello 0-3 for McManamon, E Lowndes for Small, D Daly for O'Sullivan.
Mayo: R Hennelly, B Harrison, D Vaughan, K Higgins, L Keegan 1-0, C Boyle, P Durcan 0-2, S O'Shea, T Parsons, K McLoughlin 0-1, A O'Shea, D O'Connor 0-1, J Doherty, A Moran 0-1, C O'Connor 0-9f. **Subs:** S Coen for Keegan (bc), C O'Shea for Vaughan, D Clarke for Hennelly (bc), B Moran for A Moran, A Dillon for Doherty.
Referee: M Deegan (Laois).

2017

Leinster quarter-final
Saturday, 3 June 2017, O'Moore Park, Portlaoise (attendance 13,238)
Dublin 0-19 Carlow 0-7
Dublin: S Cluxton; E Lowndes, J Cooper, M Fitzsimons; J McCaffrey 0-2, C O'Sullivan, J McCarthy; B Fenton, C Kilkenny 0-3; N Scully 0-1, C O'Callaghan 0-2f, D Connolly 0-1 45; P Mannion 0-1, D Rock 0-6f, K McManamon. **Subs:** B Brogan 0-2 for McManamon, S Carthy for McCaffrey, M Schutte for Scully, C McHugh 0-1 for Rock, D Byrne for O'Sullivan, D Bastick for Fenton.
Carlow: C Kearney; C Lawlor, S Redmond, J Murphy; C Crowley, D St Ledger, G Kelly; B Murphy 0-1, S Murphy 0-1; E Ruth, D Foley 0-1f, A Kelly; D Moran 0-1, P Broderick 0-3f, S Gannon. **Subs:** M Rennick for A Kelly, S Clarke for Ruth, J Clarke for G Kelly, K Nolan for Crowley, BJ Molloy for Moran, C Moran for Broderick.
Referee: S Hurson (Tyrone).

Leinster semi-final
Sunday, 25 June 2017, Croke Park (attendance 33,370)
Dublin 4-29 Westmeath 0-10
Dublin: S Cluxton; M Fitzsimons, C O'Sullivan, J Cooper; D Daly, E Lowndes, J McCaffrey; B Fenton 0-2, J McCarthy; C Kilkenny 1-3, C O'Callaghan 0-3, N Scully; D Rock 1-5 (0-3f, 0-2 45), P Andrews 0-3, P Mannion 0-8. **Subs:** E O'Gara 1-0 for Andrews, S Carthy 0-2 for Cooper, D Byrne for Fitzsimons, B Brogan 0-2 (1f) for Rock, K McManamon 1-1 for Scully, B Howard for O'Callaghan.
Westmeath: D Quinn; J Gonoud, K Maguire, F Boyle; D Lynch, K Daly, J Dolan; A Gaughan, G Egan 0-1; J Egan 0-2, P Sharry, C McCormack; M McCallon, J Heslin 0-4 (3f), K Martin 0-3. **Subs:** N Mulligan for Gaughan, K Reilly for McCormack, C Boyle for Daly, S Corcoran for J Egan, D Glennon for Sharry, A Stone for Lynch.
Referee: C Lane (Cork).

Leinster final
Sunday, 16 July 2017, Croke Park (attendance 66,734)
Dublin 2-23 Kildare 1-17
Dublin: S Cluxton; P McMahon, C O'Sullivan, M Fitzsimons; E Lowndes, J Small, J McCaffrey; J McCarthy 1-0, B Fenton; N Scully, C Kilkenny 0-2, P Mannion 0-1; C O'Callaghan 0-12 (6f), P Andrews 0-1, D Rock 1-0. **Subs:** B Brogan 0-5 for Rock (bc), S Carthy 0-1 for Scully, D Daly for McMahon, K McManamon for Andrews, D Byrne for O'Sullivan, B Howard 0-1 for Fenton.
Kildare: M Donnellan; M O'Grady, D Hyland, O Lyons; J Byrne 0-1, E Doyle, K Cribbin 0-1; K Feely 0-5 (4f), T Moolick; F Conway, N Kelly 0-1, D Slattery 0-1; P Brophy 1-3 (0-1f), D Flynn 0-2, C McNally 0-2. **Subs:** P Cribbin for Conway, F Dowling 0-1 for Moolick, P Kelly for Doyle, B McCormack for McNally, E Bolton for Byrne, E O'Callaghan for Feely (bc).
Referee: A Nolan (Wicklow).

All-Ireland quarter-final
Saturday, 5 August 2017, Croke Park (attendance 82,300)
Dublin 1-19 Monaghan 0-12
Dublin: S Cluxton; P McMahon, C O'Sullivan, M Fitzsimons; J Cooper, J Small 0-1, E Lowndes; B Fenton, J McCarthy 0-1; C Kilkenny, C O'Callaghan 0-1, J McCaffrey 0-1; P Mannion 0-3, P Andrews 0-3, D Rock 1-7 (0-6f, 0-1 45). **Subs:** B Brogan for Lowndes, D Daly for Small, P Flynn 0-1 for McCarthy, E O'Gara 0-1 for Andrews, MD Macauley for Kilkenny, D Byrne for Cooper.
Monaghan: R Beggan 0-1f; F Kelly, D Wylie, R Wylie; C Walshe 0-1, K Duffy, K O'Connell 0-1; K Hughes, D Hughes 0-1; G Doogan, D Ward, S Carey; R McAnespie 0-1, J McCarron, C McManus 0-4f. **Subs:** C McCarthy 0-3 for Doogan, O Duffy for Ward, D Mone for O'Connell, V Corey for R Wylie, D Malone for Carey, N McAdam for D Hughes.
Referee: C Lane (Cork).

All-Ireland semi-final
Sunday, 27 August 2017, Croke Park (attendance 82,300)
Dublin 2-17 Tyrone 0-11
Dublin: S Cluxton; P McMahon, C O'Sullivan, M Fitzsimons; J Cooper, J Small, J McCaffrey 0-1; B Fenton 0-1, J McCarthy; C Kilkenny 0-1, C O'Callaghan 1-2, N Scully; P Mannion 0-1, P Andrews 0-2, D Rock 0-5 (4f). **Subs:** P Flynn 0-3 for N Scully, K McManamon for Andrews, D Daly for Small, E O'Gara 1-1 for Rock, E Lowndes for Mannion, D Connolly for O'Callaghan.
Tyrone: N Morgan; A McCrory, R McNamee, C McCarron; T McCann 0-1, P Hampsey, P Harte 0-4 (3f); C Cavanagh 0-2, C McCann; D Mulgrew, N Sludden 0-2, K McGeary; M Bradley, S Cavanagh 0-1f, M Donnelly. **Subs:** D McClure 0-1 for C McCann, R Brennan for McGeary, D McCurry for Mulgrew, R O'Neill for Bradley, C Meyler for S Cavanagh, P McNulty for McNamee.
Referee: D Coldrick (Meath).

All-Ireland final
Sunday, 17 September 2017, Croke Park (attendance 82,300)
Dublin 1-17 Mayo 1-16
Dublin: S Cluxton; J Cooper, P McMahon, M Fitzsimons; J Small 0-1, C O'Sullivan, J McCaffrey; B Fenton 0-1, J McCarthy 0-2; D Rock 0-7 (3f), C O'Callaghan 1-0, C Kilkenny; P Mannion 0-3, E O'Gara 0-1, P Andrews. **Subs:** P Flynn for McCaffrey, D Connolly 0-1 for Andrews, K McManamon 0-1 for O'Gara, B Brogan for Flynn, N Scully for O'Callaghan, C Costello for Mannion.
Mayo: D Clarke; C Barrett, B Harrison, P Durcan; L Keegan 1-0, C Boyle 0-1, K Higgins; S O'Shea, T Parsons; K McLoughlin 0-2, A O'Shea, D Vaughan 0-1; A Moran 0-3, C O'Connor 0-7 (4f), J Doherty 0-2. **Subs:** D O'Connor for S O'Shea, S Coen for Boyle, C Loftus for Moran, D Drake for Doherty, D Kirby for McLoughlin, G Cafferkey for Higgins.
Referee: J McQuillan (Cavan).

2018

Leinster quarter-final
Sunday, 27 May 2018, O'Moore Park, Portlaoise (attendance 11,786)
Dublin 4-25 Wicklow 1-11
Dublin: S Cluxton; E Lowndes, P McMahon 0-1, M Fitzsimons; J McCarthy, J Cooper, B Howard 0-1; MD Macauley 0-1, B Fenton 1-3; N Scully, C Kilkenny 1-7, C O'Callaghan 1-3; D Rock 1-2 (0-2f), P Mannion 0-1 45), P Andrews 0-3. **Subs:** E Murchan for Fitzsimons, C McHugh 0-2 (1f) for Rock, P Flynn for Macauley, D Daly for Mannion, C Basquel 0-1 for Andrews, K McManamon for O'Callaghan.
Wicklow: M Jackson 0-2f; E Murtagh, R O'Brien, C Hyland; J Crowe, D Healy 0-1, S Kearon; R Finn 0-1, J Stafford 1-1; D Hayden 0-2, K Murphy, T Smyth 0-2; S Furlong 0-1, J McGrath, M Kenny 0-1. **Subs:** C Magee for Murphy, D Fitzgerald for McGrath, C Healy for Kearon, P Merrigan for Crowe, B Kennedy for Stafford, D Keane for Smyth.
Referee: C Branagan (Down).

Leinster semi-final
Sunday, 10 June 2018, Croke Park (attendance 39,028)
Dublin 2-25 Longford 0-12
Dublin: S Cluxton; E Lowndes, P McMahon 0-1, M Fitzsimons; J McCarthy 0-1, J Cooper, B Howard 0-1; B Fenton 0-4, MD Macauley; N Scully 0-1, C O'Callaghan 0-2, P Mannion 1-2; D Rock 1-6 (0-5f), C Kilkenny 0-4, P Andrews 0-1. **Subs:** E Comerford for Cluxton (bs), D Daly for Fitzsimons, J McCaffrey for Cooper, C Basquel 0-2 for Mannion, K McManamon for Andrews, C O'Sullivan for McCarthy, P Flynn for Macauley.
Longford: P Collum 0-1 45; P Fox, P McCormack, D Masterson; D McElligott 0-1, D Mimnagh, M Quinn 0-1; D Gallagher, C Berry; L Connerton, D McGivney, D Reynolds; R Smyth 0-5 (3f), J McGivney, R Brady. **Subs:** S McCormack 0-1 for Connerton, B Gilleran for Quinn (bc), M Nally for D McGivney, P Foy for Reynolds, D Quinn for Masterson, S Donohoe for Mimnagh.
Referee: M Deegan (Laois).

THE GAMES: (ABOUT) A DECADE OF THE DUBS

Leinster final
Sunday, 24 June 2018, Croke Park (attendance 41,728)
Dublin 1-25 Laois 0-10
Dublin: E Comerford; E Lowndes, P McMahon, M Fitzsimons; J McCarthy 0-1, J Cooper, B Howard 0-1; B Fenton 0-1, MD Macauley; N Scully 0-1, C O'Callaghan 0-2, C Kilkenny 1-4; P Mannion 0-1, D Rock 0-8 (5f, 1 45), P Andrews 0-2. **Subs:** J McCaffrey for Lowndes, C Costello 0-4 for Andrews, J Small for Macauley, P Flynn for O'Callaghan, D Daly for Mannion, C McHugh for Rock.
Laois: G Brody; D Strong, M Timmons, G Dillon; F Crowley, C Begley, T Collins; J O'Loughlin, K Lillis 0-1; A Farrell 0-2, P Kingston, N Donoher; E O'Carroll 0-1, D Kingston 0-4 (2f), Damien O'Connor. **Subs:** B Carroll for Donoher, R Munnelly for Crowley, E Keogh for Brody, D Holland for Strong, B Glynn for Farrell, G Walsh 0-2 for P Kingston.
Referee: B Cassidy (Derry).

Super 8s Rd1
Saturday, 14 July 2018, Croke Park (attendance 53,501)
Dublin 2-15 Donegal 0-16
Dublin: S Cluxton; M Fitzsimons, C O'Sullivan, J Cooper; J McCarthy 0-1, E Murchan, J McCaffrey; B Fenton, MD Macauley; N Scully 2-0, C O'Callaghan, B Howard 0-2; P Mannion, C Kilkenny 0-1, D Rock 0-7 (5f, 1 45). **Subs:** C Costello 0-2 for Macauley, K McManamon for Mannion, P Flynn 0-2 for Howard, E Lowndes for McCaffrey, C Basquel for O'Callaghan, D Daly for Fitzsimons.
Donegal: S Patton; S McMenamin, F McGlynn 0-1, E Bán Gallagher; E Doherty 0-1, P Brennan, P McGrath; H McFadden, O MacNiallais; R McHugh 0-2, M Murphy 0-6 (3f, 1 45), C Thompson 0-1; L McLoone, M Langan 0-2, J Brennan 0-3. **Subs:** N McGee for McGrath, D Ó Baoill for MacNiallis, C Mulligan for Thompson, C Ward for Doherty, A Thompson for P Brennan, S McBrearty for J Brennan.
Referee: C Lane (Cork).

263

Super 8s Rd2
Saturday, 21 July 2018, Healy Park, Omagh (attendance 16,205)
Dublin 1-14 Tyrone 0-14
Dublin: S Cluxton; E Murchan, P McMahon 0-1, J Cooper; B Howard 0-1, C O'Sullivan, J Small 0-1; J McCarthy 1-0, B Fenton; N Scully, C Kilkenny 0-2, C O'Callaghan; D Rock 0-6 (4f), P Mannion, J McCaffrey 0-1. **Subs:** C Costello for Mannion, K McManamon 0-1 for Scully, M Fitzsimons for McMahon, P Flynn 0-1 for Howard, D Daly for Small, MD Macauley for McCarthy.
Tyrone: N Morgan; M McKernan 0-1, R McNamee, HP McGeary; T McCann 0-1, M Donnelly, F Burns 0-1, C Cavanagh, P Hampsey; N Sludden, P Harte 0-3 (2f) C Meyler; C McShane 0-2, R Donnelly, C McAliskey 0-2 (1 45). **Subs:** R Brennan for McNamee, M Bradley 0-1 for McAliskey, K McGeary 0-2 for Burns, D McClure for Cavanagh, H Loughran 0-1 for Meyler, R O'Neill for Sludden.
Referee: D Coldrick (Meath).

Super 8s Rd3
Sunday, 5 August 2018, Croke Park (attendance 33,240)
Dublin 4-24 Roscommon 2-16
Dublin: S Cluxton; M Fitzsimons, C O'Sullivan, P McMahon 0-1; E Lowndes, J Small 0-1, D Daly; P Flynn 1-3, MD Macauley 1-1; J McCaffrey, E O'Gara 2-2, C Costello 0-9 (1 45, 1f); K McManamon 0-3 (2f), C Basquel, P Andrews 0-2. **Subs:** C Mullally for O'Sullivan, J McCarthy for McCaffrey, M Schutte 0-1 for Small, P Small 0-1 for Costello, C McHugh 0-2 for O'Gara, A McGowan for Daly, B Brogan for Schutte (bs), Schutte for Brogan.
Roscommon: J Featherstone; D Murray, P Domican, N McInerney; J McManus, D Petit, R Timothy; T O'Rourke, E Smith; N Kilroy 0-1, C Murtagh 0-1f, C Devaney 0-1; D Murtagh 0-6 (2f), B Stack, C Lennon 0-2. **Subs:** G Patterson 1-0 for Timothy, P Kelly 0-2 for Kilroy, D Smith 1-3 (0-1 45) for Domican, I Kilbride for Stack, C Cregg for C Murtagh, S McDermott for McManus.
Referee: C Reilly (Meath).

THE GAMES: (ABOUT) A DECADE OF THE DUBS

All-Ireland semi-final
Saturday, 11 August 2018, Croke Park (attendance 54,715)
Dublin 1-24 Galway 2-12
Dublin: S Cluxton; E Murchan, P McMahon, J Cooper; J Small, C O'Sullivan, J McCaffrey; B Fenton 0-2, J McCarthy; N Scully, C Kilkenny 0-3, B Howard 0-1; D Rock 0-5 (4f), P Mannion 0-4, C O'Callaghan 1-3. **Subs:** M Fitzsimons for O'Sullivan, C Costello 0-3 (1f) for Scully, K McManamon 0-2 for Rock, MD Macauley for Murchan, D Daly for Small, P Flynn 0-1 for McCaffrey.
Galway: R Lavelle; D Kyne, SA O Ceallaigh, E Kerin; C Sweeney, G Bradshaw, S Kelly; C Duggan, T Flynn 0-1; E Brannigan, S Walsh 1-5 (0-3f), J Heaney 0-1; S Armstrong, D Comer 1-1, I Burke 0-2. **Subs:** M Daly 0-1 for Armstrong, P Cooke for Brannigan, G O'Donnell 0-1 for Sweeney, A Varley for Heaney, K Molloy for Kerin, J Duane for Bradshaw.
Referee: B Cassidy (Derry).

All-Ireland final
Sunday, 2 September 2018, Croke Park (attendance 82,300)
Dublin 2-17 Tyrone 1-14
Dublin: S Cluxton; P McMahon, C O'Sullivan, J Cooper; J Small, E Murchan, J McCaffrey 0-1; B Fenton 0-2, J McCarthy; N Scully 1-0, C O'Callaghan, B Howard 0-1; P Mannion 1-0 pen, C Kilkenny 0-4, D Rock 0-7 (2f, 1 45). **Subs:** M Fitzsimons for O'Sullivan, C Costello for Scully, K McManamon 0-1 for Mannion, D Daly for Murchan, E Lowndes for Cooper, MD Macauley 0-1 for Rock.
Tyrone: N Morgan; R McNamee, T McCann 0-1, P Hampsey 0-1; M Donnelly, M McKernan, R Brennan; C Cavanagh, C McShane 0-2; K McGeary 0-1, N Sludden, C Meyler; M Bradley 0-2, P Harte 1-1 (1-0 pen, 0-1f), C McAliskey 0-3 (1f). **Subs:** L Brennan 0-3f for Meyler, F Burns for Sludden, H Loughran for McGeary (bc), R Donnelly for McAliskey, D McClure for McShane, R O'Neill for Bradley.
Referee: C Lane (Cork).

2019

Leinster quarter-final
Sunday, 26 May 2019, O'Moore Park, Portlaoise (attendance 14,380)
Dublin 5-21 Louth 0-10
Louth: F Sheekey; F Donohoe, E Carolan, J Craven; A Williams, B Duffy, J Clutterbuck; T Durnin, J Califf; A McDonnell 0-1, J McEneaney 0-2, C McKeever 0-1; C Downey 0-1, R Burns 0-4 (2f), D Byrne. **Subs:** D Corcoran for Donohoe, S Mulroy for Byrne, C Early for Califf, D Maguire for Clutterbuck, E Callaghan 0-1 for Craven (bc), E Duffy for McEneaney.
Dublin: S Cluxton; D Byrne, C O'Sullivan, M Fitzsimons 0-1; J McCaffrey, J Small, J McCarthy; B Fenton 1-1, D Gavin; N Scully 0-2, C Kilkenny 0-1, B Howard; P Mannion 0-2, C O'Callaghan 1-0, C Costello 1-12 (0-10f, 0-1 45). **Subs:** MD Macauley 1-0 for Gavin, P McMahon 1-0 for O'Sullivan, R O'Carroll for McCaffrey, P Small 0-1 for O'Callaghan, K McManamon 0-1f for Scully, S Bugler for Costello.
Referee: J Henry (Mayo).

Leinster semi-final
Sunday, 9 June 2019, Croke Park (attendance 36,126)
Dublin 0-26 Kildare 0-11
Dublin: S Cluxton; D Byrne, M Fitzsimons, J Small, J McCarthy, C O'Sullivan, J McCaffrey, B Fenton 0-2, MD McAuley, N Scully, C Costello 0-9 (3f, 1 45), B Howard 0-1, C Kilkenny 0-3, C O'Callaghan 0-3, P Mannion 0-7. **Subs:** P Small 0-1 for McAuley, P McMahon for O'Sullivan, E Murchan for McCaffrey, P Andrews for O'Callaghan, R O'Carroll for Fitzsimons.
Kildare: M Donnellan; M Dempsey, M O'Grady 0-1, D Hyland 0-1, P Kelly, E Doyle, K Cribbin, K Feely 0-1, T Moolick, D Slattery, C Healy, F Conway, A Tyrrell 0-4 (3f), B McCormack 0-3, N Flynn 0-1f. **Subs:** K O'Callaghan for Flynn, C O'Donoghue for Moolick, J Hyland for Healy, E O'Flaherty for Cribbin, C Hartley for Slattery.
Referee: C Lane (Cork).

THE GAMES: (ABOUT) A DECADE OF THE DUBS

Leinster final
Sunday, 23 June 2019, Croke Park (attendance 47,027)
Dublin 1-17 Meath 0-4
Dublin: S Cluxton; P McMahon 0-1, M Fitzsimons, J McCaffrey 0-2; D Byrne, C O'Sullivan, J Small; B Fenton 0-1, J McCarthy; N Scully, C Kilkenny 0-1, B Howard 0-1; C Costello 0-3 (2f, 1 45), P Mannion 0-3, C O'Callaghan 1-0. **Subs:** MD Macauley for McCarthy, D Rock 0-4 (1f) for Howard, K McManamon for Costello, P Small for Kilkenny, P Andrews 0-1 for P Small, R O'Carroll for McCaffey.
Meath: A Colgan; C McGill, S Lavin, S Gallagher; J McEntee, D Keogan, R Ryan; B Menton 0-1, S McEntee; C O'Sullivan, B McMahon, G Reilly; B Brennan, J Conlon, M Newman 0-3 (1f). **Subs:** S Tobin for Brennan, E Devine for Reilly, T O'Reilly for Conlon, B Dardis for S McEntee, S Curran for Gallagher, T McGovern for McMahon.
Referee: S Hurson (Tyrone).

All-Ireland Group 1
Saturday, 13 July 2019, Croke Park (attendance 30,214)
Dublin 5-18 Cork 1-17
Dublin: S Cluxton; P McMahon 0-3, M Fitzsimons, D Byrne; J McCaffrey 1-0, C O'Sullivan, J Small 0-1; B Fenton 1-1, MD Macauley 1-0; N Scully 1-0, C Kilkenny 1-2, B Howard; P Mannion 0-3, C Costello 0-1, C O'Callaghan 0-4. **Subs:** D Rock 0-5 (1 45, 3f) for Costello, P Small for O'Callaghan, K McManamon for Mannion, J Cooper for O'Sullivan, E Murchan for McCaffrey, J McCarthy for Fenton.
Cork: M White; T Clancy, K Flahive, J Loughrey; L O'Donovan 0-1, T Clancy, M Taylor 0-1; I Maguire, K O'Driscoll 0-1; L Connolly 1-3 (0-1 45, 1-0 pen), S White 0-1, R Deane 0-1; P Kerrigan 0-2, B Hurley 0-4 (1f), M Collins 0-1f. **Subs:** M Hurley 0-2 for Kerrigan, K O'Donovan for Loughrey, S Sherlock for Connolly, C Kiely for L O'Donovan, J O'Rourke for Maguire.
Referee: D Gough (Meath).

All-Ireland Group 2
Saturday, 20 July 2019, Croke Park (attendance 36,530)
Dublin 2-26 Roscommon 0-14
Dublin: S Cluxton; J Cooper, P McMahon, M Fitzsimons; J McCaffrey 0-1, J McCarthy, J Small; B Fenton 0-2, MD Macauley 1-0; N Scully 0-1, C Kilkenny 0-2, B Howard; C O'Callaghan 0-2, P Mannion 0-3, D Rock 1-11 (0-10f). **Subs:** K McManamon 0-1 for Kilkenny, P Small 0-3 for Mannion, R O'Carroll for Fitzsimons, E Lowndes for McCaffrey, P Andrews for O'Callaghan, D Byrne for Macauley.
Roscommon: D O'Malley; S Mullooly 0-1, D Murray, C Daly; R Daly, C Hussey 0-3, N Daly 0-1; E Smith, S Killoran; B Stack, C Cregg, N Kilroy; D Murtagh 0-1, C Cox 0-7 (4f), C Compton 0-1. **Subs:** F Cregg for Killoran, A Lyons for Compton, J McManus for C Cregg, C McKeon for D Murtagh, G Patterson for Murray, C McKeon for Kilroy.
Referee: B Cassidy (Derry).

All-Ireland Group 3
Sunday, 4 August 2019, Healy Park, Omagh (attendance 15,315)
Dublin 1-16 Tyrone 0-13
Dublin: E Comerford; D Byrne, R O'Carroll, A McGowan; E Lowndes, J Cooper, E Murchan; J McCarthy, D Connolly 0-1; R McDaid, K McManamon 0-2, S Bugler 0-3; P Small 0-2, P Andrews 0-1, C Costello 0-6 (4f). **Subs:** MD Macauley for McCarthy, P McMahon for Byrne, B Brogan 0-1 for Cooper, E O'Gara 1-0 for Small, C O'Connor for O'Carroll, P O Cofaigh Byrne for Costello.
Tyrone: B Gallen; A McCrory, P Hampsey, C McLaughlin; T McCann, M Cassidy, L Rafferty; R Donnelly 0-2, D McClure; B McDonnell, K Coney 0-2f, C Grugan 0-1; D Mulgrew, C McAliskey 0-5 (2f), C McCann 0-1. **Subs:** HP McGeary for Hampsey, R Brennan for Cassidy, B Kennedy for Donnelly, D McCurry 0-1 for C McCann, M McKernan for T McCann, N Sludden 0-1 for Mulgrew.
Referee: J McQuillan (Cavan).

THE GAMES: (ABOUT) A DECADE OF THE DUBS

All-Ireland semi-final
Saturday, 10 August 2019, Croke Park (attendance 82,300)
Dublin 3-14 Mayo 1-10
Dublin: S Cluxton; D Byrne, J Cooper, M Fitzsimons; J McCaffrey, J McCarthy, J Small; B Fenton 1-1, MD Macauley; N Scully 0-1, C O'Callaghan 2-0, B Howard 0-1; P Mannion 0-5, D Rock 0-6f, C Kilkenny. **Subs:** C O'Sullivan for Macauley, E Murchan for Small, C Costello for Mannion, P McMahon for Cooper, D Connolly for Scully, P Andrews for O'Callaghan.
Mayo: R Hennelly; C Barrett, B Harrison, S Coen 0-1; L Keegan 1-0, C Boyle 0-1, P Durcan 0-2; A O'Shea, S O'Shea 0-1; F McDonagh, D Vaughan, M Ruane; C O'Connor 0-3 (2f), D O'Connor, J Carr 0-1. **Subs:** K Higgins for Vaughan, K McLoughlin for McDonagh, A Moran for Carr, E O'Donoghue for Boyle, T Parsons for Séamus O'Shea, F Boland 0-1f for D O'Connor.
Referee: C Lane (Cork).

All-Ireland final
Sunday, 1 September 2019, Croke Park (attendance 82,300)
Dublin 1-16 Kerry 1-16
Dublin: S Cluxton; D Byrne, J Cooper, M Fitzsimons; J McCaffrey 1-3, J McCarthy, J Small; B Fenton, MD Macauley; N Scully, C O'Callaghan 0-1, B Howard; P Mannion 0-2, D Rock 0-10 (6f, 1 45), C Kilkenny. **Subs:** P Small for Macauley, D Connolly for Howard, C Costello for Mannion, K McManamon for Scully.
Kerry: S Ryan; J Foley, T Morley, T O'Sullivan; P Murphy, G Crowley 0-1, B Ó Beaglaoich; D Moran, A Spillane; G White, S O'Shea 0-10 (4f, 3 45), S O'Brien 0-1; D Clifford 0-2, P Geaney, J Barry. **Subs:** K Spillane 1-1 for A Spillane, J Sherwood for White, T Walsh 0-1 for Ó Beaglaoich, J Lyne for Crowley, D Moynihan for Barry, M Griffin for O'Brien.
Referee: D Gough (Meath).

All-Ireland final replay
Saturday, 14 September 2019, Croke Park (attendance 82,300)
Dublin 1-18 Kerry 0-15
Dublin: S Cluxton; E Murchan 1-0, D Byrne 0-1, M Fitzsimons; J Cooper, J Small, J McCaffrey; B Fenton, J McCarthy 0-1; N Scully 0-1, C Kilkenny 0-4, B Howard; P Mannion 0-4, C O'Callaghan 0-4, D Rock 0-3 (1 45).
Subs: D Connolly for McCaffrey, P McMahon for Murchan, C Costello for Scully, C O'Sullivan for Byrne, K McManamon for Mannion, MD Macauley for Howard.
Kerry: S Ryan; J Foley, T O'Sullivan, T Morley; P Murphy, G Crowley, B Ó Beaglaoich; D Moran, J Barry, D O'Connor, S O'Shea 0-5 (3f), A Spillane 0-1; D Clifford 0-5 (1f), P Geaney 0-4, S O'Brien. **Subs:** G White for Spillane, J Sherwood for Ó Beaglaoich, T Walsh for O'Connor, K Spillane for Murphy, J O'Donoghue for Barry, D Moynihan for G Crowley.
Referee: C Lane (Cork).

2020

Leinster quarter-final
Saturday, 7 November 2020, O'Moore Park, Portlaoise
Dublin 0-22 Westmeath 0-11
Dublin: S Cluxton; M Fitzsimons, J Cooper 0-1, E Murchan 0-1; J McCarthy 0-1, J Small, R McDaid 0-1; B Fenton, T Lahiff; N Scully 0-1, C Kilkenny 0-5, S Bugler 0-2; P Small 0-2, C O'Callaghan 0-1, D Rock 0-7 (6f). **Subs:** B Howard for Bugler, C Costello for P Small, D Byrne for Fitzsimons, A Byrne for Scully, E Lowndes for Murchan.
Westmeath: J Daly; B Sayeh, K Maguire, J Smith; J Gonoud, R Wallace 0-1, J Dolan; R Connellan 0-2, S Duncan; D Lynch, J Heslin 0-2 (1f), K Daly; R O'Toole 0-1, L Loughlin 0-2, K Martin 0-3 (2f). **Subs:** C Slevin for K Daly, C McCormack for Lynch, L Dolan for Martin, A McGivney for Loughlin, B Kelly for O'Toole.
Referee: M McNally (Monaghan).

THE GAMES: (ABOUT) A DECADE OF THE DUBS

Leinster semi-final
Sunday, 15 November 2020, Croke Park
Dublin 2-23 Laois 0-7
Dublin: S Cluxton; M Fitzsimons, J Cooper, E Murchan; J McCarthy, J Small, R McDaid 0-1; B Fenton 0-4, T Lahiff; N Scully 0-3, C Kilkenny 1-4, S Bugler 1-0; P Small 0-1, C O'Callaghan 0-1, D Rock 0-2 (1f, 1 45). **Subs:** P Mannion for P Small, C Costello 0-7 (2f) for Rock, D Byrne for Lahiff, B Howard for Bugler, P McMahon for Murchan.
Laois: N Corbet; T Collins, M Timmons, R Pigott; S O'Flynn, P O'Sullivan, E Buggie; D O'Reilly, J O'Loughlin; G Dillon, K Lillis, B Byrne 0-1; E O'Carroll 0-1 P Kingston 0-2, Walsh 0-2 (1f). **Subs:** M Barry for O'Reilly, M Keogh for Dillon, R Munnelly 0-1 for Walsh, D Whelan for Byrne.
Referee: C Branagan (Down).

Leinster final
Saturday, 21 November 2020, Croke Park
Dublin 3-21 Meath 0-9
Dublin: S Cluxton; E Murchan, M Fitzsimons, D Byrne; J Cooper, J Small 0-1, R McDaid; J McCarthy, B Fenton; N Scully 1-1, C Kilkenny 0-4, S Bugler 1-2; P Small 0-3 (2m), C O'Callaghan 0-2, D Rock 1-7 (5f, 1 45). **Subs:** B Howard for Cooper, P Mannion 0-1f for Small, E Lowndes for J Small, C Costello for O'Callaghan, K McManamon for Kilkenny.
Meath: M Brennan; R Ryan, C McGill, D Toner; S Lavin, D Keogan, M Costello; B Menton 0-1, R Jones; B McMahon, C O'Sullivan 0-1, S McEntee; T O'Reilly 0-1f, S Walsh, J Morris 0-4 (1f). **Subs:** C Hickey for Toner, E Harkin for McGill, E Devine for Costello, J Scully 0-1 for McMahon, J Wallace 0-1m for O'Reilly.
Referee: D O'Mahoney (Tipperary).

All-Ireland semi-final
Saturday, 5 December 2020, Croke Park
Dublin 1-24 Cavan 0-12
Dublin: S Cluxton; M Fitzsimons, D Byrne, J Cooper; E Murchan, J Small, R McDaid 1-2; B Fenton 0-4, J McCarthy; N Scully, C Kilkenny 0-4 (1m),

S Bugler; P Small 0-2 (1m), C O'Callaghan 0-4, D Rock 0-6 (2f). **Subs:** B Howard 0-1 for Bugler, P McMahon for Cooper, P Mannion for P Small, C Costello 0-1 for Scully, C Basquel for Rock.
Cavan: R Galligan; K Clarke, P Faulkner, K Brady; L Fortune, Ciaran Brady 0-1, J McLoughlin; G McKiernan 0-1f, J Smith 0-2; G Smith, C Conroy 0-1f, O Kiernan 0-2; M Reilly 0-3, T Galligan 0-1, C Madden 0-1. **Subs:** C Smith for K Brady, S Murray for Conroy, N Murray for Clarke, Conor Brady for C Smith, S Smith for Madden.
Referee: C Branagan (Down).

All-Ireland final
Saturday, 19 December 2020, Croke Park
Dublin 2-14 Mayo 0-15
Dublin: S Cluxton; M Fitzsimons, D Byrne, E Murchan; J Cooper, J Small 0-1, R McDaid; B Fenton 0-1, J McCarthy; N Scully 0-1, C Kilkenny 0-3, S Bugler 0-1; P Small, C O'Callaghan 1-1, D Rock 1-4 (0-4f). **Subs:** B Howard 0-1 for Bugler, P Mannion 0-1f for P Small, C Basquel for Cooper, C Costello for Scully, P McMahon for Murchan.
Mayo: D Clarke; P Durcan, C Barrett, L Keegan; S Coen 0-1m, O Mullin 0-1, E McLoughlin; D O'Connor, M Ruane; K McLoughlin, R O'Donoghue 0-2, C Loftus 0-1; T Conroy, A O'Shea, C O'Connor 0-9 (5f, 2m). **Subs:** M Plunkett for Durcan, J Carr for Conroy, D Coen 0-1 for O'Donoghue, J Flynn for Loftus, J Durcan for McLaughlin.
Referee: D Coldrick (Meath).

2021

Leinster quarter-final
Sunday, 4 July 2021, Wexford Park (attendance 500)
Dublin 0-15 Wexford 0-7
Wexford: D Brooks; L O'Connor, G Sheehan, E Porter; B Malone, M O'Connor, M Furlong; D Waters, L Coleman; P Hughes 0-1, T Byrne, K O'Grady; M Rossiter 0-2 (1f), J Tubritt 0-1, N Hughes. **Subs:** S Nolan for Tubritt, A Tobin for Waters, D Shanley 0-2 for Hughes, R Brooks for

Rossiter, C Carthy for O'Grady.
Dublin: E Comerford; M Fitzsimons, D Byrne, S McMahon; J McCarthy 0-1, B Howard 0-2, R McDaid; B Fenton 0-1, P O'Cofaigh Byrne; P Small, C Kilkenny 0-1, N Scully; R Basquel, C O'Callaghan, C Costello 0-7 (6f). **Subs:** T Lahiff 0-1 for McDaid, S Bugler for R Basquel, C Basquel 0-1 for Scully, A Byrne for Small, D Rock 0-1 for A Byrne.
Referee: D O'Mahoney (Tipperary).

Leinster semi-final
Sunday, 18 July 2021, Croke Park (attendance 18,000)
Dublin 2-16 Meath 1-13
Dublin: E Comerford; M Fitzsimons, D Byrne, J Cooper; P Ó Cofaigh-Byrne, B Howard, S McMahon; B Fenton 0-1, J McCarthy; D Rock 0-2 (1f), C Kilkenny 0-5, N Scully; P Small 0-1, C O'Callaghan 1-3, C Costello 1-4 (1-0 pen). **Subs:** T Lahiff for Ó Cofaigh-Byrne, S Bugler for Small, C Basquel for Rock, C Murphy for McMahon.
Meath: H Hogan; S Lavin, C McGill, D Keogan; C Hickey, S McEntee, F Reilly; B Menton, P Harnan; E Wallace 0-2, B McMahon 0-1, M Costello 1-2 (0-1f); J Morris 0-3 (1f), C O'Sullivan 0-1, J Wallace 0-2. **Subs:** R Jones for Reilly, T O'Reilly 0-1f for McMahon, J McEntee 0-1 45 for Hickey, E Devine for Costello.
Referee: C Lane (Cork).

Leinster final
Sunday, 1 August 2021, Croke Park (attendance 18,000)
Dublin 0-20 Kildare 1-9
Dublin: E Comerford; M Fitzsimons, D Byrne, J Cooper; B Howard 0-1, J Small, S McMahon; J McCarthy 0-1, B Fenton; P Small 0-1, C Kilkenny 0-4 (1m), N Scully 0-2 (1m); C Costello 0-4, C O'Callaghan 0-1, D Rock 0-5 (3f). **Subs:** E Murchan for J Small (bs), C Basquel for Rock, S Bugler for P Small, T Lahiff for Cooper, R Basquel 0-1 for O'Callaghan, E O Conghaile for Kilkenny.
Kildare: M Donnellan; M O'Grady, M Dempsey, D Malone; K Flynn, D Hyland, R Houlihan; L Flynn, A Masterson; S Ryan, F Conway, N Flynn

0-1; B McCormack, D Flynn 1-2 (0-1m), J Hyland 0-4 (2f). **Subs:** N Kelly for Houlihan, A Beirne 0-1 for Conway, D Kirwan for Hyland, B McLoughlin 0-1 for N Flynn, S O'Sullivan for McCormack.
Referee: M McNally (Monaghan).

All-Ireland semi-final
Sunday, 14 August 2021, Croke Park (attendance 24,000)
Dublin 0-14 Mayo 0-17 (AET)
Mayo: R Hennelly 0-3 (2f, 1 45); P O'Hora, L Keegan (0-1), S Coen; M Plunkett, P Durcan, E McLaughlin; M Ruane 0-1, D O'Connor; D McHale, K McLoughlin 0-1, C Loftus 0-1; T Conroy 0-3, A O'Shea, R O'Donoghue 0-5 (2f, 1m). **Subs:** E Hession for McHale, B Walsh for Plunkett, J Carr for O'Shea, J Flynn 0-1 for E McLaughlin, C O'Shea for Loftus, D Coen 0-1 for S Coen, S Coen for C O'Shea, C Loftus for K McLoughlin, J Durcan for Carr, B Harrison for O'Connor, A O'Shea for D Coen.
Dublin: E Comerford; E Murchan, D Byrne, M Fitzsimons; J McCarthy, J Cooper, J Small; B Fenton, B Howard; P Small 0-2, C Costello, N Scully; C O'Callaghan 0-1, C Kilkenny 0-3 (1m), D Rock 0-7 (5f). **Subs:** C Basquel for Costello, T Lahiff for Cooper, S Bugler 0-1 for Scully, S McMahon for Murchan, P McMahon for S McMahon, R McDaid for J Small, A Byrne for Howard, C Costello for P Small.
Referee: C Lane (Cork).

Total, 2015–2021: Played 46, Won 42, Drew 3, Lost 1

* * *

THE GAMES: (ABOUT) A DECADE OF THE DUBS

2022

Leinster quarter-final
Saturday, 30 April 2022, Wexford Park
Dublin 1-24 Wexford 0-4
Dublin: D O'Hanlon; E Murchan, M Fitzsimons, L Gannon; J Small 0-1, J Cooper, R McDaid; B Fenton 0-5, T Lahiff 0-1; S Bugler, B Howard 0-2, C Kilkenny 0-1; C Costello 0-2, D Rock 0-5 (1 45, 1m), C O'Callaghan 1-6. **Subs:** J McCarthy for McDaid, N Scully for Bugler, S MacMahon for Murchan, A Byrne for Costello, L O'Dell 0-1 for Small.
Wexford: D Brooks; L O'Connor, E Porter, D Furlong; M O'Connor, G Malone, K O'Grady; N Hughes 0-1m, L Coleman; A Tobin, D Shanley, P Hughes 0-1; M Rossiter, E Nolan 0-1, B Brosnan 0-1. **Subs:** T Byrne for Shanley, R Brooks for Rossiter, M Furlong for Tobin, J Tubritt for Brosnan, S Ryan for Nolan.
Referee: B Cassidy (Derry).

Leinster semi-final
Sunday, 15 May 2022, Croke Park (attendance 38,081)
Dublin 1-27 Meath 1-14
Dublin: E Comerford; E Murchan, M Fitzsimons, L Gannon; J Small, L O'Dell 0-2, J McCarthy 0-2; B Fenton, T Lahiff 0-2; S Bugler 0-1, B Howard 0-1, C Kilkenny 0-5; C Costello 0-3, C O'Callaghan 0-2, D Rock 1-8 (1-6f). **Subs:** J Cooper for Murchan, N Scully for O'Dell, P Small 0-1 for O'Callaghan, S Clayton for Fenton, B O'Leary for Costello.
Meath: H Hogan; R Clarke, C McGill, E Harkin; J McEntee, D Keogan 0-1, R Ryan; B Menton 0-3, R Jones; M Costello, C O'Sullivan, J O'Connor 0-3 (2f); J Morris 1-3 (1-2f), T O'Reilly 0-1, J Wallace 0-1. **Subs:** C Hickey for McEntee, S Walsh for O'Reilly, S McEntee 0-1 for Ryan, J Flynn 0-1 for Jones, B McMahon for O'Sullivan.
Referee: D O'Mahoney (Tipperary).

275

Leinster final
Saturday, 28 May 2022, Croke Park (attendance 38,000)
Dublin 5-17 Kildare 1-15
Dublin: E Comerford; E Murchan, M Fitzsimons, L Gannon 0-2; J McCarthy, J Small 1-0, B Howard; B Fenton 0-3, T Lahiff; S Bugler, L O'Dell, C Kilkenny 1-0; C Costello 2-1, D Rock 0-4f, C O'Callaghan 1-5 (0-1m). **Subs:** N Scully 0-1 for O'Dell, C Murphy for Murchan, A Byrne 0-1 for Rock, J Cooper for Lahiff, B O'Leary for Costello.
Kildare: M Donnellan; M O'Grady, S Ryan, R Houlihan; K Flynn 0-1, J Murray, T Archbold; K Feely 0-1, K O'Callaghan; A Beirne, B McCormack 0-5 (1m), P Cribbin 0-1; D Kirwan 0-1, D Flynn 0-1m, J Hyland 1-4 (0-3f). **Subs:** D Hyland for Murray, P Woodgate 0-1f for Kirwan, P McDermott for Cribbin, D Malone for Archbold, F Conway for Beirne.
Referee: P Neilan (Roscommon).

All-Ireland quarter-final
Saturday, 25 June 2022, Croke Park (attendance 50,874)
Dublin 0-21 Cork 0-10
Dublin: E Comerford; E Murchan, M Fitzsimons, L Gannon 0-2; J Small, J Cooper, S Bulger 0-1; B Fenton 0-2, T Lahiff 0-1; N Scully, B Howard, C Kilkenny 0-3; C Costello 0-1, D Rock 0-9f, P Small 0-1. **Subs:** L O'Dell for Bugler, C Murphy for Cooper, A Byrne 0-1 for Small, E O'Connell for Murchan, D Byrne for Small.
Cork: MA Martin; S Powter, M Shanley, K O'Donovan; J Cooper, R Maguire, M Taylor; I Maguire, C O'Callaghan; P Ring, E McSweeney 0-1, J O'Rourke 0-1; S Sherlock 0-3 (2f), B Hurley 0-2, C O'Mahony 0-3 (1f, 1m). **Subs:** S Meehan for Ring, D Dineen for McSweeney, B Hayes for Sherlock, C Kiely for Cooper, B Murphy for O'Callaghan.
Referee: S Hurson (Tyrone).

THE GAMES: (ABOUT) A DECADE OF THE DUBS

All-Ireland semi-final
Sunday, 10 July 2022, Croke Park (attendance 73,609)
Dublin 1-13 Kerry 1-14
Kerry: S Ryan; G O'Sullivan, J Foley, T O'Sullivan 0-1; B Ó Beaglaioch, T Morley, G White; D Moran, D O'Connor; J Barry, S O'Shea 1-4 (1-2f), S O'Brien; P Clifford 0-2, D Clifford 0-6 (1f, 1m), P Geaney. **Subs:** D Moynihan 0-1 for O'Brien, K Spillane for Geaney, A Spillane for Moran, J O'Connor for White.
Dublin: E Comerford; E Murchan, M Fitzsimons, L Gannon 0-1; J Small 0-1, J Cooper, S Bugler 0-1; B Fenton 0-1, T Lahiff; J McCarthy 0-1, B Howard 0-1, C Kilkenny 0-3; C Costello 1-0, D Rock 0-3 (3f), L O'Dell. **Subs:** P Small 0-1 for O'Dell, D Byrne for Cooper, S McMahon for Murchan, C Murphy for Fitzsimons.
Referee: P Neilan (Roscommon).

2023

Leinster quarter-final
Sunday, 23 April 2023, O'Moore Park, Portlaoise
Dublin 4-30 Laois 2-9
Dublin: D O'Hanlon; D Byrne, D Newcombe, S McMahon; C Murphy 0-1, J McCaffrey, L Gannon 1-0; B Fenton 0-3, J McCarthy; C Kilkenny 1-4, S Bugler 0-1, R McGarry 0-2; P Mannion 0-3 (1f), C O'Callaghan 1-7 (0-2m, 0-1f), C Basquel 1-5. **Subs:** B Howard 0-1 for McCarthy, E Murchan for McCaffrey, C Costello for O'Callaghan, D Rock 0-3 for Mannion, C Dias for Fenton.
Laois: S Osborne; S Greene, T Collins, R Pigott; S O'Flynn, M Timmons 0-1, P Kirwan 0-1; K Lillis, D Larkin; K Swayne, P Kingston 0-3 (1f, 1m), P O'Sullivan; E Lowry 2-1 (0-1m), E O'Carroll 0-2 (1f, 1m), M Barry 0-1. **Subs:** S Lacey for Greene, D Kavanagh for Pigott, C Murphy for Barry, J Finn for Swayne, A Mohan for O'Flynn.
Referee: B Judge (Sligo).

Leinster semi-final
Sunday, 30 April 2023, Croke Park (attendance 30,499)
Dublin 0-14 Kildare 0-12
Dublin: S Cluxton; D Newcombe, D Byrne, L Gannon 0-1; J Small, C Murphy 0-1, T Lahiff; B Fenton, J McCarthy; R McGarry 0-1, S Bugler 0-1, C Kilkenny 0-1; P Mannion 0-3, C O'Callaghan 0-2 (1f), C Basquel 0-1.
Subs: C Costello 0-1f for McGarry, J McCaffrey 0-1 for Lahiff, L O'Dell 0-1 for Basquel, P Small for Mannion, D Rock for Bugler.
Kildare: M Donnellan; E Doyle, M O'Grady, P McDermott; D Hyland, K Flynn, S Ryan; K O'Callaghan, A Masterson; A Beirne, B McCormack 0-2, J Sargent; P Woodgate 0-4 (2f, 1 45), D Kirwan 0-2, J Robinson 0-3f. **Subs:** P Cribbin for Beirne, N Flynn 0-1 for Robinson, D Flynn for Kirwan, K Feely for Masterson, J Hyland for McCormack.
Referee: F Kelly (Longford).

Leinster final
Sunday, 14 May 2023, Croke Park (attendance 40,115)
Dublin 5-21 Louth 0-15
Dublin: S Cluxton; D Newcombe, D Byrne, L Gannon; B Howard, J Small 0-1, J McCaffrey 0-2; B Fenton, J McCarthy 1-0; N Scully, C O'Callaghan 0-4 (1m), C Kilkenny 0-3; P Mannion 1-1 (0-1f), S Bugler 1-3, C Costello 0-5 (3f, 1 45). **Subs:** C Murphy for McCaffrey, P Small 1-0 for Scully, D Rock 0-1 for Costello, C Basquel 1-0 for Mannion, S MacMahon 0-1 for Howard.
Louth: J Califf; D Corcoran, P Lynch, D McKenny; L Grey, N Sharkey, C Murphy; T Durnin, C Early; C McKeever, S Mulroy 0-10 (7f, 1 45), C Grimes 0-2; D McConnon, C Downey 0-1, L Jackson 0-1. **Subs:** C Lennon 0-1 for McConnon, A Williams for Murphy, C McCaul for Jackson, P Matthews for Early, R Burns for Corcoran.
Referee: C Lane (Cork).

THE GAMES: (ABOUT) A DECADE OF THE DUBS

All-Ireland Group 3, Round 1
Sunday, 28 May 2022, Croke Park (attendance 30,802)
Dublin 1-11 Roscommon 0-14
Dublin: S Cluxton; D Newcombe, M Fitzsimons, D Byrne; B Howard, J Small 1-0, L Gannon; B Fenton, J McCarthy; N Scully, S Bugler 0-2, C Kilkenny; P Mannion, C O'Callaghan 0-2, C Costello 0-7 (2f, 2 45). **Subs:** C Murphy for Byrne, C Basquel for Mannion, L O'Dell for Scully, D Rock for Kilkenny, T Lahiff for McCarthy.
Roscommon: C Carroll; C Hussey, B Stack, D Murray; N Daly 0-1, E McCormack, D Ruane; E Nolan, E Smith 0-1; C Murtagh 0-5 (2f), C Lennon 0-2, C McKeon; D Murtagh 0-3 (2f), D Smith 0-1f, B O'Carroll. **Subs:** K Doyle for Lennon, C Daly for Ruane, C Connolly for O'Carroll, C Cox 0-1f for McKeon, R Fallon for Nolan.
Referee: B Cassidy (Derry). Sub: B Cawley (Kildare) for Cassidy ht.

All-Ireland Group 3, Round 2
Saturday, 3 June 2023, Nowlan Park, Kilkenny (attendance 8,216)
Kildare 0-13 Dublin 0-22
Dublin: S Cluxton; D Newcombe, M Fitzsimons, S McMahon; B Howard, J Small, L Gannon; B Fenton 0-1, J McCarthy; N Scully 0-1, S Bugler 0-3, C Basquel 0-5; D Rock 0-4 (2f), C O'Callaghan 0-4, K O'Gara 0-1. **Subs:** P Mannion 0-2 for O'Gara, L O'Dell for Rock, T Lahiff 0-1 for O'Callaghan, C Murphy for Small, G McEneaney for MacMahon.
Kildare: M Donnellan; M O'Grady, S Ryan, E Doyle; D Hyland, K Flynn, J Sargent; K O'Callaghan 0-1, A Masterson 0-1; P McDermott, B McCormack 0-3, A Beirne; N Flynn 0-5 (2f, 1 45), D Kirwan 0-1, P Woodgate 0-1f. **Subs:** R Houlihan for Doyle, T Archbold for Sargent, K Feely 0-1m for Masterson, P Cribbin for McCormack.
Referee: S Hurson (Tyrone).

All-Ireland Group 3, Round 3
Sunday, 18 June 2023, Breffni Park, Cavan
Dublin 3-23 Sligo 0-8
Dublin: S Cluxton; D Newcombe, M Fitzsimons, E Murchan 1-0; B Howard 0-1, J Small 0-1, L Gannon 0-3; B Fenton, J McCarthy; N Scully, S Bugler 0-2, C Basquel 1-3 (0-1f); P Small 0-5 (3f), C O'Callaghan 1-5, C Kilkenny 0-1. **Subs:** T Lahiff for McCarthy, C Murphy for J Small, P Mannion 0-2 for Scully, L O'Dell for O'Callaghan, J McCaffrey for Murchan.
Sligo: A Devaney; L Nicholson, B Cox, E Lyons; L Towey, J Lavin, D Cummins 0-1; C Lally, P Kilcoyne; P McNamara, F Cawley, A Reilly; N Murphy 0-2, S Carrabine 0-4 (2f, 1 45), P Spillane. **Subs:** M Gordon for Towey, G O'Kelly Lynch for Lally, M Walsh for Cummins, P O'Connor 0-1 for Reilly, K Cawley for Lavin.
Referee: N Cullen (Fermanagh).

All-Ireland quarter-final
Sunday, 2 July 2023, Croke Park (attendance 82,300)
Dublin 2-17 Mayo 0-11
Dublin: S Cluxton; D Byrne, M Fitzsimons, L Gannon; J McCarthy 0-1, J Small, E Murchan; B Fenton, B Howard; P Mannion 0-2, S Bugler, N Scully; C Costello 0-5 (3f), C O'Callaghan 0-2, C Basquel 2-2. **Subs:** J McCaffrey for Murchan, C Kilkenny 0-1 for Bugler, P Small 0-1 for Scully, T Lahiff for Costello, D Rock 0-1 for Basquel.
Mayo: C Reape 0-1 45; J Coyne, D McBrien, P O'Hora; P Durcan 0-1, S Coen, E McLaughlin; M Ruane, D O'Connor; S Callinan, J Carney, J Flynn 0-1; A O'Shea 0-1f, T Conroy 0-2, R O'Donoghue 0-5 (2f). **Subs:** E Hession for O'Hora, C O'Connor for O'Shea, K McLoughlin for McLaughlin, J Carr for Ruane, D McHugh for Coen (bs), J Doherty for Callinan.
Referee: D Gough (Meath).

THE GAMES: (ABOUT) A DECADE OF THE DUBS

All-Ireland semi-final
Saturday, 15 July 2023, Croke Park (attendance 82,300)
Dublin 1-17 Monaghan 0-13
Dublin: S Cluxton; E Murchan, M Fitzsimons, D Byrne; J McCarthy, J Small, L Gannon 0-1; B Fenton 0-2, B Howard; P Mannion 0-2 (1f, 1m), P Small 0-1, N Scully; C Costello 0-7 (3f, 1m), C O'Callaghan 0-2, C Basquel. **Subs:** C Kilkenny for Scully, J McCaffrey 0-1 for Basquel, L O'Dell for P Small, D Rock 1-1 (0-1f) for Mannion, T Lahiff for Costello.
Monaghan: R Beggan 0-3 45; D Hughes, K Duffy, R Wylie; K O'Connell, C Boyle, C McCarthy; K Hughes, K Lavelle; S O'Hanlon 0-1, M Bannigan 0-1, R McAnespie 0-1; C McManus 0-5 (3f, 1m), G Mohan 0-1, D Ward. **Subs:** K Gallagher for Ward, J McCarron 0-1 for K Hughes, C Lennon for D Hughes (bs), D Hughes for Lennon, R O'Toole for Boyle, S Jones for McAnespie, Lennon for Lavelle.
Referee: S Hurson (Tyrone).

All-Ireland final
Sunday, 30 July 2023, Croke Park (attendance 82,300)
Dublin 1-15 Kerry 1-13
Dublin: S Cluxton 0-2 (1 45, 1f); E Murchan, M Fitzsimons, D Byrne; J McCarthy, J Small, L Gannon; B Fenton 0-2, B Howard 0-1; P Small 1-1, P Mannion 0-5 (1f), C Kilkenny; C Costello 0-1f, C O'Callaghan, C Basquel 0-2. **Subs:** J McCaffrey for Gannon, N Scully for Costello, S MacMahon for Howard, C Murphy for Murchan, D Rock 0-1 for P Small.
Kerry: S Ryan; G O'Sullivan, J Foley, T O'Sullivan; P Murphy, T Morley, G White; D O'Connor, J Barry; D Moynihan, S O'Shea 0-5 (4f), S O'Brien; P Clifford 0-3, D Clifford 0-3 (1f), P Geaney 1-1. **Subs:** B Ó Beaglaoich for Murphy, A Spillane for Moynihan, M Burns for O'Brien, K Spillane 0-1 for Geaney, M Breen for Barry.
Referee: D Gough (Meath).

2024

Leinster quarter-final
Sunday, 14 April 2024, Croke Park (attendance 21,445)
Dublin 3-19 Meath 0-12
Dublin: S Cluxton; E Murchan, M Fitzsimons, S MacMahon; S Bugler 1-0, J Small 0-2, C Murphy 0-1; T Lahiff, B Howard; R McGarry, C Basquel 0-2, C Kilkenny 0-3; P Mannion 1-6 (0-3f), C O'Callaghan 1-2 (0-1m), N Scully 0-1m. **Subs:** J McCarthy for Basquel, P Small 0-1 for Scully, C Costello 0-1 for Mannion, K McGinnis for McGarry, P Ó Cofaigh Byrne for J Small.
Meath: B Hogan 0-1 45; H O'Higgins, D Keogan, A O'Neill; S Coffey, R Ryan, C Caulfield 0-1; R Jones 0-1m, D McGowan; M Costello 0-1f, D Campion 0-1, C Hickey; E Frayne 0-3 (2f), J Conlon 0-1, J Morris 0-3.
Subs: J O'Connor for Campion, C McBride for McGowan, K Curtis for Morris, R Kinsella for Ryan, A Lynch for Conlon.
Referee: T Murphy (Galway).

Leinster semi-final
Sunday, 28 April 2024, Croke Park (attendance 21,957)
Dublin 3-22 Offaly 0-11
Dublin: S Cluxton; S MacMahon 0-1, M Fitzsimons, E Murchan; J McCarthy, J Small 0-2, C Murphy 0-1; B Fenton 0-1, T Lahiff; C Costello 0-4 (2f), C Kilkenny 0-1, N Scully 1-1; P Mannion 0-3, C O'Callaghan 1-2, C Basquel 1-3 (0-1f). **Subs:** L O'Dell 0-2 for O'Callaghan, K McGinnis 0-1 for Costello, R McGarry for Mannion, D Newcombe for Murchan, T Clancy for McCarthy.
Offaly: I Duffy; L Pearson 0-1, D Dempsey, J Furlong; C Egan, D Hogan, P Cunningham; E Carroll, J McEvoy; D Hyland 0-5 (2f 1 '45), R McNamee, J Hayes 0-1; N Poland, K O'Neill 0-3 (1m), J Bryant. **Subs:** C Flynn 0-1 for McNamee, R Egan for Poland, K McDermott for Bryant, C Donoghue for McEvoy, J O'Brien for O'Neill.
Referee: P Faloon (Down).

THE GAMES: (ABOUT) A DECADE OF THE DUBS

Leinster final
Sunday 12 May 2024, Croke Park (attendance 23,113)
Dublin 1-19 Louth 2-12
Dublin: S Cluxton; C Murphy, M Fitzsimons, E Murchan; T Lahiff 0-1, J Small, S Bugler 0-1; B Fenton 0-3, J McCarthy; C Kilkenny 0-1, C Costello 0-6 (4f), N Scully; P Mannion 0-1, C O'Callaghan 1-4 (1m), C Basquel 0-1. **Subs:** J McCaffrey for Scully, P Small 0-1 for Basquel, B Howard for Lahiff, R McGarry for Bugler, K McGinnis for Mannion.
Louth: N McDonnell; D Corcoran, P Lynch, D McKenny; N Sharkey, A Williams, C McKeever; T Durnin 0-1, B Duffy; C Downey 0-1, C Keenan 1-0, C Grimes 0-4; L Grey, S Mulroy 0-6 (5f), C Lennon 1-0. **Subs:** D Campbell for Sharkey, C Early for Williams, C Byrne for Durnin, R Burns for Keenan, L Jackson for Grey.
Referee: N Mooney (Cavan).

All-Ireland Group Stage, Round 1
Saturday 25 May 2024, Croke Park (attendance 11,176)
Dublin 2-19 Roscommon 0-13
Dublin: S Cluxton; S MacMahon, E Murchan, M Fitzsimons; B Howard, C Murphy 0-2, J Small 0-1; B Fenton 0-2, T Lahiff 0-1; R McGarry 0-2, C Costello 0-2f, C Kilkenny; P Mannion 0-2, C O'Callaghan 1-4, N Scully 0-2. **Subs:** S Bugler 0-1 for Mannion, J McCaffrey for Lahiff, C Basquel 1-0 for Scully, P Small for McGarry, T Clancy for Murphy.
Roscommon: C Carroll; R Dolan, B Stack, D Murray; N Higgins, N Daly, E McCormack; E Smith, T O'Rourke; D Ruane, D Smith, C Lennon; D Murtagh 0-5 (2f), D Cregg 0-4 (1f), C Cox 0-4 (1f). **Subs:** S Cunnane for O'Rourke, U Harney for D Smith, R Fallon for Daly, B O'Carroll for Ruane, K Doyle for Cox.

All-Ireland Group Stage, Round 2
Saturday 1 June 2024, Breffni Park (attendance 9,028)
Cavan 0-13 Dublin 5-17
Cavan: L Brady 0-1 45; C Reilly, K Brady, L Fortune; P Faulkner, N Carolan, O Kiernan; C Brady, B O'Connell; O Kiernan, C Madden 0-2, G Smith 0-1; R O'Neill, J Smith 0-1, O Brady 0-7 (4f). **Subs:** M Magee for Reilly, M Meade for Brady, T Madden for Kiernan, R Brady for Kiernan, D Lovett for O'Neill.
Dublin: S Cluxton; E Murchan, M Fitzsimons, D Newcombe; B Howard, J Small, S Bugler 1-1; B Fenton 0-3, K McGinnis 1-0; N Scully 0-1, C Costello 2-5 1-0 pen, 1 45, C Kilkenny; P Mannion 0-2f, C O'Callaghan, P Small 0-2. **Subs:** C Basquel 0-3 for O'Callaghan, T Clancy for Murchan, L O'Dell for J Small, P Ó Cofaigh-Byrne for Fenton, G McEneaney for P Small.

All-Ireland Group Stage, Round 3
Sunday 16 June 2024, Dr Hyde Park (attendance 16,870)
Dublin 0-17 Mayo 0-17
Dublin: S Cluxton; E Murchan, M Fitzsimons, S McMahon; B Howard, J Small, S Bugler 0-1; B Fenton, T Lahiff, N Scully 0-1, C Costello 0-7 (3f), C Kilkenny 0-1; P Small 0-1, C O'Callaghan 0-1, C Basquel 0-2. Subs: K McGinnis for Lahiff, J McCaffrey 0-1 for Scully, P Mannion for P Small, R McGarry for McGinnis, J McCarthy for Bugler.
Mayo: C Reape 0-1 '45; J Coyne, D McBrien, R Brickendenc; S Callinan, S Coen 0-1, E McLaughlin; J Carney, M Ruane 0-2; D McHugh, D McHale, J Flynn 0-1; A O'Shea 0-1f, T Conroy 0-3, R O'Donoghue 0-7 (5f). Subs: C Loftus 0-1 for McLaughlin, C O'Connor for McHale, D O'Connor for Coen, B Tuohy for Ruane, P Towey for Carney.
Referee: M McNally (Roscommon)

THE GAMES: (ABOUT) A DECADE OF THE DUBS

All-Ireland quarter-final
Saturday 29 June 2024, Croke Park (attendance 49,896)
Dublin 0-16 Galway 0-17
Dublin: S Cluxton; E Murchan, S MacMahon, M Fitzsimons; J Small 0-1m, B Howard, J McCaffrey; B Fenton 0-1, J McCarthy; N Scully, S Bugler 0-2, C Kilkenny 0-2; P Mannion 0-1, C O'Callaghan 0-4 (2m,1f). C Costello 0-4 (2f), 1 45. Subs: C Basquel for Mannion, R McGarry 0-1 for Scully, T Lahiff for McCaffrey, P Small for Costello, L O'Dell for Murchan.
Galway: C Gleeson; J McGrath, S Fitzgerald, J Glynn; D McHugh 0-1, L Silke, S Mulkerrin; P Conroy 0-1, S Kelly; M Tierney 0-1m, J Maher 0-1, C McDaid 0-3; R Finnerty, D Comer, S Walsh 0-7 (4f). Subs: C Darcy 0-1 for Kelly, L O Conghaile for Finnerty, J Heaney 0-1 for Tierney, C Hernon for Fitzgerald, T Culhane 0-1 for Walsh.
Referee: Sean Hurson

* * *

Dublin in National League 2013–2024

2013 Played 9, Won 7, Drew 1, Lost 1
Rd1: Dublin 1-18 Cork 2-9; Rd2: Derry 0-4 Dublin 1-11; Rd3: Dublin 2-14 Mayo 0-16; Rd4: Dublin 2-20 Kildare 2-9; Rd5: Dublin 1-14 Tyrone 0-18; Rd6: Dublin 1-15 Down 0-9; Rd7: Donegal 1-10 Dublin 0-13; Semi-final: Dublin 2-16 Mayo 0-16; Final: Dublin 0-18 Tyrone 0-17 (Dublin's ninth NFL title).

2014 Played 9, Won 6, Drew 1, Lost 2
Rd1: Dublin 2-8 Kerry 1-10; Rd2: Westmeath 1-7 Dublin 0-14; Rd3: Dublin 0-18 Cork 1-17; Rd4: Dublin 1-22 Kildare 0-12; Rd5: Derry 1-16 Dublin 0-13; Rd6: Dublin 3-14 Mayo 2-17; Rd7: Tyrone 1-15 Dublin 3-10; Semi-final: Cork 2-13 Dublin 2-20; Final: Dublin 3-19 Derry 1-10 (Dublin's 10th NFL title).

2015 Played 9, Won 6, Drew 1, Lost 2
Rd1: Cork 1-15 Dublin 0-16; Rd2: Dublin 2-10 Donegal 0-11; Rd3: Kerry 0-15 Dublin 1-10; Rd4: Dublin 1-9 Tyrone 0-12; Rd5: Mayo 0-10 Dublin 2-18; Rd6: Dublin 0-8 Derry 0-4; Rd7: Monaghan 1-11 Dublin 1-22; Semi-final: Dublin 0-17 Monaghan 0-16; Final: Dublin 1-21 Cork 2-7 (Dublin's 11th NFL title).

2016 Played 9, Won 9, Drew 0, Lost 0
Rd1: Dublin 2-14 Kerry 0-14; Rd2: Mayo 0-7 Dublin 0-9; Rd3: Dublin 1-14 Monaghan 0-16; Rd4: Dublin 2-14 Cork 2-10; Rd5: Down 1-7 Dublin 1-15; Rd6: Dublin 1-10 Donegal 1-7; Rd7: Roscommon 1-12 Dublin 1-13; Semi-final: Dublin 1-20 Donegal 0-13; Final: Dublin 2-18 Kerry 0-13 (Dublin's 12th NFL title).

2017 Played 8, Won 4, Drew 3, Lost 1
Rd1: Cavan 0-11 Dublin 0-18; Rd2: Dublin 0-10 Tyrone 1-7; Rd3: Donegal 2-5 Dublin 1-8; Rd4: Dublin 1-16 Mayo 0-7; Rd5: Kerry 0-13 Dublin 0-13; Rd6: Dublin 2-29 Roscommon 0-14; Rd7: Monaghan 1-15 Dublin 2-15; Final: Kerry 0-20 Dublin 1-16.

2018 Played 8, Won 6, Drew 1, Lost 1
Rd1: Dublin 2-17 Kildare 2-10; Rd2: Tyrone 1-11 Dublin 2-13; Rd3: Dublin 0-20 Donegal 0-15; Rd4: Mayo 0-12 Dublin 2-10; Rd5: Dublin 2-17 Kerry

0-11; Rd6: Galway 0-13 Dublin 0-13; Rd7: Dublin 0-17 Monaghan 2-12; Final: Dublin 0-18 Galway 0-14 (Dublin's 13th NFL title).

2019 Played 7, Won 4, Drew 0, Lost 3

Rd1: Monaghan 2-13 Dublin 1-13; Rd2: Dublin 1-15 Galway 0-7; Rd3: Kerry 1-18 Dublin 2-14; Rd4: Dublin 1-12 Mayo 0-7; Rd5: Roscommon 1-12 Dublin 2-14; Rd6: Dublin 1-11 Tyrone 1-14; Rd7: Cavan 1-10 Dublin 1-16.

2020 Played 7, Won 4, Drew 2, Lost 1

Rd1: Dublin 1-19 Kerry 1-19; Rd2: Mayo 0-8 Dublin 1-11; Rd3: Dublin 1-15 Monaghan 1-15; Rd4: Dublin 1-15 Donegal 1-14; Rd5: Tyrone 1-10 Dublin 1-7; Rd6: Dublin 1-20 Meath 0-19; Rd7: Galway 0-15 Dublin 2-15.

2021 Played 4, Won 3, Drew 1, Lost 0

Rd1: Roscommon 0-16 Dublin 1-22; Rd2: Dublin 4-9 Kerry 1-18; Rd3: Galway 1-15 Dublin 2-16; Final: Donegal 1-14 Dublin 1-18 (Dublin's 14th NFL title, split with Kerry).

2022 Played 7, Won 2, Drew 0, Lost 5

Rd1: Dublin 1-13 Armagh 2-15; Rd2: Kerry 1-15 Dublin 0-11; Rd3: Dublin 0-12 Mayo 2-11; Rd4: Kildare 1-12 Dublin 0-12; Rd5: Tyrone 0-8 Dublin 0-13; Rd6: Dublin 2-15 Donegal 2-11; Rd7: Monaghan 3-13 Dublin 1-18 (Dublin relegated to Div2).

2023 Div2: Played 8, Won 7, Drew 0, Lost 1

Rd1: Dublin 1-11 Kildare 0-13; Rd2: Limerick 1-11 Dublin 2-17; Rd3: Cork 2-10 Dublin 0-18; Rd4: Dublin 0-16 Clare 1-12; Rd5: Derry 1-11 Dublin 0-13; Rd6: Meath 1-11 Dublin 2-19; Rd7: Dublin 0-16 Louth 1-6; Final: Dublin 4-6 Derry 0-11 (Dublin win NFL Div2).

2024 Div 1: Played 8, Won 5, Drew 0, Lost 3

Rd1: Dublin 1-14 Monaghan 3-9; Rd2: Mayo 1-12 Dublin 0-14; Rd3: Dublin 1-19 Roscommon 1-12; Rd4: Dublin 3-18 Kerry 1-14; Rd5: Derry 1-11 Dublin 1-16; Rd6: Galway 0-14 Dublin 0-22; Rd7: Dublin 5-18 Tyrone 0-12. Final: Dublin 2-21 Derry 3-18 AET (Derry win on pens)

Overall NFL Record, 2013–2024:
Played 93, Won 63, Drew 10, Lost 20

* * *

'Streak' All Star Awards 2015–2021

2015 (7): Rory O'Carroll, Philly McMahon, Cian O'Sullivan, Jack McCaffrey (Footballer of the Year), Brian Fenton, Ciarán Kilkenny, Bernard Brogan.

2016 (6): Jonny Cooper, Philly McMahon, Brian Fenton, Diarmuid Connolly, Ciarán Kilkenny, Dean Rock.

2017 (7): Michael Fitzsimons, Cian O'Sullivan, Jack McCaffrey, James McCarthy, Con O'Callaghan, Paul Mannion, Dean Rock.

2018 (7): Jonny Cooper, James McCarthy, Jack McCaffrey, Brian Fenton (Footballer of the Year), Brian Howard, Paul Mannion, Ciarán Kilkenny.

2019 (7): Stephen Cluxton (Footballer of the Year), Michael Fitzsimons, Brian Howard, Jack McCaffrey, Brian Fenton, Paul Mannion, Con O'Callaghan.

2020: (9): Michael Fitzsimons, James McCarthy, John Small, Eoin Murchan, Brian Fenton (Footballer of Year), Niall Scully, Ciarán Kilkenny, Con O'Callaghan, Dean Rock.

2021 (1): Ciarán Kilkenny.

* * *

Index

Abbeylara GAA club, 114
All-Ireland camogie championship, 241
All-Ireland club championship, 28, 64–5, 74, 110
All-Ireland ladies' football championship, 94, 161, 182, 228, 240
All-Ireland minor football championship, 46–7, 103
All-Ireland senior football championship
   quarter-finals/super 8s
      2009, 74, 208, 229
      2014, 20
      2015, 37–8
      2016, 61–3, 66
      2017, 84–90
      2018, 105–6, 116–23, 242
      2019, 135, 142–9, 242
      2022, 213–14
      2023, 224–5
      2024, 220, 229–30, 231
   semi-finals
      1977, 127
      1994, 124
      2002, 99
      2006, 201
      2007, 74
      2011, 79
      2012, 200
      2013, 74, 86
      2014, 17–25, 38, 44, 50, 156, 206
      2015, 38–45, 79
      2016, 63–6, 74
      2017, 90–3
      2018, 123–4
      2019, 149–53
      2020, 175–9
      2021, 195–204
      2022, 214
      2023, 225–6
      2024, 230
   finals
      1951, 196–7
      1992, 150
      1995, 207–8
      2004, 180
      2006, 180
      2020, 230
      2011, 32–3
      2013, 21, 88, 180, 205
      2014, 46, 61
      2015, 46–9
      2016, 66–72, 242
      2017, 50, 78, 94–103, 235–6
      2018, 125–31
      2019, 153–63
      2021, 204
      2022, 214–15
      2023, 28, 226–29
      2024, 230
All-Ireland senior hurling championship, 87, 241
All-Ireland U-20 football championship, 75, 223
All-Ireland U-21 football championship, 75, 119, 164, 166, 223
All Stars, 48, 72, 74, 57, 99, 103, 104, 109, 130–1, 132, 163, 172, 182, 198, 228
Andrews, Paddy, 21, 23, 45, 51, 59, 62, 70, 89, 107, 154, 190, 235, 244
Andrews, Peadar, 140, 141
Armagh senior football team, 20, 84, 93, 99, 114, 221, 230
Aughrim, 107
Austin Stack Park, 73
Australia, 34, 226–7

Ballina GAA club, 224
Ballina Herald, 196–7
Ballyboden St Enda's GAA club, 104, 152, 172
Ballymun Kickhams GAA club, 28, 107, 147, 160, 172, 180, 192–3
Barr, Keith, 32, 150
Barrett, Chris, 99, 237, 239
Barry, Jack, 154
basketball, 47
Basquel, Colm, 52, 75, 104–5, 110, 114, 119, 220, 222, 224–5
Basquel, Ryan, 190, 193
Bastick, Denis, 39, 40, 42, 109
Bealin, Paul, 140, 150
Becton, Gavan, 142
Beggan, Rory, 238–39
Beijing Sinobo Guoan FC, 61
Bernard Brogan Podcast, 168
Bogue, Declan, 87
Bohan, Mick, 94, 161, 182
Bonner, Declan, 118, 119, 144
Boston, 110, 111, 125, 145
Boston senior football championship, 125
Boyle, Colm, 40–1, 42, 67, 95, 96–7, 237, 239
Boyle, Donnchadh, 20–1, 136
Boyle, Marty, 79
Brady, David, 183
Brady, Tomás, 39
Branagan, Ciarán, 79, 112
Brannigan, Eamonn, 124
Breaffy GAA club, 180
Breffni Park, 187, 222, 231
Brennan, Ger, 33, 220, 223
Brennan, John, 61
Brennan, Paul, 75
Britain, 61
Brogan, Alan, 17, 23, 28–9, 30, 37–8, 40, 45, 47–8, 51, 53, 72, 122, 127, 210
Brogan, Bernard, 29, 31–2, 35, 39, 45, 47–8, 56, 57, 58, 63–5, 67, 69–70, 71–2, 78, 81, 88, 93, 97, 98, 102, 106–7, 110, 111, 122–3, 125–30, 132, 149, 154, 162–3, 168, 177, 206, 211, 234–6, 243
Brogan, Bernard Snr., 127
Brogan, Jim, 128
Brolly, Joe, 46–7, 101–2, 116, 157–9, 174, 202, 220
Brophy, Paddy, 83
Bugler, Seán, 182, 190, 219, 222
Burns, Jarlath, 165, 230–1
Byrne, David, 52, 70, 108, 140, 199, 222, 234

Caffrey, Leah, 228
Caffrey, Paul 'Pillar', 146–7, 167
Cahill, Barry, 209
Cahill, Des, 28
Callinan, Sam, 224
camogie, 241
Canavan, Peter, 59
Canning, Ger, 67
Canning, Joe, 85
Cantwell, Joanne, 158
Carlow senior football team, 76–9, 113
Carr, Tommy, 63, 208
Carthy, Shane, 81
Cassidy, Kevin, 87, 92
Castlebar, 39, 94, 107, 144, 168
Castleknock GAA club, 145, 172
Cavan senior football team, 115, 116, 174, 175–9, 231
Cavanagh, Colm, 130
Cavanagh, Sean, 91–2, 234
Central Appeals Commitee, 44
Central Competitions Committee, 81
Central Hearings Committee, 44
Charlotte Independence FC, 61
China, 61
Clare senior football team, 83–4, 86, 94, 188
Clarke, David, 67, 70–1, 95, 100, 180, 200

INDEX

Clarke, Jamie, 221
Clarke, Paul, 104–5, 109
Clerkin, Dick, 137
Clifford, David, 46–7, 153, 157–9, 161, 168, 186, 214, 227, 228, 229, 237, 238–39
Clifford, Paudie, 237
Clones, 58–9, 74, 135
Clontarf GAA club, 143, 244
Cluxton, Stephen, 18, 20, 30, 31, 37, 40, 41–2, 65, 76, 83, 86–8, 91–2, 102, 107, 113–14, 115, 124, 129, 137, 140–1, 151, 157, 162, 163, 187, 188–90, 191, 193, 215–16, 219, 227, 229, 233–6, 241, 243
Cody, Brian, 106, 241
Coen, Darren, 182
Comer, Damien, 229–30
Comerford, Evan, 75, 113, 119, 187, 189, 192–3
Community Sports Engagement, 210
Competitions Control Committee, 44
Connacht senior football championship, 59, 70, 84, 116, 144, 175
Connacht Tribune, 203
Connellan, Ray, 172
Connelly, Noel, 38, 54
Connerton, Denis, 113, 114
Connerton, Liam, 114
Connolly, Diarmuid, 17–18, 22, 29, 31–2, 34, 42, 44, 48, 51, 53, 56, 57, 59, 61, 62, 65, 67–9, 71, 72, 79–81, 88, 93, 97–8, 100–1, 107, 109, 110, 111, 125, 136–7, 144–7, 148, 154, 159, 161–2, 177, 233–6, 243
Connolly, Luke, 238
Connolly, Mike, 135
Cooper, Colm 'The Gooch', 63–5, 74–5, 86, 112, 237
Cooper, Jonny, 72, 78, 90–1, 108, 112, 129, 131, 144, 148, 152, 157–9, 173, 193, 233–6, 241

Cork ladies football team, 182, 240
Cork senior football team, 19, 26, 29, 84, 94, 142–7, 172, 175, 213–14, 230, 238
Cork senior hurling team, 87, 139
Corrigan, Thomas, 37
Cosgrove, Ray, 99, 150
Costello, Cormac, 17–18, 27, 37, 119, 122, 123–4, 130, 134, 137, 138, 154, 159, 162, 186, 187, 190, 191, 193, 213, 220, 222, 224–5, 231, 235–6, 244
Costello, John, 164
Covid pandemic, 169, 184–5, 187
Cribbin, Keith, 83
Cribbin, Paul, 33–4, 194–5
Cribbin, Tom, 59, 81
Croke Park, 17, 27, 30–49, 57–72, 74, 75, 80–103, 106–7, 108, 110, 113–31, 134–5, 137–63, 168, 173–82, 185, 190–204, 216–21, 229, 231
Crossmaglen GAA club, 221
Crowley, Peter, 65, 155
Cuala GAA club, 56, 82, 91, 95, 182, 214, 241
Culhane, Tomo, 229
Cullen, Bryan, 32–3
Cunningham, Anthony, 147
Curran, Paul, 28, 35
Curtis, Roy, 111, 125, 140, 147, 198

Daly, Darren, 63, 109, 130, 243
Darby, Seamus, 241
Darcy, Declan, 24
'Decades of the Dubs' series, 69, 103, 205–7, 209
Delaney, Rory, 56
Devenney, Brendan, 20–2, 23, 24
Derry minor football team, 103
Derry senior football team, 20, 29, 57, 74, 84, 94, 220, 225, 226, 230–1
Dillon, Alan, 67
Dingle GAA club, 65

291

Disputes Resolution Authority (DRA), 44–5, 79
Dr Crokes GAA club, 74
Dr Cullen Park, 79
Dr Hyde Park, 186, 231
Dolan, Dessie, 40, 96, 97, 98, 193
Donaghy, Kieran, 46–7
Donegal Boston GAA club, 125, 145
Donegal senior football team, 17–25, 27, 50, 58–9, 61–3, 79, 84, 87, 106–7, 116, 117–20, 135, 144, 150, 156, 168, 175, 187, 206, 239, 244
Dowd, Tommy, 140
Down senior football team, 53, 84, 93, 230
Doyle, Johnny, 216
Dublin camogie team, 241
Dublin City University (DCU) GAA club, 28, 52
Dublin club championship, 107, 145, 152
Dublin County Board, 164, 165
Dublin ladies football team, 94, 161, 182, 228
Dublin masters football team, 141
Dublin minor football team, 223
Dublin U-21 football team, 75, 119–20, 164, 166, 223
Dubs TV, 144–5
Duffy, Joe, 20, 185
Dungiven, 57
Durcan, Paddy, 45, 71, 97, 151, 237
Durcan, Paul 'Papa', 18, 22

Earley, Dermot, 216, 218, 219
Ennis, 94, 188
Enniscorthy, 105
Enniskillen, 116
Enright, Shane, 154
Evans, John, 112–13
Evening Herald, 33, 35, 69, 81, 103, 145, 186, 188, 205–7, 209, 246

Fanning, Dion, 220
Farrell, Dessie, 75, 145, 164, 166–7, 184–5, 189, 190–1, 212–13, 215, 229, 231–2, 240
Feely, Kevin, 83
Fennin, Tadhg, 218, 219
Fenton, Brian, 47, 48, 61, 67, 72, 109–10, 111, 131, 137, 143, 151–2, 163, 171, 173, 174, 177, 179, 182, 213, 214, 225, 227, 229, 233–4, 236, 241, 243
Fermanagh senior football team, 37–8, 60, 119
Fermanagh Herald, 37
Fingal Ravens GAA club, 243
Fingallians GAA club, 102, 132, 234
Fitzgerald, Maurice, 63, 186
Fitzgerald Stadium, 144
Fitzmaurice, Éamonn, 48, 75, 155, 158
Fitzsimons, Michael, 52, 65–6, 70, 103, 107, 130, 157, 163, 182, 227, 228–29, 233–6, 241–2
Flanagan, Ger, 135
Flynn, Daniel, 192–3
Flynn, Jordan, 168
Flynn, Paul, 37–8, 41, 53, 57, 64, 69, 70, 93, 97, 102–3, 119, 130, 132, 177, 205–7, 211, 233–6, 246
Fogarty, John, 221
Foley, Darragh, 78
Football Review Committee, 165
Footballer of the Year award, 26–7, 48, 63, 66, 72, 94, 163, 182, 210, 228
Free State podcast, 220
Freeman, Alan, 42, 43

Gaelic Grounds, 116
Gaelic Life, 92
Gaelic Players Association, 132–3
Gallagher, Rory, 61–2, 220
Galvin, Mick, 186, 187
Galway senior football team, 59, 70, 75, 84–5, 94, 108–9, 110, 116,

INDEX

123–4, 134, 170, 187, 214, 226, 229–30
Galway senior hurling team, 85
Game On, 167
Gartland, Niall, 120
Gavin, Darren, 144, 242
Gavin, Jim, 17, 19–21, 23–7, 31, 32, 48–9, 52–3, 59, 62, 69, 70, 76, 79–83, 86–8, 89, 90, 100, 104, 106, 108–9, 112, 121–3, 125–30, 136–9, 144–7, 148–9, 154, 156, 159, 162–5, 166, 195, 206–8, 235
Geaney, Paul, 48, 65, 73, 75, 153, 157, 161, 227, 238–39
Geraghty, Graham, 140
Giles, Trevor, 140
Gilroy, Pat, 28, 32, 165, 167, 208–10, 216, 220
Glasgow Celtic FC, 61
Glenbeigh-Glencar GAA club, 65
Gough, David, 65–6, 155–6, 157–9
Graham, Mickey, 176
Griffin, Tony, 214–15

Handy, Niall, 55–6
Harte, Mickey, 54, 59, 90, 116, 219–20
Harte, Peter, 239
Healy Park, 148–9, 168, 242
Heery, Eamonn, 207–8
Heffernan, Kevin, 49, 128
Hennelly, Rob, 70, 150–1, 198, 199
Henry, David, 109–10
Heslin, John, 35–6, 52, 60, 81–2, 171, 228, 238
Hickey, David, 209
Higgins, Keith, 41, 200
Hogan, Vincent, 20, 71, 85, 86–8, 179–80, 203
Hogan Cup, 223
Holmes, Pat, 38, 54
Horan, James, 38, 133–4, 150, 152–3, 179, 198, 201, 214
Howard, Brian, 75, 104–5, 109–10, 119, 124, 131, 154, 163, 182, 213, 236
Hurley, Brian, 238
hurling, 55, 85, 87, 106, 139, 241, 242

Irish Examiner, 124, 155, 221
Irish Independent, 20–1, 24–5, 31, 33, 54, 59, 68, 71, 77, 80–1, 83, 85, 86, 108, 111, 124, 136, 137, 149, 155, 156, 161, 179–80, 184–5, 186, 203, 210–11, 218, 224, 229
Irish News, 77
Irish Times, 196–7

Japan, 191
Johnstownbridge GAA club, 194
Joyce, Pádraig, 170, 229, 231

Kavanagh, Gerry, 56
Keane, Mark, 172
Keane, Peter, 153, 185
Kearns, Eoin, 173
Keaveney, Jimmy, 27–8
Keegan, Lee, 41, 42, 44, 66, 67, 71, 95, 97–8, 100–1, 134, 150, 151–2, 200–1, 237, 239
Kelly, Seán, 229
Kennedy, Martin, 54
Kernan, Joe, 99
Kerry ladies football team, 94, 228, 240
Kerry minor football team, 46–7, 103
Kerry senior football team, 23, 28, 33, 38, 44, 46–9, 51–2, 53–4, 59, 61, 63–6, 73–5, 83–4, 86, 92, 94, 108, 115, 127, 133, 135, 136, 139, 143, 144, 153–63, 167–8, 172, 175, 185, 186, 187, 204, 208, 214–15, 225–8, 230, 237–39, 241, 244
Kerryman, 75
Keys, Colm, 31, 54, 108, 124, 197, 203, 212
Kiely, John, 87, 241
Kildare County Board, 115–16
Kildare minor football team, 223

Kildare senior football team, 30, 31–4, 60, 78, 82–4, 106, 114, 115–16, 137–9, 173, 176, 188, 192–5, 213, 216–19, 222–3, 242
Kilkenny, Ciarán, 35, 48, 56, 68, 78, 81, 91, 101, 106, 108, 110, 111, 123, 130, 131, 143, 145, 151–2, 154, 160, 162, 172, 173, 174, 179, 181, 182, 191, 193, 198, 200, 213, 214, 222, 233, 235, 236, 241, 243
Kilkenny senior hurling team, 106, 139, 241
Kilkerrin-Clonberne GAA club, 110
Killarney, 39, 74
Kilmacud Crokes GAA club, 48, 62, 110, 114, 136, 152, 176, 242

Lacey, Brian, 216
Lahiff, Tom, 172
Lancaster, Stuart, 121–2
Laois County Board, 55–6
Laois senior football team, 20, 30, 55–6, 115–18, 173, 215–16, 223, 244
Lavin, Colm, 186
Leinster club championship, 28, 107
Leinster Express, 56
Leinster GAA Council, 117
Leinster minor football championship, 223
Leinster rugby team, 121–2
Leinster senior football championship
    1944, 78
    1991, 30, 140
    1997, 140
    1999, 140
    2000, 218, 219
    2001, 141
    2002, 30
    2003, 30
    2004, 30, 113–14
    2005, 30
    2009, 34
    2010, 30
    2013, 31
    2014, 20, 27
    2015, 30–6, 242
    2016, 55–60
    2017, 76–84
    2018, 78, 111–18
    2019, 136–42, 219, 242
    2020, 170–4
    2021, 188–95, 242
    2022, 213
    2023, 215–20
    2024, 223, 231
Leitrim senior football team, 79, 124
Lillis, Mick, 56
Limerick, 94
Limerick senior football team, 116
Limerick senior hurling team, 87, 241
Liston, Bomber, 108
London senior football team, 70, 77, 79
Longford senior football team, 30–1, 105, 113–14, 137, 167, 238
Loughnane, Ger, 86
Louth senior football team, 76, 136–7, 216, 219–20, 223, 231, 242
Lowndes, Eric, 40, 53, 54, 59, 93, 243
Lucan Sarsfields GAA club, 242
Lynch, Fergal, 57
Lyons, Tommy, 30, 81, 215
Lyster, Michael, 129

Macauley, Michael Darragh, 40, 45, 58, 70, 93, 130, 137, 143, 162, 171, 190, 235–6, 243–4
McBrearty, Paddy, 119
McCaffrey, Jack, 26–7, 31, 35, 38, 39, 40, 48, 51–3, 102, 103, 119, 124, 131, 143–4, 145, 151, 157, 159, 162, 163, 168, 177, 178, 215–16, 222, 229, 233–6, 244
McCarthy, James, 41, 43, 47, 54, 98, 100, 103, 120, 131, 144, 148, 171, 180, 182, 192–3, 200, 214, 215, 219, 224, 227, 229, 233–6, 243

INDEX

McCarthy, Ronan, 143
McConville, Oisin, 124
McCoy, Niall, 99
McDaid, Robbie, 52, 144, 172, 178, 181
McDonald, Ciaran, 180
McEntee, Andy, 142
McGee, Neil, 51, 63
McGill, Gerry, 240
McGinley, Mark Anthony, 62
McGivney, James, 113
McGoldrick, Sean, 118
McGrane, Paul, 99
McGrath, Pat, 18
McGrath, Pete, 37
McGuinness, Jim, 17, 19, 20, 22, 61, 76, 87, 117, 170
MacHale Park, 59, 60, 107
McHugh, Barry, 108
McHugh, Conor, 73
McHugh, Ryan, 18, 62, 119
McIntyre, John, 203
McIver, Brian, 20
McKenna Cup, 220
McKeon, Conor, 33, 103, 142–3, 156, 205–6, 218
McLaughlin, Eoghan, 198
McLoughlin, Kevin, 42, 67, 98, 116, 199, 200
McMahon, Philly, 25, 40, 41, 43, 45, 48, 52, 53–4, 72, 129, 131, 137, 154, 162, 200, 210–11, 218, 224, 233–6, 237, 244
McMahon, Seán, 75, 104–5
McManamon, Kevin, 37, 45, 56, 58, 65, 78, 81, 97, 99, 124, 130, 154, 155, 162, 190–1, 220, 234–6, 243
McManus, Conor, 237
McNamee, Ronan, 91, 239
McQuillan, Joe, 42, 98
McShane, Cathal, 237
McStay, Kevin, 18, 38–9, 151, 225, 226
Madden, Conor, 176–9
Magee, Jonny, 33

Magill magazine, 211
Maloney, Darragh, 41
Mannion, Paul, 52, 56, 62, 70, 73–5, 81, 89, 93, 98, 103, 107, 110, 114–15, 129, 131, 137, 138, 145, 151–2, 154, 161–3, 172, 182, 190, 191, 215–16, 219, 222, 224–5, 229, 234–6
Mayo County Board, 134–5
Mayo International Supporters' Foundation, 134
Mayo News, 134–5
Mayo senior football team, 23, 38–45, 52, 54–5, 59, 60, 62, 66–72, 78, 79, 84–5, 92, 94–103, 107, 115–16, 133–5, 137, 144, 149–53, 168, 175, 179–83, 187–8, 195–204, 214, 224–5, 226, 230, 231, 235, 237–39, 242, 244
Meath senior football team, 20, 30–1, 57–8, 105, 139–42, 144, 170, 173–4, 190–2, 194, 196–7, 213, 231, 242
Meath Chronicle, 57, 142, 197
Miller, Liam, 121
Monaghan senior football team, 20, 61, 74, 79, 84–90, 109, 124, 135, 168, 212, 225–6, 230–1, 238–39
Moran, Andy, 40, 41–2, 43, 67, 94, 95, 98, 238–39
Moran, Barry, 42
Moran, David, 158, 160, 239
Moran, Kevin, 136
Morgan, Niall, 91, 129–30, 238
Morning Ireland, 102
Morrissey, Marty, 62
Mortimer, Conor, 180
Mullally, Conor, 52, 242
Mullin, Oisin, 239
Mullinalaghta GAA club, 176
Mullins, Brian, 107, 211, 234
Munster senior football championship, 59, 83–4, 115, 143, 172, 174, 175

295

Murchan, Eoin, 75, 109, 110, 119, 120, 124, 130, 144, 154, 160, 161, 182, 222
Murphy, Brendan, 77–8
Murphy, Brian, 113
Murphy, Cian, 75, 242
Murphy, Michael, 239
Murphy, Ollie, 140–1
Murtagh, Diarmuid, 237–8

Na Fianna GAA club, 39, 73, 109, 112, 130, 157, 161, 164, 166, 187, 193
Naas CBS GAA club, 223
National League
   2013, 27
   2014, 19–20, 27, 29, 156
   2015, 26–9, 39, 156
   2016, 50–5
   2017, 73–5
   2018, 106–11
   2019, 132–5
   2020, 167–70, 176
   2021, 184–8
   2022, 212–13
   2023, 216
   2024, 220, 223
New York, 197
New Zealand, 48, 51
Newbridge, 176
Ní Chuilinn, Evanne, 166
Ní Mhuircheartaigh, Louise, 228
Nowlan Park, 55–6, 217–18, 222

O'Brien, Ross, 111–12
O'Brien, Stephen, 153, 162
O'Byrne Cup, 104–5, 167, 226
O'Callaghan, Con, 56, 57, 75, 82–3, 91, 93, 95, 103, 111, 119, 123–4, 137, 143–4, 150, 151–2, 154, 157, 162, 163, 179, 180–2, 186, 187, 191, 213–14, 222, 233–6, 242–3
O'Carroll, Rory, 48, 51, 53, 136
Ó Ceallaigh, Seán Andy, 108
Ó Cofaigh-Byrne, Peadar, 190
Ó Conghaile, Emmett, 242
O'Connor, Cian, 242
O'Connor, Cillian, 40, 42, 68, 71, 94, 96, 99, 107, 152, 181, 188, 200, 237, 239
O'Connor, Diarmuid, 94, 199
O'Connor, Jack, 192, 214–15, 227–8
O'Connor, Turlough, 76
O'Donoghue, Ryan, 181
O'Dwyer, Mick, 30, 155
Ó Fearghail, Aogán, 44–5
Offaly senior football team, 104, 231, 241
O'Gara, Eoghan, 57–8, 61, 73, 81, 93, 99, 106, 108, 122, 149, 163, 235, 243, 244
O'Gara, Killian, 104, 226
O'Hehir, Michael, 127, 161
Olympic Games, 169, 191
Omagh, 106, 120–1, 148–9, 168, 170
O'Moore Park, 55, 76–9, 111–13, 136–7, 170–2, 215–16
O'Neill, Cian, 83, 106, 116
O'Neill, Pat, 207
O'Rourke, Colm, 80, 138–9, 140, 141–2, 168, 202
Ó Sé, Darragh, 234
Ó Sé, Marc, 83
Ó Sé, Páidí, 81, 113
Ó Sé, Tomás, 80–1, 83, 119, 155, 180, 191
O'Shea, Aidan, 41, 42, 68, 96, 180, 198, 200
O'Shea, Conor, 199
O'Shea, Jack, 234
O'Shea, Seánie, 153, 159, 214, 237, 239
O'Sullivan, Cian, 27, 32–3, 48, 103, 148, 154, 156, 162, 234, 236
O'Sullivan, Darran, 65
O'Toole, Anton, 136
O'Toole, Kevin, 134

INDEX

Páirc Tailteann, 156
Páirc Uí Chaoimh, 121, 143, 175
Parnell Park, 88, 135, 152, 170, 173
Parnells GAA club, 65, 113, 189
Parsons, Tom, 42, 98
Patton, Shaun, 187
Pearse Park, 114, 167
Pearse Stadium, 108
Poacher, Steven, 76–7, 97
Portumna GAA club, 85

Quigley, Sean, 37
Quinlivan, Michael, 175
Quinn, Darren, 238
Quinn, Tomás 'Mossy', 30
Quirke, Mike, 173

Raheny GAA club, 109–10, 152, 174
Rainbow, Anthony, 216
Rathnew GAA club, 107
Reape, Colm, 224
Redmond, Charlie, 125, 136, 150
Reilly, Dermot, 197
Riley, Pat, 127
Robinson, Jack, 216
Roche, Frank, 224
Rochford, Stephen, 54, 69, 70, 94, 116, 133–4
Rock, Dean, 26, 27–9, 31, 50, 55–7, 58, 62, 65, 67, 72, 73, 75, 78, 82, 89, 95–6, 98, 100, 103, 107, 111, 114, 129, 137, 147, 148, 150, 151, 154, 159, 160, 162, 168, 172, 179, 180, 181, 182, 185–6, 193, 214, 220, 222, 225–6, 233–6, 241, 242
Roscommon senior football team, 59, 74, 84, 85, 94, 121–3, 144, 147–8, 176, 186, 187, 221–3, 230–1, 237–8, 242
Round Towers Clondalkin, 100, 217
Rowe, Carla, 228
RTÉ, 18, 28, 40, 41, 44, 46, 62, 67, 80, 98, 102, 129, 130, 140, 151, 157–9, 166, 167, 193, 202, 210, 225
Ruane, Matty, 239
rugby, 121–2, 184
Ruislip, 79
Ryan, Glenn, 216–19, 223
Ryan, Jason, 31
Ryan, Shane, 153, 161

St Brigid's GAA club (Dublin), 21, 45, 70, 145, 209–10
St Brigid's GAA club (Roscommon), 28
St Conleth's Park, 115–16, 217–18
St Jude's GAA club, 99, 172, 243
St Ledger, Daniel, 77, 78
St Oliver Plunkett Eoghan Ruadh GAA club, 28, 31, 64, 107, 122, 222
St Peregrine's GAA club, 93, 243
St Vincent's GAA club, 18, 35, 61, 98, 107, 145, 186, 208
Salthill, 108, 170
Schutte, Mark, 122–3
Scully, Niall, 33, 106, 107, 108, 110, 118, 129, 143–4, 151, 154, 180–1, 182, 235–6, 243
Semple Stadium, 63, 94, 116, 186
Shannon, Kieran, 102
Sherlock, Jason, 29, 88, 108–9
Shiel, Michael, 186
Sigerson Cup, 28, 52
Skerries Harps GAA club, 32
Sky Sports, 77, 79, 117
Slaughtneil GAA club, 74
Sligo senior football team, 59, 84, 222
Sludden, Niall, 91, 124
Small, John, 41–2, 67, 96–7, 110, 182, 198, 213, 234, 236
Small, Paddy, 75, 105, 119, 172, 179, 182, 187, 219–20, 227
Smith, Enda, 59
Smyth, Robbie, 114, 238
soccer, 30, 57, 61, 121, 169, 184, 226
South Africa, 104
Spillane, Killian, 154, 159

Spillane, Pat, 79, 80, 115, 136, 158–9, 164–5, 213
Stanley, Seán, 163–4
Sunday Game, 80, 81, 102, 119, 139, 159, 168
Sunday Independent, 51, 101–2, 139, 141–2, 202
Sunday World, 61, 111, 115, 118, 125, 129, 147, 183, 197–8, 213
Sweeney, Conor, 175
Sweeney, Eamonn, 149, 186
Sweeney, Mickey, 43

Tailteann Cup, 223
Templeogue Synge Street GAA club, 42, 57, 106, 118, 136, 244
TG4, 46, 170
TG4 Underdogs, 46
Thomas Davis GAA club, 242
Tipperary senior football team, 59, 66, 85, 116, 174, 175, 179
Tohill, Anthony, 234
Toye, Christy, 18
Tralee, 73
Tuam, 187
Tullamore, 75, 222–3
Tyrrell, Hannah, 228
Tyrone Herald, 120
Tyrone senior football team, 27, 39, 54, 58–9, 60, 61, 66, 84, 85, 90–3, 106, 115, 116, 120–1, 124–31, 148–9, 168, 187, 204, 226, 237, 238–39, 242, 244

Ulster senior football championship, 58–9, 61, 84, 119, 144, 174, 175–6
United States, 61, 110, 111, 125, 145, 168, 197, 207
University College Dublin (UCD) GAA club, 52, 171, 228

Vaughan, Donie, 68, 96–7

Walsh, David, 211
Walsh, Donnchadh, 65
Walsh, Shane, 110, 152, 214, 230
Walsh, Tommy, 154, 159
Westmeath senior football team, 30, 34–6, 52, 58–60, 80–2, 105, 113, 170–2, 192, 238
Westport GAA club, 97, 200
Wexford Park, 188–90, 213
Wexford senior football team, 20, 27, 76, 78, 104–5, 188–90, 213, 219
Whelan, Ciarán, 109–10, 158, 186, 207–8, 234
Whelan, Mickey, 207
White, Gavin, 153
White, Mark, 144
Whitehall Colmcille GAA club, 17, 105, 138
Wicklow senior football team, 55, 111–13, 226
Wolfe Tones GAA club, 125

Acknowledgements

It's hard to know where to start when it comes to acknowledging all the tips, tricks, pointers and called-in favours involved during the two or so years I spent messing around on this project in the hope that this blind squirrel would eventually stumble his way upon a nut.

For the genesis of this book, I really have long-time *Sunday World* chief sportswriter and doyen of Dublin fans Roy Curtis to thank/blame. In the very early days of what turned into interminable lockdown, the bould Roy recommended Richard Ben Cramer's fantastic biography of baseball icon Joe DiMaggio among a shortlist of 'Must Read' books. Needless to say, I took Roy's advice and picked up a copy. As is often the case, reading Cramer's masterpiece led me happily to another DiMaggio book, Michael Seidel's *The Streak*, a deep-dive into the immortal New York Yankee's legendary 56-game hitting streak ('as they say in the States') of 1941. I happened to read Seidel's game-by-game, day-by-day, chronological account of one of American sport's most talked-about achievements during the sporting shutdown of summer 2020. The Dubs, at the time, had been unbeaten since 2015.

The Dubs will lose one of these days, I told myself. Everyone gets beat eventually. And when they do – why not give this a go? And here we are.

Actually, in truth, the seed for a project such as this was planted around 1995 when, as a basketball-mad 13-year-old, my eldest sister brought me back a copy of Sam Smith's *The Jordan Rules* from a trip to the States. The year-long diary of the Chicago Bulls' breakthrough NBA Championship-winning 1991 season opened my eyes to the wild and wonderful behind-the-scenes world of elite sportspeople. Since then, I have always felt that the real story of sport takes place far away from the pitch, court, course, table, racetrack or wherever your favourite game takes place. The dynamic of team sportspeople at the very top of their game will be eternally fascinating.

If Roy Curtis unwittingly provided the trigger for the book, he and many of our colleagues also provided a magnificent historical body of work that helped me piece together the evolution of the greatest football team we've ever seen. From the *Irish Independent*, the writings of Vincent Hogan, Colm Keys and Conor McKeon were a non-stop fountain of information and entertainment. My old *Evening Herald* colleague, Kevin 'Sniper' Nolan (Mr Dublin Gah), filled in an endless amount of blanks, as did the work of another Talbot Street veteran, Frank Roche, as well as John Fogarty of the *Irish Examiner* and too-many-to-mention sports writers from regional papers and websites around the country. We are indebted to the professional men and women who cover our sports on a daily basis. Your work has never been more crucial.

I have loved the written word and newspapers for as long as I can remember, and working my way through this project via the Irish Newspaper Archives has seen that appreciation only grow. Many an afternoon was spent gleefully diving down one rabbit-hole after another as my easily distracted mind found an endless treasure trove of archived gems from one of our many fine publications. The unavoidable demise

ACKNOWLEDGEMENTS

of printed news is something we should all lament. We'll miss newspapers when they're gone.

My thanks to the many characters of the RTÉ online sports desk, in particular Anthony Pyne for sitting patiently through many an incoherent voice note – and generally replying in kind; and Armagh's own Niall McCoy, whose excellent book *Kings For a Day*, about the Orchard County's 2002 All-Ireland triumph, is a must-read for football fans.

I am also grateful to the writers and subjects of several GAA books, including the autobiographies of Bernard Brogan, Jason Sherlock, Jim McGuinness and Philly McMahon, as well as works by David Walsh, Niall Cotter and Tom Humphries.

I am indebted to the entire team at The O'Brien Press for their patience, support, good humour and unyielding professionalism – and to Ivan O'Brien for occasional tips for a rookie cyclist. On our original meeting, Ivan assured this first-time author that when it comes to books, it's all in the editing. To that end, the fingerprints of Donny Mahoney's guiding hand are all over *Unbeatable*. The quintessential details man, Donny helped turn thousands of words of inane ramblings into something, well, readable! Once our initial edit had been dumped in her lap, the endlessly patient Nicola Reddy proved the perfect candidate for our final draft.

GAA folk don't exactly queue up to talk to journalists in the year 2024. However, the candid contributions of Brendan Devenney, Steven Poacher, Dan St Ledger, Paul Cribbin, Conor Madden and John Heslin provided an insight into the world of elite Gaelic football that quite simply made this book possible. Our conversations sent this project in directions it otherwise could not have gone. My eternal gratitude to you all.

Speaking of elite footballers, in my early years being lifted over the turnstiles to Hill 16, there were few more elite than former Dublin goalkeeper John O'Leary. When John agreed to contribute to this project with a wonderful foreword it was, quite honestly, a dream come true.

To my pals in the Dublin Journalists' Golf Society: see you Monday – we'll never grow old!

The Dublin football team that dominated the decade of the 2010s amassed unimaginable riches on the playing field. Their achievements, when measured in the pounds, shillings and pence of gold medals, will most likely never be matched. However, we dearly hope that Pat Gilroy, Jim Gavin, Dessie Farrell and all of those players realise that they gave us, the fans, so much more than mere trinkets.

Following this team became a huge part of my life during this spell, and I count myself exceptionally lucky to have a daughter who enjoys football as much as I do. Abbie, we've been very lucky in life. We walked on the Great Wall of China on Christmas Day; dined al fresco on a dairy farm in Xi'an; caught the races at the Meadowlands in New Jersey; cheered a New York Mets game-winning home run in Citi Field almost as loudly as Clucko's 2011 winner; saw some World Cup football in Brisbane; got soaked by Niagara Falls and by a geyser in Reykjavik; and we've whiled away an afternoon watching regular folk play softball in Central Park. But wrapping up warm and pointing the car at some obscure provincial ground for our O'Byrne Cup roadtrips every January is among my favourite things in this world. 'What d'ya make of that

ACKNOWLEDGEMENTS

wing-back, seems handy.' 'Yeah, quick too. Like to see him on a dry sod.' 'Yeah. Might see him in the league.'

As I'm sure you know, it's really all about unspoken things that are infinitely more important than football.

These are the good old days.

Up the Dubs.

Eric Haughan

Enjoying life with
O'BRIEN
Hundreds of books for all occasions

From beautiful gifts to books you won't want to be parted from! Great writing, beautiful illustration and leading design. Discover books for readers of all ages.

Follow us for all the latest news and information, or go to our website to explore our full range of titles.

TheOBrienPress TheOBrienPress
OBrienPress TheOBrienPress

Visit, explore, buy
obrien.ie